Jan '96

Matt,
Wishing you all the
best for '96.
Peace, health and happiness.
Darren

SLAM DUNK

SLAM DUNK

THE RAPTORS AND THE NBA IN CANADA

BRENDAN CONNOR
NANCY RUSSELL

PRENTICE HALL CANADA INC.
SCARBOROUGH, ONTARIO

Canadian Cataloguing in Publication Data

Connor, Brendan
    Slam dunk: the Raptors and the NBA in Canada

Includes index.
ISBN 0-13-455700-X

1. Toronto Raptors (Basketball team).   2. National Basketball Association.
3. Basketball – Canada.
I. Russell, Nancy, 1963–   . II. Title.

GV885.8.C3C65   1995   796.323'64'0971   C95-932310-4

© 1995 Brendan Connor and Nancy Russell

ALL RIGHTS RESERVED.

No part of this book may be reproduced in any form without permission in writing from the publisher.

Prentice-Hall, Inc., Englewood Cliffs, New Jersey
Prentice-Hall International (UK) Limited, London
Prentice-Hall of Australia, Pty. Limited, Sydney
Prentice-Hall Hispanoamericana. S.A., Mexico City
Prentice-Hall of India Private Limited, New Delhi
Prentice-Hall of Japan, Inc., Tokyo
Simon & Schuster Asia Private Limited, Singapore
Editora Prentice-Hall do Brasil Ltda., Rio de Janeiro

ISBN 0-13-455700-X

Managing Editor: David Jolliffe
Copy Editor: Tanya Long
Production Editor: Avivah Wargon
Production Coordinator: Anita Boyle-Evans
Permissions/Photo Research: Marijke Leupen
Cover Design: Bruce Bond
Cover Image: Balvis Rubess
Page Layout: Arlene Edgar

1 2 3 4 5   99 98 97 96 95

Printed and bound in U.S.A.

To Baba and Dede, who were always so proud.
Nancy

To my son Adam. I love you and hope you will someday enjoy basketball as I do. It's a great game. Be happy it has come to Canada.
Brendan

CONTENTS

CHAPTER

ONE	Winners and Losers	1
TWO	The State of the NBA	28
THREE	Canadian Roots	44
FOUR	The Expansion Experience	62
FIVE	The Gamble on Gambling	87
SIX	There's No Place Like Home: The Search for an Arena	96
SEVEN	The Name Game	112
EIGHT	The Television Deal	120
NINE	It's Showtime	131
TEN	The Ducats Dilemma	139
ELEVEN	Who's in Charge? Hiring a General Manager	149
TWELVE	Selling the Sizzle: The Toronto Market	157
THIRTEEN	The Draft	180
FOURTEEN	John Bitove Jr.: Answering the Critics	190
FIFTEEN	The Labour Situation	204
SIXTEEN	Vancouver	228
SEVENTEEN	Conclusion	236

ACKNOWLEDGEMENTS

Special thanks to my mother Joanne Ahearn who has read and judiciously edited everything that I have written since I first put Jumbo pencil to paper. My dad, David Russell, and my brother, John, are the real sports fans in the family. Thanks for the advice.

My grandpa, George Russell, taught me a lot about writing over the years. Thanks to my sister, Jodi, for all the late-night phone calls to cheer me on. To Bronte: I owe you about a million long walks that you missed while I was sitting at the computer. And, of course, thanks to Joanne Ahearn for letting me borrow the cottage to write.

Thanks to my agent, Daphne Hart, who put up with all my rookie questions, to Chris and Barb for introducing me to the world of publishing and to Jeff for legal advice!

My friends, especially Bob, Sharon, Tricia, James and March in Toronto, and Shary and Danny in Vancouver, were always helpful during the writing. Thanks to everyone at CBC Charlottetown and all the people on the Island who were wonderfully supportive of my endeavour.

Finally, to Brendan. Thanks, love always.

Nancy

My thanks go to Rick Brace, Scott Moore, Mike Day, Michael Landsberg and my other colleagues at TSN who were supportive and encouraging.

Thanks also to Chuck Johnston who put up with the mess over the summer in our humble abode, to Tanya Long, my gentle reader and copy editor, to David Jolliffe and his staff at Prentice Hall for their help, to Daphne Hart of the Helen Heller Agency for her guidance and to John Lashway of the Raptors and Steve Frost of the Grizzlies for their co-operation. Thanks as well to Wade Harper of Canadian Airlines and Bob Lavelle of Bell Mobility.

To my son Adam, thanks for putting up with a distracted dad for much of our time together this summer.

Thanks also to my parents, Mike and Lynn Connor, who continue to be "great sports" and continue to keep me "rooted" in Sudbury, where I first fell in love with basketball.

Thanks mostly to Nancy. It's been a pleasure working with you. I continue to admire and respect you, and your dedication and thoroughness as a journalist. I'm proud of you. Thank you for coming to me with this project and for coming into my life. You know what you mean to me, and I will take the Bard's advice in old Sonnet 29 and will "hap'ly think on thee...then scorn to change my state with kings."

Truly, madly, deeply Nance . . . and always.

Brendan

INTRODUCTION

The presentations took place at Manhattan's Omni Berkshire Hotel. The Bitove group was the last of the four Canadian bids to appear before the expansion committee. Its two Toronto rivals had appeared in the morning, and the Vancouver group was to make its presentation just before the final Toronto bid would be heard. The Bitove partners spent the day rehearsing in another room, waiting for their turn. The proceedings were behind schedule, so it was late afternoon before the group made it to the second-floor meeting room to deliver its one-hour pitch. None of the group had ever been better in rehearsal. The group capped off its presentation with a tape, which ended with "a fantastic crescendo of crowd noise and courtside commentators shouting over opening night excitement, describing the arena and the incredible wisdom and foresight of the NBA for picking this facility." A proud John Bitove Sr., who was there as an adviser to the group, sat at the back of the room and wept as he saw his son's dream of owning an NBA team about to become a reality.

It is fitting that the arrival of the NBA in Canada should be full of drama. After all, the league prides itself on its ability to market the personalities and the images of the sport of basketball. At the time the Canadian bidders began their lobbying efforts to bring the prestigious league north of the border, an NBA franchise was "the" hot sports commodity. But it has been anything but smooth sailing for John Bitove Jr. and his partners since they joined the elite NBA family.

Slam Dunk traces the history of the NBA's arrival in Canada, beginning with the high-stakes competition among the three rival groups in Toronto who sought to get the franchise. Ironically, the consortium that did the most groundwork, and pressed the NBA the hardest to look towards Canada, ended up losing that competition. Behind the scenes, the Bitove family and associates used skills honed through years of successful deal-making, politicking and the occasional backroom arm-twist in the cutthroat world of the Toronto business scene, and, in the end, they triumphed over some of Canada's top corporate powers.

The people behind the Raptors have gambled almost $400 million Canadian ($170 million for the franchise fee, $200 million for a new arena, a team payroll of $20 million) that basketball will sell in Canada. John Bitove Jr. and his partners, Allan Slaight, Phil Granovsky, Scotiabank, David Peterson and Isiah Thomas, believe it will, but they have endured numerous struggles and setbacks, some of their own doing, some that were out of their control. In the Pro-Line debate, the Bitove group learned a tough lesson about the kind of control the NBA likes to exert. It almost cost Toronto the franchise. The Raptors have also run into organizational problems ranging from slow ticket sales to bureaucratic red tape at Toronto City Hall, from getting TV coverage to the summer-long NBA lockout. It sometimes seemed as if Murphy's law was at work for the rookie owners: everything that could go wrong did go wrong.

The short and bumpy history of the Raptors to date mirrors the up-and-down history of the sport of basketball in this country. In spite of the fact the game was invented by a Canadian, basketball has never really caught on in Canada. Toronto's first foray into the NBA lasted only one season, and as the chapter on the history of Canadian basketball demonstrates, the sport has always been a tough sell here beyond a small following of loyal fans. This time, however, the marvellous NBA marketing machine is behind the new franchises in Toronto and Vancouver, and a chapter is devoted to a concept on which the NBA prides itself—"selling the sizzle."

The Vancouver Grizzlies have gone through growing pains of their own, and some people question whether the NBA and the NHL can co-exist in a city with Vancouver's population and lifestyle. The original ownership group, the Griffiths family, was forced to restructure its finances and turn over equity control to a rich American investor in order to make the basketball venture fly. Like the Raptors, the Grizzlies are hoping the NBA marketing magic will help to overcome some of the skepticism about how basketball will sell in Vancouver.

Slam Dunk also looks closely at the revival of the NBA from a league that was seen, as recently as the early 1980s, as drug infested and garnering only marginal interest among fans, sponsors and TV networks to the sports juggernaut it is now, commanding the attention of 125 million Americans. We look closely as well at some of the most recent expansion experiences in the NBA. Even the most successful of the expansion franchises, the Orlando Magic, have had to overcome some difficulties to get where they are today. The Magic had the benefit of something the Canadian teams will not have: a number one position in the NBA Draft. Orlando has been a success on the court and off since the arrival of Shaquille O'Neal. Toronto and Vancouver can't hope for such a windfall, but they can hope to enjoy at least a portion of the success at the gate that has been seen in Orlando, Charlotte and even Miami. At best, the Raptors and the Grizzlies will want to avoid the pitfalls of the Minnesota Timberwolves, who are in ongoing turmoil, on the court and off, after more than six years in the NBA.

The Raptors also face the additional challenge of selling themselves in the already complicated marketplace that is Toronto. As the recent experience of the Blue Jays has proved, the fans will come when the team is winning, but they can be fickle, and they demand their sports be "big league." The Raptors will be hard pressed to duplicate the gate success of the Toronto Maple Leafs, and may, in fact, find themselves competing with that venerable team, which is the city's most popular sports franchise.

There has been plenty of criticism and jealousy directed at John Bitove Jr. and his group, and a chapter in *Slam Dunk* is devoted to laying these criticisms out for Bitove to answer. He answers with candour and with passion, and his dynamism and sense of purpose become clear.

A chapter is also devoted to the 1995 NBA Draft, which was held at Toronto's SkyDome, and which allowed the Raptors a look at what kind of excitement and response they'll receive from fans when they hit the court.

The first five years of the Raptors and the Grizzlies will be filled with challenges. As their early history has shown, being part of a wildly successful league is not a guarantee of good fortune for either team. Both will need a combination of management savvy, lots of money, marketing acumen and a bit of luck to help them through their growing pains, and maybe then they will someday justify the significant investment they've made in bringing the NBA to Canada.

Slam Dunk is a must-read for people who are already fans of the game, people who are not and are wondering about it, and for people interested in the synergy of big-league sports and big business.

WINNERS AND LOSERS

"The NBA is all about sweat, pain, fouling, elbowing, shoving and brutal aggression. And that's just to get a franchise."

That's the caption on a video put together by the Bitove group when they were pursuing the NBA franchise for Toronto. The words turned out to be prophetic. Referring to the latest efforts to get the NBA to come to Canada, John Bitove Jr. says he and his father were the first ones to encourage the league to think about it. They say it all began with a meeting at the NBA office in New York in 1989. Toronto construction magnate and multimillionaire Larry Tanenbaum says *he* was the architect of the NBA coming to Canada, through his persistent efforts to acquire a team.

Observers in the know say Tanenbaum did do the groundwork and turned the NBA's head. But he got scooped by a slicker, more dynamic Bitove, who got the nod because he was willing to do the NBA's bidding while Tanenbaum had some of his own ideas on how a uniquely Canadian franchise in the NBA should be run. Tanenbaum has been trying to become a sports entrepreneur for years. He has money, a good reputation and a passion for sports. As far back as the 1970s, Tanenbaum was interested in getting the NFL to Toronto, along with publisher Paul Godfrey and the Bassetts of broadcasting fame. That effort was scuttled when it was made clear that neither the NFL nor the government of Canada wanted to see it happen. At the beginning of the 1990s, Tanenbaum and his friends were busy trying to buy an ailing NBA team and bring it to Toronto, and it was their work that led to the NBA finally agreeing to look towards Canada for expansion.

In March 1991, Tanenbaum, along with his cousin Joel Rose, a Toronto lawyer, and Richard Peddie, then president of SkyDome, were part of a group called Palestra. Palestra was engaged in serious talks with the owners of the NBA's Denver Nuggets, with a view to buying the team and transferring it to Toronto.

"We put in a proposal to build a facility at the Exhibition site, and to move the Nuggets here," said Tanenbaum. "Our condition was that we got the transfer rights from the NBA. That was our first meeting with Commissioner David Stern, when we presented ourselves as potential buyers of the Nuggets, who wanted to sell to us. But Stern didn't want to lose the Denver market and asked the team's ownership to reconsider, and basically it became clear to us that it was politically unacceptable."

The Denver sale died in the fall of 1991. At that point, Stern and the NBA were not considering Canada for expansion, but Stern did tell the Palestra group he would give them his blessing if the group wanted to buy the New Jersey Nets and move them to Toronto.

"We explored that, but the problem was, the Nets had eight different owners, and we could never get them all to agree on a deal to sell to us," said Tanenbaum.

After that, there were talks about buying the Indianapolis franchise, and a March 1992 pitch from Palestra to Stern on the possibility of expansion to Toronto. The pitch was politely turned down, with Stern saying the league's latest expansion was still relatively new and, until the weak had a chance to get strong, there would be no more. So the Palestra people went shopping again, and this time hooked a big one in May 1992, effectively cutting a deal to buy the San Antonio Spurs.

"They were in financial trouble and a group of New York speculators had a deal to buy the Spurs from the owners at the time, McCombs and Woods. That New York group agreed to sign over to us, for a price, a deal to give us the transfer rights so we could move them to Toronto. However, it needed majority approval from the NBA owners for it to fly," said Tanenbaum.

The Palestra group hired the high-profile Cleveland lawyer, Irv Leonard, who was an expert in sports transactions, to attend another meeting in New York with David Stern.

"We got to Stern's office, and he was beside himself with anger," said Tanenbaum. "He didn't want to lose San Antonio, I think because the NBA was the only pro sports franchise in that market at the time. He promised the owners any help he could give if they would stay."

Tanenbaum and company were in the Commissioner's face again, trying to achieve something he didn't want to see happen. But Stern must have recognized Palestra's interest and persistence, and saw an opportunity to make some money for the NBA from the huge expansion fees rather than the smaller transfer fee. So in the fall of 1992, he said he'd consider expansion to Toronto if Palestra would drop its pursuit of existing teams.

"He said if we could get the approval of the owners, he'd say yes to expansion," said Tanenbaum.

The Tanenbaum group put its machinery to work. Richard Peddie was a key member of the team because of his hugely successful background in packaged goods. Working from his position of strength as president of SkyDome, Peddie took on the job of developing the business plan and doing the financial analysis of building and running an arena—the ticketing, the marketing and so on. Joel Rose handled the legal aspects and Tanenbaum looked after the money.

"We spent over a million dollars on our bid, but first we had to get around to see as many of the owners as we could. We saw most of them. In the fall of 1992, the Toronto sports scene was right in their faces anyway, with the Blue Jays winning the World Series and pictures of a packed SkyDome all over the TV. They agreed to expansion to Toronto, and would make it official that winter at the 1993 All-Star Game," said Tanenbaum.

The NBA had finally agreed to expand to Toronto, and Palestra figured it would be the guaranteed choice to win the new franchise. But it didn't quite work out that way. Along came another powerful business force from Toronto, led by John Bitove Jr. The Bitoves were not strangers to the NBA, even before the bidding started for a Toronto team. In 1989, John Bitove Sr. had been part of a five-member group that travelled to the NBA head offices in New York to talk to league Commissioner David Stern about acquiring a team to play at SkyDome. But it was son John Jr. who was the basketball nut in the family and who would eventually propel the Bitoves into the NBA.

"My dad went to see David Stern in 1989 at my insistence..." Bitove Jr. later recalled, "...for the very reason that I was too young."

By now, the story of John Bitove Jr.'s roots in basketball has become part of the popular mythology surrounding the Toronto team. The story has been repeated hundreds of times: how Bitove Jr. started subscribing to *Sports Illustrated* at age eight, and has collected every issue of the magazine since 1969. By age 12, he was designing sports complexes and planning corporate takeovers on paper. The basketball bug bit Bitove Jr. during his teens when the Buffalo Braves came to Toronto to play.

"He and his buddies made a point of taking in the games and while some imagined themselves at centre court, John's focus was on the owner's box," reported a 1993 profile in *The Toronto Sun*.

Years later, the Bitoves, John Jr. and John Sr., were sitting at an NBA playoff game, and that dream returned. The elder Bitove says that his son turned to him and said, "We've got to get a franchise, Dad."

The fire of John Jr.'s basketball passion was stoked while he was away at university. Basketball-crazy Indiana University seemed an odd choice for a kid growing up in North Toronto, but his mother, Dotsa, was originally from Fort Wayne, Indiana, and John Jr. had aspirations of being a student–athlete at IU. The family would have preferred that he go to school in Canada, but agreed to let him go after Johnny, as he was called then, worked three jobs during the summer to earn the $15,000 tuition to go to the American school.

John Jr. was there in 1981 when Isiah Thomas led the Indiana Hoosiers to the NCAA basketball championship; this was a connection that would be rekindled in later years. Bitove Jr. met his wife, Randi, while in Indiana, and she would later say that it was during those years that the roots of his NBA ambitions were planted.

"It all started there. That's a basketball-crazy place. We'd go to basketball games and have a ball. We were hooked. It's like a lifetime he's been working on this search for a franchise," she told *The Toronto Star.*

In 1987, after two degrees and a stint in the Ottawa political circles, Bitove Jr. rejoined the family catering and food services business. Shortly thereafter, John Bitove Sr. divided the company into five equal shares, each going to one of his five children: sons Jordan, Tom, Nick and John Jr., and daughter Vonna. By the time Bitove Sr. retired, according to the trade magazine *Foodservice and Hospitality*, the family catering business was worth an estimated $45 million in annual revenue and employed 1,200 people. (That figure, published in 1989, was the last time that the Bitoves revealed publicly how much the company was earning. In 1994, *The Financial Post* estimated that the annual revenue had probably increased to about $200 million.)

All five children have remained in the business in one area or another. They all learned their business acumen sitting around the table in the family home. The children were allowed to attend the business meetings that their father held at home, but it was John Jr. who was present most often, asking questions about various business deals. Family friend Senator Trevor Eyton has said: "The Bitoves are very competitive with each other, but John Jr. is the tiger. John Jr. is motivated by enormous ambition. He wants to do great things. He'll work any number of hours and travel anywhere to achieve that."

While his siblings had found their own places in the company, John Jr. never really found his niche until basketball came along. Since then, he has become the most high-profile member of the family. In this regard, he seems to take after the man he is named for, his father John Sr.

The story of John Bitove Sr. has also been raised to the level of mythology, though a few of the more messy details have been glossed over, such as his ongoing court problems, which date back to the 1970s. Otherwise, it's the classic North American tale of a hard-working immigrant who tranforms his humble beginnings into a family dynasty. In 1949, John Bitove Sr., the son of a Macedonian butcher, opened a 12-stool coffee shop, the Java Shoppe, on Avenue Road in Toronto. He was in his early 20s. During the 1960s, he added five more coffee shops and then four supper clubs in Toronto and Hamilton. In 1969, Bitove Sr. became the Canadian franchise holder for the Big Boy and Roy Rogers restaurant chains, which eventually grew to 40 restaurants across Canada.

In the late 1970s, the sons started getting into the business. In 1978, Nick and Tom opened the first Hard Rock Cafe in Toronto. They now have two more in Toronto and Montreal, and another opened in Vancouver in the summer of 1995. In 1983 a real turning point came for the company. Under the name York Quality Food, the Bitoves put in a tender on the contract for the food concession at Pearson Airport. The concession had long been held by Cara Operations, but it was the tiny upstart company that won the bid with the promise of a favourable lease arrangement for the government reportedly set at a minimum of $4.3 million a year, plus an annual increase of $500,000. It's ironic that the Bitoves won the deal at Pearson by offering such good terms to the federal government, considering the Bitoves' later problems over the lease arrangements at the airport, where the company ended up being sued by the government for not paying their rent.

The deal at Pearson led to other government contracts. In 1990, the Bitoves added exclusive food services at Terminal 3 to their list of concessions, but this was a deal that would later come back to haunt them.

In 1983, when the Bitoves first outbid Cara to win the food and drink concessions at Pearson, they promised the government a minimum annual guaranteed rent or a fixed percentage of gross revenue, whichever was greater. According to the *Globe and Mail*, the minimum was originally set at $4.325 million in 1984–85, with the amount rising to $10.2 million by the final year of the deal, 1993–94. After that, the Bitoves would have to bid again for a new lease running from 1994–2004.

When the government announced in 1986 that it was allowing private investors to build a third terminal at Pearson and that it would make renovations to Terminals 1 and 2, the Bitove Corporation allegedly threatened to sue unless it was compensated for loss of business to the new Terminal 3, and for lost revenues during the renovations. Court documents reportedly show that there was finally a deal made between the Bitoves and Transport Canada in the fall of 1988. According to reports, the government agreed to amend the lease and extend it for five years, to April 1999. Under the amended deal, the government would get more rent if passengers spent more at the airport and less if passenger traffic and spending was down. In the four years from 1988 to 1992, a combination of factors including an economic recession, the introduction of the goods and services tax, and the Persian Gulf war had people flying less and, therefore, there was less spending at the airport. The Bitoves made reduced rent payments until May 1992, when they suddenly announced that they didn't have to make any rent payments at all. According to the Bitoves, the amended lease "would replace completely the rent payment provisions under the lease, once Terminal 3 was opened," and so they were no longer required to pay a minimum rent. This amendment had been made by an outside accountant retained by the government to work on the Pearson file. The amendment was never approved by the federal government's Treasury Board.

In the fall of 1993, the federal government went to court to sue the Bitoves for payment of the minimum rent, which it argued was still due. Once all the calculations were done, the government filed a statement of claim in April 1994 asking for over $21 million. In documents filed in its defence, the Bitove Corporation said that it had been "within its rights in withholding rent payments since May 1992, and that it has further accumulated 'rent credits' totalling 'approximately $4.2 million'." The Bitoves said that their profits from Terminals 1 and 2 have dropped by $4.2 million. The statement of defence further argued that the Bitoves should not have to pay any rent for the remainder of the lease, and that the "rent credits" can be applied against any future obligations, should the contract at Pearson be renewed. Bitove Corporation filed a counterclaim against the government and also launched an action against Goodman and Goodman, a Toronto law firm with Tory connections that drew up the amended deal for the Bitoves that was signed in 1989.

During the trial, it was revealed that there was some political pressure involved in getting the amended lease deal for the Bitove Corporation. A senior Transport Canada official confirmed that John Bitove Sr. called then Prime Minister Brian Mulroney on the eve of his re-election in 1988. According to the official, Mulroney then called a deputy transport minister in July 1988 telling him to resolve the dispute. The new deal was signed within six months, after two years of wrangling.

(The Bitove roots in the Conservative party run deep. John Bitove Jr. worked for the party in Ottawa after graduating from law school. Bitove Sr. had been a long-time fund raiser for the party. During the 1988 election, he was credited, along with friend and business partner Senator Trevor Eyton, with raising about $9 million for the Mulroney campaign as co-chair of the Toronto fund-raising efforts.)

In September 1995, the Ontario Court's General Division ruled against the Bitoves, finding for the federal government in the Pearson rent dispute, and ordered Bitove Corporation to pay $22.7 million for past and future rent. In his 86-page ruling, Mr. Justice Sydney Lederman struck down the 1989 amendment to the lease because it was never approved by Treasury Board. "Treasury Board approval was a condition precedent to a binding agreement between the parties. Without such approval [the amendment] cannot have binding effect," said Judge Lederman in his ruling.

He also pointed out that the amended lease would have seen the Bitove Corporation pay no rent at Pearson until 1999, and that the amended lease would have allowed the company to make $6 million a year, rent free for seven years. So the company was ordered to pay $7.1 million in back rent from June 1991 to April 1994, and $15.7 million for the period until the contract expires in April 1999. Judge Lederman also dismissed the Bitove Corporation counterclaim against the government and dismissed the action against the law firm of Goodman and Goodman. In mid-September, Bitove Corporation said it would appeal the decision on the rent at Pearson.

The Bitoves also fought with Metro Toronto over almost $500,000 in back rent and taxes on the Guild Inn, a property in Scarborough that they leased as partners in Giant Step Realty. The matter was settled out of court to everyone's satisfaction, in August 1995.

There are other court actions under way and pending. Some suppliers have reportedly decided, however, not to pursue unpaid debts with the Bitoves because of the business potential of the NBA team. Even Richard Peddie, who became a competitor of the Bitoves for the NBA bid, shakes his head at the memory of their business style: "When I was at SkyDome, we had to chase them for money all the time. They didn't pay TSN for a year on the World Track and Field account."

One of the other potentially damaging lawsuits involving the Bitove family revolves around the luxury boxes at SkyDome, which will be the temporary home for the Raptors in their first couple of seasons. The Bitoves have made quite a name for themselves among sports fans through their catering business at the Dome. In 1989, they joined the consortium of private companies at SkyDome that was being put together by Senator Trevor Eyton. The Bitoves were given a 99-year monopoly on what are called the high-end concessions at both SkyDome and the SkyDome hotel. They control all the food in the complex except the fast-food rights, which are owned by McDonald's. The deal also includes rules that restrict luxury boxholders from bringing their own liquor or food into the SkyDome, giving the Bitoves the ability to charge whatever prices they want for food and drink. Those prices have been so exorbitant ($80 for a case of beer, $75 for chicken fingers to serve six) that some boxholders have formed an association and are now suing the Bitoves over their alleged price-gouging.

Stories like these, and countless others that never make it to court are out there along with the perception that the Bitoves play "hardball" and can wait out many a plaintiff. Somehow, though, the Bitoves always seem to shake off any damage to their image.

While not willing to discuss any actions against the Bitove Corporation, John Jr. rolls his eyes and sighs with resignation when asked about the court cases and the "word on the street" concerning his family's way of doing business. "It goes with the territory. There are professional jealousies, unhappy former employees and suppliers who may or may not have a legitimate claim. That's what the courts are for. If people feel they haven't been dealt with fairly, they have that recourse."

As general counsel to, chairman of, and part owner of the organization, David Peterson, former Premier of Ontario, concurs: "I sit on boards of a dozen companies, and I don't know one that doesn't have somebody suing it. You look at any big organization, the banks, big financial firms, all have litigation against them that makes these cases look like small potatoes."

Still, the reputation of the Bitoves has been established, especially in Toronto, and it is not necessarily a positive one in all corners. The other thing that everyone says about the Bitoves is that the family is very "defensive and protective." If you pick a fight with one Bitove, you have picked a fight with the entire family. Many people in the Toronto business community have learned this lesson the hard way. Nevertheless, it is that same ability to make powerful connections and form strategic alliances that ultimately won the Bitoves a piece of the lucrative NBA pie.

As was discussed above, the Palestra people had pretty much pressured the NBA into putting Canadian expansion onto the front burner. After lobbying the owners throughout the league, Palestra sent a bid application and a non-refundable $100,000 cheque to the NBA's league expansion committee. The league accepted the bid, and that got the ball rolling.

"We weren't necessarily in 'expansion mode' unless a particular city brought something unique to the table," said Expansion Committee Chair Jerry Colangelo, who also owns the Phoenix Suns. But Colangelo said his committee decided that they "looked favourably upon expansion for 1995–96" and that "we looked favourably towards Canada."

By April 1993, there were three parties interested in bidding for a franchise. Besides the Palestra group, there was a bid from Tampa–St. Petersburg, despite the fact that American applicants were being discouraged by the league, and there was a bid from Vancouver. In April, the Northwest Arena Corporation, led by President Arthur Griffiths of the Vancouver Canucks, had put in its application for a team, along with the $100,000 deposit. The NBA was already familiar with the group through its reputation in the NHL, and the NBA made it clear from the outset that the Vancouver and Toronto bids were not rivals, that there could be room for both cities if all worked out.

"We expect a second application from Toronto," said Colangelo at the time. "There's a lot of jockeying going on."

One of the other interested groups was headed by Bruce McNall, who at the time owned both the Los Angeles Kings and the Toronto Argonauts. In February, he had stated that he was "very interested in a Toronto NBA franchise," but by April, he had developed cold feet. A spokesperson for McNall said that he was not interested in another long-distance ownership situation. "Bruce has seen a proximity problem in terms of owning the Argos and being based in Toronto. And he knows that local ownership is also a priority for the NBA," said McNall aide Scott Carmichael.

BCL Enterprise was another potential bidder for a Toronto team. BCL was made up of Bill Ballard, Michael Cohl and Labatt Breweries, who were planning a 22,000-seat concert–sport facility at Exhibition Place. Ballard and Cohl were familiar with the NBA, as they had been involved in the last Toronto bid in the mid-1980s. This time, however, it appeared that they were more interested in finding a tenant for their facility than in actually bidding for the team themselves.

Michael Cohl told *The Globe and Mail:* "BCL won't be bidding, but Billy and I have the facility and we'd love to have either Tanenbaum or Bitove come into the building as tenants and work in what we feel is the superior site."

The Tanenbaum group, however, was now cool to the idea of Exhibition Place and of teaming up with BCL. Joel Rose said Palestra would be building its own basketball venue and not at the site it had proposed when it was looking to move the Denver Nuggets north. "We talked with Ballard six months ago and we're not prepared to go to the Canadian National Exhibition. If we were, we'd do it ourselves. But without mass transit [a subway stop] or a better road infrastructure, we're not going to do it."

Everyone in the NBA knew that in addition to bids from Palestra and BCL, the Bitoves would make a move, but that move didn't come right away. John Bitove Jr. had attended the league meetings in Salt Lake City in February 1993 when Canadian expansion was tabled, but Bitove Jr. was biding his time before making his plan public. The NBA brass were familiar with the

Bitove family by now. They had met John Bitove Sr. in 1989, but even more recently, the Bitoves had done the sport of basketball an enormous favour by bidding for and becoming the successful Toronto hosts of the 1994 World Championship of Basketball. The event had been originally planned for Belgrade, but the political situation in what was then Yugoslavia made it too dangerous, especially for the players of Dream Team II, who would represent the U.S. at the World Championship. The original Dream Team at the Barcelona Olympics had made a tremendous worldwide impact on the popularity of the NBA, and the league was hoping for similar results from the World Championship. So they wanted nothing to get in the way of their plans. There were, in the end, two possible replacements for Belgrade: Toronto or Athens. Though it was Europe's turn to host the Worlds, the NBA felt more comfortable with a North American city, so in the fall of 1992 the Bitoves got the nod. It was a stroke of good fortune and good timing that many feel guaranteed the Toronto NBA franchise for the Bitove group, as they had found a way into the inner sanctum of the league powers.

The road to hosting the World Championship of Basketball had, however, been a bumpy one for the Bitoves. Both John Jr. and John Sr. had been on the organizing committee for the Toronto bid for the 1996 Summer Olympics, which they had lost to Atlanta. But watching the Atlanta committee in action was a valuable learning experience for the younger Bitove. Shortly after Toronto lost the Olympic bid, Primo Nebiolo, President of the International Amateur Athletic Federation, suggested to John Bitove Jr. that Toronto should get some experience hosting international sports events, and he suggested the World Indoor Track and Field Championship. Bitove took the suggestion to heart. In March 1993, SkyDome played host to the international track meet, and John Bitove Jr. was at the centre of the action.

The event was only a moderate success. Bitove Jr. was not familiar with the world of track and field, and apparently made some questionable hiring decisions. Though the meet itself ran smoothly, only 80,000 tickets were sold, well short of expectations. Though Bitove says the meet "broke even," some observers behind the scene say that wasn't necessarily the case. People who worked with Bitove on the championship also commented that his style didn't make him popular.

James Worrall, Chair of the meet's organizing committee, told *The Toronto Sun:* "Bitove took charge and got things done quickly in his own way. It's not a style that everybody takes to. He's not a person who talks things over. The meet wasn't run by constant committee meetings." That seems to be the consensus on John Bitove Jr. In the same article, another former employee calls Bitove Jr. "a young Alan Eagleson. There's a lot of adrenalin and he can blow in a hurry."

Still, the World Indoor Track and Field Championship, and even the failed Toronto Olympic bid, helped Bitove position himself to host the World Championship of Basketball and, ultimately, to bring the NBA to Canada. But in April 1993, John Bitove Jr. hadn't even thrown his hat into the ring to bid for the Toronto team. It was the Palestra group that appeared, publicly at least, to be making all the right moves. Just days before a crucial meeting of the NBA expansion committee, the Palestra group announced the addition of two heavy hitters as partners in its NBA bid. John Labatt Ltd. and the Canadian Imperial Bank of Commerce became equal partners with Tanenbaum in the Palestra bid. Labatt and the Bank of Commerce had already made their names in the sports world. In 1976, they had been part of the bid that brought Major League Baseball to Toronto. In 1993, Labatt owned 90 percent of the Toronto Blue Jays and CIBC 10 percent, and they had enjoyed several decades of success on and off the field.

Tanenbaum and Joel Rose were delighted with the additions to their group. Said Rose: "I believe we've selected the greatest strategic partners possible and believe the NBA will agree with that assessment."

John Hunkin of CIBC said the bank had been talking to Palestra for months about a potential deal, which would give Palestra, CIBC and Labatt each one-third of the franchise. "We see it as a win-win situation, a good investment, good for the community and good for Canada at large. What could be better than another Blue Jays experience?"

Palestra had also brought another powerful partner on-side for the bid. Tanenbaum had struck a deal with Maple Leaf Gardens Chair Steve Stavro to combine forces on a new state-of-the-art arena, which would be shared by the NHL and NBA teams in Toronto. The arena would be ready for the basketball team's second year; the team would play its first season with home games split between Maple Leaf Gardens and SkyDome.

The decision by John Labatt Ltd. to align itself with the Palestra group signalled to some people that the Tanenbaum-led bid had the inside track, as the Labatt name had also in the past been linked to potential bids from the Ballard–Cohl group and the Bitoves. Herb England, a senior vice-president for Labatt, discussed the decision to go with Palestra at the media conference announcing the new partnership: "I'd say we turned our front to Larry as opposed to turning our backs on anyone else. We believe this is the group that can bring basketball to Toronto."

The day after the Palestra group announcement, the Toronto bidding took another unexpected twist. There would be another bid, but it was still not from the Bitove group. The BCL group was back in the running, but they had a very high-profile investor joining them: former NBA star Magic Johnson. Johnson had recently re-retired from the league, and though he was rumoured to be in the running for the job as coach of the Los Angeles Lakers, he had been perfectly clear as to what his intentions were: "I want to own a team, that's my goal." Even with the clout of a Magic Johnson, the Ballard–Cohl bid still had to be considered the underdog. This approach had been tried before in the mid-80s when another version of a Ballard–Cohl alliance enlisted the aid of ex-NBA superstar Wilt Chamberlain in an unsuccessful attempt to get an expansion team.

Meanwhile, John Bitove Jr. was putting the final pieces in place to unveil his group's entry in the bidding sweepstakes. On April 26, 1993, he was ready. While he may at some point have toyed with the idea of going for the franchise himself, that could only be a dream.

"The family is very substantial, but I don't think the family wanted to do 100 percent of the deal—or I don't know whether they could," said family friend Ralph Lean. "You're talking a $300 million deal for the franchise and arena. There's not many people who could do it all. Ego only goes so far in sports enterprises."

It was an impressive group that John Bitove Jr. had pulled together. Through Ralph Lean, a Toronto lawyer in the firm Cassels Brock & Blackwell, he had met David Peterson, a senior partner in the firm and the former premier of Ontario. Peterson would go on to become an integral part of the bid, as Chair of the Professional Basketball Franchise (Canada) Inc., often acting as co-spokesperson with John Bitove Jr. Peterson admits he got into the basketball venture without being much of a fan, but he was intrigued by the business opportunity and acted on the basis of some advice from his two teenaged sons. "They told me the NBA was the greatest thing in the world. That was the extent of my market research. Kids understand the power of basketball far more than adults."

Peterson says he asked the traditional questions right away. "Who's in, how much does it cost, who decides, where would you play? Those sorts of things. John had an answer for everything. He's incredibly dynamic and bright. He had a hundred balls in the air at once."

So Peterson agreed to join the Bitove team, saying: "I was not afraid to fail, although everyone predicted we would. A lot of my friends thought we didn't have a chance, and that Palestra was the shoe-in. Larry Tanenbaum is an extremely fine human being—rich, smart—and looked to be the insider on this. But I considered it an extremely interesting project . I mean it's a huge undertaking, a $300 to $400 million deal really. I knew nothing about basketball, but I do know a lot about process, about reading the road map, about the necessity for clear vision, for a set of goals, for understanding human behaviour, strategies and financial questions. And I know the media, and how you have to have thick skin in that regard. Believe me, I know that!"

In fact, Peterson was quite taken with the project, so much so that he admits to having become a fan over the next couple of years, and he bought in as a financial partner as well, purchasing a one percent share. "My suggestion was to keep the ownership group small, just a handful of people, no conflicts of interest, and I was sure it would be successful," says Peterson.

Peterson played a practical and critical role in the early days of the bid through his presence and bearing. Very corporate, a familiar face and voice in the media from his days running the province of Ontario, he was valuable as a spokesperson. Rumour has it that Bitove Jr. was worried that his age would be a factor and would discredit his group's bid, to the point where he wouldn't publicly reveal his birthdate until the NBA deal was done.

"He was self-conscious about it," Ralph Lean told *The Toronto Star*. "One of the reasons he brought David Peterson on board was because of David's gray hair."

Peterson also brought along some very important connections, the first of whom was Peter Godsoe, who had just taken over as chairman and CEO at the Bank of Nova Scotia. Godsoe agreed to become part of the bid, to the tune of 10 percent of the equity investment. The equity investment of the shareholders is $65 million US, with the other $60 million US to be financed. So Scotiabank is in for about $6.5 million and will help finance the rest, along with a U.S. company, Nation's Bank. The $60 million "mortgage" is to be paid back over seven years by the team, not by the investors.

"We had been involved for a time with the Montreal Forum, but had no other current sports interests to speak of," said Borden Osmak, Vice-President of Corporate Banking for Scotiabank. "We looked at this, and saw that there was a salary cap in the NBA, that there was no farm system, that the costs are basically fixed. We did find out in our due diligence research that owning the arena was key. But, in the the end, we decided it was a good enough investment that we would be part of it."

Scotiabank is not entirely new to the sports game, as the bank has done some financing for Gulf & Western, the one-time owners of the NHL's New York Rangers and the NBA's New York Knicks. "We feel if we can get some good promotional opportunities out of this, and thereby derive some intrinsic value and possibly some economic return as well, we will have made a good investment. We'll give it five years before we evaluate," says Osmak.

Even if the returns are not there, at $6.5 million US or $10 million Canadian, the bank is hardly in deep, and this could never be called a bad investment. (The $600 million it put into Olympia and York *was* a bad investment.)

The Scotiabank connection then led to one of the bank's corporate customers, Allan Slaight, President and CEO of Standard Broadcasting. "I was not an NBA fan, watched it casually and only occasionally on TV," barks Slaight, a man known for his direct and sometimes gruff style. "But I know a good deal when I see one. I obviously saw the synergies with broadcasting and media and how they'd be involved in all this. So I had some accounting people work out some rough numbers, and decided to jump in. I really didn't know John Bitove Jr. He was a golfing buddy of my son Gary, who runs our radio division."

Slaight has been somewhat of an enigma in the ownership group. He has a major share in the Toronto Raptors, the biggest, in fact, equalling John Bitove Jr. at 44 percent, yet he has, since the beginning, played very much a backseat role in the whole endeavour and has said little. "Why should I? We have a very competent chairman in Peterson, and a competent president and CEO in John; why should I be a spokesman? I'm just a majority shareholder. I care about my investment, and if I have concerns I raise them, but not in the media."

The last member of the bidding group was Phil Granovsky who, along with his brother Irving, owns Atlantic Packaging Products Ltd. He was involved in an unsuccessful bid for the Blue Jays when Major League Baseball was coming to Toronto. This time, he ended up on the winning team. Granovsky's contribution, besides his money, was a personal relationship with several of the NBA owners.

Looking back, John Bitove Jr. describes the group as the perfect combination of talents and assets. "What my family brought was an understanding of the stadium business. Scotia brought some stability in the fact that you had a bank as an equity partner, not just a debt holder. Broadcasting is such a critical component and Allan brought that element."

But it was always John Bitove Jr. who was at the centre of the bid. He was, above all, the edge that this group had over its competitors. NBA Deputy Commissioner Russ Granik said the league's familiarity with the Bitoves counted for a lot. "That certainly gave us some comfort in terms of knowing who we were dealing with," said Granik.

Though nobody knew it at the time, in February 1993, at the first NBA meeting to talk about expansion, David Stern had already given his tentative stamp of approval to the Bitove group. Sources say that Stern said then, of John Bitove Jr. and his bid, "It's his to lose." But John Bitove Jr. and his group were not going to let that happen. On July 23, 1993, the Bitove–Peterson group put their next building block in place, as they unveiled the plans for a 20,000-seat arena at Bay and Dundas, adjacent to the Eaton Centre. The $100 million arena was a meaningful part of the Bitove bid because it was one of the league's requirements, but also because it gave a new momentum to the campaign. The arena, called the Centre Court project, was impressive: 3,000 club seats, 150 corporate boxes, rapid escalators and elevators, bars, restaurants, underground parking...it was all there. The arena was modelled on existing facilities in Orlando, Minneapolis, Detroit and Phoenix, so the design was familiar to many of the current owners in the NBA who would be deciding on the winning franchise.

In contrast, the Palestra group, still at this point considered the front-runners in the bidding, refused to reveal publicly the site for their proposed arena. They also planned on building a basketball-friendly facility—in other words, a multi-purpose arena with a view to having a second tenant, but a building that would not compromise the sightlines and enjoyment of basketball. It would seat 21,500, would cost an estimated $125 million and it would also be in downtown Toronto. The group had also already announced that the Toronto Maple Leafs would be sharing the facility should Palestra win its bid. But Palestra certainly had not developed its plans for an arena to the degree that the Bitove people had, and some said at the time that that might cost Tanenbaum and his partners in the bid war.

The Palestra group had stumbled in other ways. Right from the beginning of its bid, the group's approach had been marked by a certain brash style that wasn't necessarily appropriate for dealing with the NBA. First of all, the Tanenbaum bid was presented to the league without anyone asking for it, though the two parties had some prior discussions about possible Canadian expansion. That just isn't the way that the NBA, or Commissioner David Stern, works, and so the Palestra group was off to a bad start. Jean Sonmor wrote in *The Toronto Sun:* "Insiders speculate Tanenbaum's end run might have cost him the franchise. This 'plausible scenario' is floated: Stern doesn't like being crowded, and perhaps he said to himself: 'Yes, we'll go early. Yes, we'll go to Toronto. But no, Palestra won't get the franchise.'"

It may not have been that vindictive or that deliberate, but the Palestra approach wasn't winning the group any brownie points with the NBA. Then, the Palestra group got itself into hot water in February 1993 for using the name "NBA Toronto" in some advertising. After the league announced that it was interested in moving to Canada, basketball fans wanted to get in their bids for season tickets. Many of them were calling Larry Tanenbaum because at that point, he was the person associated with Toronto's NBA bid. When two Toronto newspapers called Tanenbaum's office asking where fans could send inquiries about the NBA, they were told to address them to "NBA Toronto, 50 Ashwarren Road, Downsview, Ontario M3J 1Z5." This was, of course, the office of Larry Tanenbaum, and it made the group appear, to the public at least, to be the favoured bid for Toronto.

The NBA wasn't impressed with the move. Joel Litvin, Deputy General Counsel for the NBA, was actually called in to investigate. "No one among the interested groups from Toronto has been told he has the inside track," said Litvin. "It's not a big issue, but I can assure you, they're not using the NBA name based on anything we told them. It doesn't raise them to a higher level. Whether it's a legal matter remains to be seen."

The Palestra group was apologetic. Spokesperson Bill Wilkerson said the group had not meant to suggest that it was the Toronto NBA franchise. "That phrase originated with me on the spur of the moment when I was asked by the papers how people should address this correspondence, " said Wilkerson. "We don't want to appear presumptuous. We have not adopted a graphic or thematic line incorporating the NBA's name. It was simply a comment made over the phone to indicate where people could direct inquiries."

The Palestra group had realized the faux pas. The NBA has the most stringent controls over the use of its name and logo of any league in professional sport, and Palestra had skirted into dangerous territory. Despite the damage control, the league brass would just chalk this up as another black mark against the Palestra bid.

Still, Palestra had the momentum. Within days of the "NBA Toronto" fiasco, the group had collected two to three hundred requests for season tickets. Some fans had even sent a deposit, which the group was sending back. "All we want to do is create a list of people who are interested. If we do receive a conditional grant of franchise, there would be a condition that we sell 12,000 season tickets, so we're starting to build a list," said Palestra President Joel Rose.

But by the summer of 1993, though they didn't know it, Palestra had already been basically blown out of the water by the smooth sell of the Bitove bid. In June, the Bitove partnership sent 50 owners and league officials a presentation about the group, including a two-page letter, information about the shareholders and a video called "Canada's Dream Team," The video included a black-and-white photo of John Bitove Jr. at age 15, with his basketball teammates, with Bitove's voiceover: "I've been a basketball fan all my life."

This was just Part One of the full-court press by the Bitove group. Over the summer, at least one shareholder in Bitove's Professional Basketball Franchise group visited every NBA owner to make a personal pitch. In late July, the expansion committee members visited Toronto, and the Bitove group hit them with a well-choreographed, emotional presentation that insiders say sealed the already-certain future of the Toronto team. The Bitove group's presentation was a preview of the kind of hype and glitz that would characterize the Raptors in their early stages, and it was very much in keeping with the flashy, entertainment-based style of the league itself.

The other two groups took more traditional approaches to their meetings with the NBA expansion committee. The Bitove group decided to go for a very visual presentation, so they took the committee members on a tour. Fortunately for John Bitove Jr., it was a perfect summer day in Toronto as he took the group out on the roof of the Scotia Plaza. A sign had been put up on the Eaton Centre parking garage showing the future location of the planned downtown arena. As the NBA expansion committee members were leaving the Scotia building, about 300 employees gathered in the bank lobby and shouted, "We want the ball."

Then the group moved to the Eaton Centre area itself, where Bitove's promoters had set up basketball hoops, and were serving free hot dogs. It was picture perfect: kids and guys in suits, with their sleeves rolled up, shooting hoops. One media report says that the only unusual sight during the presentation was a member of the Palestra group, in a suit and dark glasses, who apparently lurked at the back of the group throughout the Bitove presentation.

There was, however, one more test ahead for John Bitove Jr. and the other two groups from Toronto, as well as for the Northwest Arena people from Vancouver. They were invited to make a final presentation before the NBA expansion committee in New York on September 20, 1993. This would be the final chance to woo the league before a decision would be made. The presentations took place at Manhattan's Omni Berkshire Hotel. The Bitove group was the last of the four Canadian bids to appear before the expansion committee. Its two Toronto rivals had already appeared in the morning, and the Vancouver group was to make its presentation just before the final Toronto bid would be heard. The Bitove partners spent the day rehearsing in another room, waiting for their turn. The agenda ran behind schedule, and so it was late afternoon before the group finally made it to the second floor meeting room to make its one-hour pitch.

The Toronto firm of Cossette Communication–Marketing had been working with the Bitove group in preparing for the NBA bid, and several members of the Cossette team were in New York for the final presentation. Himal Matthew, the company's Director of Account Services, describes the group's strategy going into that final meeting with the NBA.: "The focus was on the partners themselves and the vehement enthusiasm of each, and why the NBA franchise should be awarded to this particular contingent."

Phil Granovsky of Atlantic Packaging told the committee how he had borrowed $5,000 in 1949 to start his packaging business. Afterwards, Harold Katz, the owner of the Philadelphia 76ers, reportedly embraced him and told him, "I love to hear stories like that."

The observers from Cossette Marketing sat and watched the Bitove partners in action. They later told *Marketing*: "None of them had ever done better in rehearsal."

The group capped off its presentation with a audio that ended with "a fantastic crescendo of crowd noise and courtside commentators shouting over opening night excitement, describing the arena, and the incredible wisdom and foresight of the NBA for picking this facility."

A proud John Bitove Sr., who was there as an adviser to the group, sat at the back of the room and reportedly wept as he saw his son's dream of owning an NBA team about to become a reality.

It was fitting, therefore, that 10 days later when the NBA's final choice was made public, it was John Bitove Jr.'s birthday. The celebration made the perfect visual backdrop for the television camera: John Bitove Jr., about to become the youngest governor ever in league history, surrounded by his family, celebrating their entrance into the NBA elite. (The party was held at Gretzky's Restaurant, another piece of the growing Bitove sports empire.)

"It's my birthday," said Bitove, surrounded by bright television lights and reporters. "It's a heck of a birthday present."

David Peterson introduced John Bitove Jr. to the group of 100 friends, family members and media who had gathered for the announcement. "Meet Mr. Basketball, the guy who really did it for Toronto," Peterson told the crowd.

Scotiabank's Borden Osmak, who had overseen the bank's involvement all along, said of John Bitove Jr.: "He was the catalyst, the sparkplug. His heart was in it. He's a great partner to have. He's a superb marketer. He sold us, and the other investors, and he sold the NBA."

For his part, Bitove Jr. was modest. "I was just the quarterback, the point guard, the playmaker." As he spoke to the media afterwards, he sounded very much like the owner of an NBA franchise: "This is a great day for the people of Toronto and the start of a new era for the city, and for the sport and fans of basketball. We are confident that the trust placed by the committee in our community and our group will be rewarded with a highly successful NBA franchise."

As John Bitove Jr. enjoyed a victory cigar and the rest of his group celebrated, the members of the Palestra group wondered where they had gone wrong. There was no consolation in the vote of the expansion committee itself, as the selection of the Bitove bid had been unanimous. NBA spokesman Jan Hubbard said: "In Bitove's case, they liked the arena site, they liked the group, they liked his partners and they liked his presentation. People on the committee said it was a very, very difficult decision."

The Palestra group reacted bitterly to its defeat. "We're very disappointed," said Palestra spokesperson Bill Wilkerson. "My own feeling is that there's a certain irony in this that's not easily dismissed. Palestra were the pathfinders in this, they put it on the agenda for the NBA. They secured the necessary financial and business planning. But they still came up short."

Palestra had the machinery in place and the big financial backing. The group did name and logo research, registering various potential names before finally settling on Toronto Thunder. (There's still a Toronto Thunder cap in Richard Peddie's office at Labatt Communications Inc.)

"We mounted a strong campaign, perhaps too strong in hindsight," said Peddie. "We had pedigree credentials in CIBC and Labatt. I mean these were the big partners in the Blue Jays, which is the most successful expansion franchise in the history of sports. Larry Tanenbaum was clean, no dirty politics in his background, we had market research, fan base reseach, we had it all. We presumed the NBA would be thorough in looking us over, and we thought it would be 'a lay-up'."

But Peddie figures Palestra was never in the driver's seat because of the clashes with Stern. "The NBA was just not helpful to us in making data available for us to do up our profit and loss forecasts. Ticketing prices, local radio and TV deals, souvenir sales, all that stuff we needed, was incomplete and hard to get from the league. We got most of our information from the Pistons, the Knicks and the Mavericks. Still, we were there with all of it, and I have to believe our P & L (profit and loss) preparation was better than that of the Bitoves. Hell, I remember John Bitove calling SkyDome a week before the bid presentations and asking what the rent would be. That's not a question you ask with a week to go. But it was all academic I believe, because they were in already."

The BCL group and partner Magic Johnson had been also-rans in the race for a Toronto team. Still, Johnson appeared to have been in the bidding to make a point. After the announcement, the former basketball star said, "One day, I'll own an NBA team, if not in Toronto, somewhere else. I only wanted them to have an NBA team and I appreciate the support they gave to our group."

As for his partners, this was the second defeat for Bill Ballard and Michael Cohl, who had also been part of an earlier failed bid in 1985. Cohl said, "One of the things we thought we had going for us was a definite site. I guess the NBA liked the downtown site the best." Ballard and Cohl said that they would go ahead with plans to develop a concert facility at Exhibition Place, even without a secondary tenant like the NBA team.

However, Michael Cohl did tell *The Toronto Star* that the arena issue had definitely hurt the Palestra group even more than the Ballard–Cohl people. "For sure it hurt them," said Cohl about the uncertainty over where Palestra would put its arena.

Larry Tanenbaum disagrees: "The NBA knew everything it needed to know about our site. We hadn't made it public, but they knew where it was. It was downtown, east of SkyDome, at York and Simcoe streets. It was Marathon property, but we had a deal on it. We had it wrapped up. The NBA knew our plans. They also knew I wasn't going to go with a basketball-only facility. Maybe that affected us, but it was not the location of the site, or its secrecy that lost it for us."

If the loss was bitter for the individuals involved in fronting the Palestra and BCL groups, it was even more bitter behind the scenes at Labatt. Basically, the corporation had underestimated the Bitove bid, referring to John Jr. as the "little restaurateur." Labatt brass had thought they had their bases covered with essentially two bidding groups. They were openly involved in the Palestra bid, and the brewery was also a sizable investor in BCL. Afterwards, the Labatt people admitted that they had erred badly in their dealings with the NBA. They had gone into the presentation in New York looking like "a bunch of blue suits from the brewery."

In contrast, Bitove Jr. and his people were young and enthusiastic and bold, personifying the kind of spirit that the NBA likes to market. While Labatt obviously had a successful track record in pro sports with the Toronto Blue Jays, the NBA didn't want the Toronto team to be another Blue Jays. Everything about the Labatt people, it seemed, rubbed the NBA decision-makers the wrong way, clearing the path for John Bitove Jr. Long after the Bitove contingent won the bid, the Labatt group remained in shock. To this day, some Labatt people are skeptical about the Bitove group's ability to make the team work financially, but they've had to bury the hatchet and put on good corporate faces in order to build sponsorship deals with the team and the league. (If one of the Labatt partners had won the bid for the Toronto franchise, it would have been thrown into limbo in the summer of 1995, when Labatt was sold. The new owners, Interbrew of Belgium, would probably have put the NBA franchise on the auction block before its first season was over.)

While the Labatt people were quietly skeptical, some of the Palestra people were not quiet about their feelings. Still unhappy about the NBA's choice, Joel Rose suggested there was a money issue that was more critical to his group's defeat, saying the Bitove group overpaid for the franchise by agreeing to an expansion fee of $125 million. "Our view is it's going to be tough for them," said Rose. "They may make a profit but we never felt comfortable with that kind of money."

Palestra people actually say the first number tossed out in the bid presentation was by the NBA, and the number was $160 million US.

"We all gulped when we heard that," said Peddie. "But I think that was just a highball figure so that we and the other groups would think $125 million was OK. We were prepared to start at $85 million US. That was our opening position, and that was on an 85-cent dollar at the time. But we never argued about the price. I think it was more our style and our vision that the NBA couldn't live with."

The expansion fee of $125 million US, which translates to about $170 million Canadian, was almost four times the $32.5 million paid by the last four expansion teams in the late 1980s. (The fee became the second-highest ever in pro sports, after the $140 million paid by the new Charlotte team in the NFL.) The league defended the huge increase it was charging the new Canadian franchise.

Commissioner David Stern explained: "Our network TV revenues then were about a quarter of what they are now. The fee came out of a complex set of calculations designed to satisfy us and the expansion applicants that this franchise can be successfully operated."

John Bitove Jr.'s response to the $125 million fee was that he still felt the franchise could make money. "We're not in because we promised more money. We think this makes sense." However, sources say that the Bitove group did offer the most.

The Palestra group is reported to have eventually offered about $100 million US for the rights to the Toronto team. League executives suggested in 1993 when Canadian expansion was raised that $85 million would be the fee. But with three Toronto groups and one Vancouver group interested in getting in, the price went up dramatically. As David Peterson of the Bitove bid observed, "Three bidders probably drove the price up. Who knows the limits on these franchises? It's a helluva lot of dough for 12 guys in T-shirts."

There still remain strong suggestions from people who say they are in the know that John Bitove Jr. basically offered the NBA a blank cheque, saying that his group was willing to pay whatever price the league wanted to set and that it was sure the NBA would be fair. That was allegedly how the expansion fee ended up at $125 million, and became one more compelling reason to award the bid to the Bitove group over its competitors.

Bitove disputes this story, saying the league first mentioned the $125 million figure and not just to his group. "But that blank cheque story is bull," he says.

However the price got to be what it was, whether because of the competition among the Toronto groups or because of a "blank cheque" approach, it certainly proved costly for the group bidding for a team in Vancouver, which would be charged the same price for expansion. Unlike the Toronto bid, the Vancouver team was not awarded right away because of some concerns about the financial viability of the current ownership in Vancouver. (The group may also have needed to seek extra financing once it found out that the cost of expansion would be $125 million, about $25 million more than originally anticipated.) However, both the NBA and the successful group in Toronto were hoping that the Vancouver team could also be ready for the 1995–96 season.

Northwest President Arthur Griffiths told the media, in October, that he was optimistic his group would be ready. "I more or less say we have a recommendation, subject to information provided by ourselves, satisfying our ownership structure and partnership arrangement."

Of the Vancouver bid, John Bitove Jr. said he welcomed the idea, as it would boost overall interest in basketball in Canada and would provide a natural rival for the Toronto team.

Larry Tanenbaum of Palestra was not so supportive. "I think Stern has done a disservice to the NBA and to Canada by going with Vancouver prematurely. That market has not been tested. I think it's too small at 1.5 million, with a lot of that being Asian people who are not basketball fans. I think the NBA showed greed by going in there, seeing another $125 million available and grabbing it."

While the Vancouver group reshuffled its ownership and raised more money, John Bitove Jr. and his Toronto partnership basked in their glory. In early November, Bitove Jr. and his entourage travelled to New York, as the NBA board of governors voted unanimously to grant Toronto a team. Commissioner David Stern welcomed his friend John Bitove Jr. officially into the league. "We are as excited as we can get about our Canadian expansion," Stern said at the news conference. "It's a spectacular day."

John Bitove Jr. and his father and three brothers posed for photographers, holding a basketball covered in the red maple leaf. "It really does feel great," said Bitove Jr. "I kept comparing it to a high school exam. I felt good, but I had to wait for the report card."

The report card was in, and John Bitove Jr. had passed with flying colours. He had played the NBA's game, and now he was part of their game. But there would be anything but smooth sailing ahead.

Chapter Two

THE STATE OF THE NBA

"We're proud and excited to welcome the city of Toronto into the NBA family. John Bitove and his group will provide the new franchise with solid financial backing and a wide range of business experience. We are as excited as we can be about our Canadian expansion. It's a spectacular day."

—David Stern, NBA Commissioner, November 1993

Getting an NBA franchise has been compared to getting a McDonald's franchise. You're expected to stick to the successful formula, and you're virtually guaranteed a lucrative product. That has been the story, at least, of the last 10 years of the league's history. There have been a few notable exceptions, like the ever-struggling Minnesota Timberwolves. But over all, the NBA has been, as one sports columnist put it, a licence to print money. That's what the two new Canadian franchises are hoping for.

Ironically, the Raptors and Grizzlies have joined the league just as the NBA's renaissance seems to be coming to an end. The Canadian teams are part of the master plan to reinvigorate the league after a blistering decade in the U.S, and if league Commissioner David Stern has his way, Mexico City will join the North American game plan by the turn of the century. As McDonald's dabbles with new product lines to maximize profit, so too is the NBA always looking for new ways to extend and prolong its popularity.

The NBA's rise to the top of pro sports has been nothing short of miraculous. To continue the restaurant analogy, as McDonald's created the concept of "fast food," the NBA has become the sporting equivalent. It is mass marketing at its very best, and it's wildly successful. "Somewhere along the line, basketball became America's national pastime," proclaimed *Sport* magazine in March 1994.

Now, the challenge is to supplant hockey as Canada's favourite game, and already the NBA has made dramatic inroads into changing the way that Canadians watch sports. They're simply following the same game plan that paid such big dividends south of the border.

There is one name that is synonymous with the current success of the NBA, and that is the Commissioner, David Stern. Stern began his association with the league in 1967, when he handled legal work for the league through a New York law firm. He became the NBA's general counsel from 1978 until 1980. During the 1980–81 season, then Commissioner Larry O'Brien promoted him to the post of executive vice-president. At 5'9", Stern is dwarfed by most of the millionaire superstars who now populate his league. Many of them are too young to even remember a time when the NBA wasn't a hot commodity. But David Stern remembers, as do many of the owners who were around at the time.

It's ironic now to hear some of the early impressions of David Stern. Pat Williams, President and General Manager of the Orlando Magic, told *The Sporting News* in 1992 that most of the owners thought Stern was "another lawyer, trying to tread water." But what they found instead was "the heart of another P.T. Barnum.... We found out that David was an innovator, a creator, a marketer, a visionary, a hustler, a salesman and yet, still a people person." Watching Stern in action is to watch a master at work. He handles the media with aplomb. There have been few negative comments recorded about him during his decade as commissioner. He commands, and gets, it seems, absolute loyalty from those who work with him. Stern grew up in New York, a Knicks fan, and his roots in marketing are there. A 1991 profile in *Sports Illustrated* by

E.M. Swift quotes Michael Goldberg, of the National Media Group: "David's father ran a successful deli in New York. To be successful in that business, you have to have great rapport with your customers. You have to get them to come back, even if the corned beef is a little dry and the apple pie a little stale. You have to give the customer a smile, a pleasant greeting, a sense that he is being taken care of. David Stern understands that, and I don't think it would be far-fetched to say that he has applied that to the NBA."

Like any good businessperson, David Stern knew back in 1984 that he had to have something to market. By the early 1980s, the NBA was so unpopular, the product so mediocre, that Stern basically had to rebuild. The NBA had reached rock bottom. During the 1980–81 season, 16 of the 23 teams were losing money. Four were close to going out of business. Total attendance was down almost a million from the year before, and teams were playing to an average of only 10,000 fans per game, about 58 percent of capacity.

One of the lowest of many low points had come during the championship game the year before. The 1979–80 championship was televised on tape delay at 11:30 p.m. in the East. When measured against the mammoth television ratings of the NBA in the 1990s, that seems unthinkable, but the NBA was that unmarketable a commodity in the early 1980s. "NBA basketball was a sports entity that was, back then, only slightly more popular than roller derby," said Liz Comte and Dave D'Allesandro in their February 1992 article, "Star-crossed," in *The Sporting News*.

Another low point for the league came in the form of a 1982 article in the *Los Angeles Times*, which reported that 75 percent of NBA players were on drugs. "The NBA was shunned by Madison Avenue because it was perceived as a league that was drug-infested, too black and too regional."

The "too-black" argument was a particularly touchy problem for the league. During the early 1980s, the game of basketball was increasingly referred to as a "city game" or a "ghetto game." By 1982, 75 percent of the players in the league were black, while an equal percentage of the fans were white. In a 1982 interview, Paul Silas, then president of the NBA Players Association, said, "It is a fact that white people in general look disfavorably upon blacks who are making astronomical amounts of money if it appears they are not working hard for that money. Our players have become so good that it appears they're doing things too easily, that they don't have the intensity they once had." This argument is particularly ironic in light of the superstar players who subsequently contributed to the turnaround of the league, but there was no doubt, in 1982, that the NBA was in serious crisis.

"I remember the discussions we had at the All-Star Game in New Jersey in '82," said Stern in a 1992 interview. "There was talk about combining the Utah and Denver franchises, which had fallen under heavy bank debt. Cleveland was in big trouble. So were San Diego, Kansas City and Indiana. Those were dark days."

David Stern took over the league on February 1, 1984, and he has since left his mark on the NBA, and on the face of professional sports, forever. "Stern has reshaped a floundering, financially strapped league into an entity that is the envy of professional sports—an innovative, multifaceted, billion-dollar global marketing and entertainment company whose future literally knows no bounds," writes E.M. Swift in his 1991 portrait of Stern in *Sports Illustrated*.

When David Stern took over the NBA, there were only about 40 employees, including just one person in public relations and three in marketing and broadcasting. These days the league has offices in Europe, Asia, Australia and Japan, as well as enormous head offices in New York and New Jersey. In 1984, there was no entertainment division or production facilities. Now, the league has NBA Entertainment, Inc., which produces the "NBA Game of the Week," "NBA Action" and "Inside Stuff" for television markets in over 140 countries around the world.

While David Stern is primarily responsible for masterminding the reincarnation of the NBA, he had some fairly significant help from a rookie who joined the league around the time Stern took over and from a shoe company that was looking for a breakthrough product in the early 1980s. But before he could revolutionize the marketing of the NBA, David Stern had to make sure the league was still intact and financially sound.

One of Stern's first and perhaps most profound accomplishments was that of a salary cap. In April 1983, the NBA Players

Association, headed by the late Larry Fleisher, agreed, for the good of the league, to a payroll limit. The concept of a salary cap had been proposed in the NFL in 1982, but the owners had turned it down. The dire circumstances in the NBA made the league the first to try it out. In exchange for the salary cap, the players would receive 53 percent of the gross revenues, which include gate receipts and local, network and cable television fees. The original agreement gave the players a small royalty payment from NBA Properties, which, ironically, over the years would become phenomenally lucrative. (Some estimates of retail sales are as high as $3–4 billion.) "What made it happen in basketball was that the players and management were in the gutter together. Everyone saw how necessary it was for both sides to work together to survive," said Charles Grantham, then head of the NBA Players Association, in 1991.

Since then, the NBA had enjoyed a labour peace that was the envy of other pro sports. But the façade of solidarity between ownership and players in the NBA has now crumbled. The first cracks appeared when the Chicago Bulls, owned by Jerry Reinsdorf, were caught understating its revenues, thus undercompensating the players. The players received a $60 million group settlement.

Now, the NBA Players Association is reconsidering the concept of a payroll limit, just as other leagues are struggling to impose one. "There was a time when the salary cap in our business was necessary and it helped stabilize our league," Charles Grantham told *Forbes* in June 1993. "Now the business has matured.... We are all now in a position to resume as a business without restrictions."

The owners are arguing the exact opposite, and do not want to give up the salary cap. "The salary cap is the envy of every sport league," says Orlando Magic General Manager Pat Williams. "It is one of the pillars of this league. We will never let it go."

The irony of the labour turmoil in the NBA is that most teams have been getting around the salary cap for years, and the players, particularly the younger stars, are very well paid. About 60 percent of the players make at least $1 million a year, 30 players earn at least $3 million and the average salary in the league is

$1.87 million, making it the most lucrative payday in all of professional sports. In contrast, the average salary in football is $610,000 and in baseball, $1.27 million.

Back in 1984, with labour peace guaranteed, David Stern then turned to the image problem of pro basketball. Again, together with the Players Association, the league unveiled what was labelled "the most progressive drug policy in sports." A player who came forward voluntarily, admitting to using drugs, would receive treatment. The league would continue drug testing, with reasonable cause, and could suspend a player for two years if he was caught. In 1988, the policy was extended to include drug tests for all rookies.

Over the years, the NBA has continued to have cases of athletes caught and suspended for using drugs. But the problem is nowhere near what it was perceived to be in the early 1980s when the image was that 75 percent of the players were on drugs. Even after the drug policy was in place, Len Bias of the Boston Celtics died of a cocaine overdose, in 1986. The drug problems have continued. In the fall of 1994, the league suspended Richard Dumas of the Phoenix Suns indefinitely after his relapse into drug use. The speculation continues to swirl around the possible use of cocaine by Celtics guard Reggie Lewis, who died in 1993 while shooting baskets.

Still, the appearance of beating the drug problem made the league much more marketable in the mid-1980s. "A good marketing guy knows that he has to get the product right before marketing it," says Scott Creelman, head of international sales for Spalding Sports Worldwide. "That's what Stern did with basketball. He cleaned up the product first. Only then did he start marketing."

Perhaps one of the most subtle, but one of the most powerful, changes that David Stern brought to the NBA was a new groupthink mentality, which turned the entire league into a powerful marketing force. Continuing the McDonald's analogy, Stern was able to convince the teams to market the same product everywhere. One NBA employee recalls, "I was shocked, when I went to my first league meeting, at how competitive and how uncommunicative the teams were. There was a real us-against-them attitude."

Another employee says, "All the teams were islands unto themselves. What Stern did was take the islands and turn them into a continent."

A former league executive said the changes were already noticeable by 1985. "Five years ago, a league marketing meeting would have been adjourned in 10 minutes. Today, they last at least four hours." Jon Spoelstra of the Portland Trail Blazers told *Business Week*: "When one team comes up with a really innovative way to sell high-priced season tickets to corporate accounts, this is no longer a big secret. It becomes a business-school-type case study for everyone. The front office of a team in the NBA is no longer a cushy place to stash nephews and in-laws."

Those same principles are still very evident 10 years later, as the two Canadian franchises have learned. The NBA has a division called Team Services that shares information amongst the franchises, from marketing strategies to sponsor information. But the influence goes beyond an exchange of ideas. The NBA head office in New York has made sure that the Canadian teams are diligent in doing things the NBA way. For example, insiders say that the original nickname for the Toronto franchise was going to be the "T-Rex," short for the Tyrannosaurus Rex. Apparently NBA head office had given the thumbs up to the dinosaur concept, which their market research had proven would be a sure-fire hit. But the NBA suits were worried that the T-Rex image was "too fierce" for young fans and urged the team to stick with a dinosaur but go with the "Raptors" instead. When the NBA suggests an idea, it's best to comply, and so the Raptors were hatched.

Similarly, the Vancouver Grizzlies were constantly sending their arena plans to head office for the league's OK while GM Place was under construction. The NBA has what one Grizzlies employee calls the "most stringent rules" for the way the facility should be designed. In fact, the league has such specific guidelines for camera locations that the designers of GM Place had to reconfigure two skyboxes to meet the league's requirements. Ironically, the skyboxes that were taken out of commission belonged to Arthur Griffiths, Chairman of the Grizzlies, and General Motors, the company that had paid big bucks to put its name on the new facility.

In the case of the Canadian teams, the NBA has also maintained a certain uniformity of approach because many of the key employees of the Grizzlies and Raptors have previous experience with other NBA franchises. For example, Tod Leiweke, Executive Vice-President of Business for Orca Bay Entertainment, owners of the Grizzlies and the NHL's Canucks, was formerly with Houston's Rockets; Greg von Schottenstein, the Director of Game Presentations and Special Events for the Vancouver team, previously held the same position with the Golden State Warriors. The Director of Media Relations with the Toronto Raptors, John Lashway, worked most recently with the Portland Trail Blazers. The two Canadian teams are banking on people with previous expertise in the NBA to smooth the transition north of the 49th parallel.

While Canadians over the age of 30 may not be as familiar with the game of basketball as they are with hockey, there is one player who will need no introduction. Michael Jordan has been part of the NBA, other than during his brief hiatus and his fling with baseball, for over a decade. His arrival was the final building block in David Stern's reconstruction of pro basketball. Even if someone had never watched an NBA game, or didn't know the rules of basketball, chances are they'd know Michael Jordan. It's not just a North American phenomenon. A survey in China in the early 1990s found that the respondents thought the two greatest men in history were Zhou Enlai and Michael Jordan.

In 1985, when Michael arrived, the NBA already had a pair of superstars, one per coast. In 1979, Larry Bird left Indiana State for the Boston Celtics while Earvin "Magic" Johnson, who led Michigan State to the NCAA crown over Bird's Indiana State in the final, joined the NBA with the Los Angeles Lakers. As Bob Verdi wrote when Bird and Johnson retired, the two were "renaissance, bookend virtuosos if ever there were. Then along came David Stern, the best commissioner on the planet, and Michael Jordan and here we are."

What separated Michael Jordan from Bird and Johnson was not necessarily talent, but more importantly, a company called Nike. In the late 1970s, Nike was a company that made about $100 million a year. By 1991, it grossed over $3 billion in sales. Sources say that about $200 million of that can be attributed directly to Michael Jordan. In 1984, Nike was looking for a basketball superstar. All the big names currently in the NBA were wearing Converse—Larry Bird, Magic Johnson, Isiah Thomas. Nike considered a couple of up-and-coming college players, like Charles Barkley and Patrick Ewing. But the one they really liked was Michael Jordan. Trouble was, Jordan loved Adidas, though he wore Converse as part of his college uniform. He had never worn Nike.

In *Swoosh: The Unauthorized Story of Nike,* J.B. Strasser writes that Nike wanted to make Jordan "one big marketing package.... Michael Jordan couldn't be just a face or a name stamped on a bat, ball, or a pair of sneakers. The Jordan push would have to include everything from shoes to clothes to television commercials." According to the authors of *Swoosh,* Michael Jordan went to Adidas, and offered to go with them, if they would match the Nike deal. Adidas didn't, in one of the biggest marketing gaffes of recent memory, and the rest is sports marketing history.

Nike designed the Air Jordan, a then-revolutionary red and black shoe. In "Triumph of the Swoosh," an article published in *Sports Illustrated* in August 1993, Donald Katz captures the impact of the first time North Americans experienced Air Jordan, in a commercial that transformed television advertising: "Then that basketball rolled across an urban court and a handsome kid in baggy shorts standing at the center of the prime-time image caught the ball off the toe of one of his technicolor shoes. He began to move across the blacktop to the keening sound of jet engines revving before take-off, and by the time the engines had roared at critical scream, Jordan was aloft in a slow-motion tableau so magically drawn out that children who couldn't generate the vertical leap to touch a doorknob could climb right inside the moment."

Unbelievable as it is, in retrospect, the first night Jordan wore the shoes, the Bulls got a $1,000 fine. The NBA had warned Jordan that the shoes violated the NBA "uniformity of uniform" clause. The league threatened to fine him $5,000 if he wore them again, and the third time, the Bulls would forfeit the game. After the first fine, the people from Nike set up a meeting with Commissioner David Stern. Strasser writes: "Stern realized that Air Jordan was going to help the league, and gave his okay." What an understatement that has proven to be. In the first year, sales of Air Jordan were over $100 million. Michael Jordan revolutionized sports marketing. Said Dusty Kidd, of Nike public relations: "Michael was the first athlete to be the corporate focus of a footwear product. He was also really the first athlete marketed on TV."

But Michael Jordan also carried the NBA to the peak of professional sports. "Jordan couldn't have been more perfect if Stern had created him out of sheer wishful thinking. Urbane, articulate, handsome and immensely charismatic, he was also perceived as clean-living, drug-free and well adjusted, and he proved remarkably unthreatening to white people, perhaps because his image was heavily marketed from the beginning of his pro career," writes Pamela Swanigan in her May 1993 article in *The Toronto Star*, "The Selling of Basketball."

Similarly, Kevin O'Malley, Senior Vice-President of Sports Programming for TNT, said recently that Jordan has "had as marked an effect on ratings as any individual in sports."

It has been over a decade since the simultaneous arrival of Michael Jordan, the player, and Air Jordan, the product. These days, savvy marketers come up with annual tabulations of the appeal of athletes. Not surprisingly, basketball players dominate the Q ratings in the 1990s. The Q ratings are determined by surveys and reflect the recognizability and likability of the athletes. The top five from 1994: Michael Jordan, Shaquille O'Neal (who has been carefully groomed by the NBA as Jordan's successor), Scottie Pippen, Charles Barkley and Magic Johnson. Seven of the top nine are from basketball. The other two are baseball's late Mickey Mantle (number six) and Jerry Rice (number eight), of the San Francisco 49ers of the NFL. No current baseball player even makes the top 100.

The results are similar in Canada. In *Teen Trends, A Nation in Motion*, sociology professor Reginald Bibby records his discovery that basketball players have already replaced hockey stars as teen heroes. While the Great One, Wayne Gretzky, made it into the top three, Michael Jordan was number one, with Magic Johnson third in popularity, according to Bibby's survey. He also found that while only about five percent of adult Canadians follow the NBA, that number jumps to almost one-third of Canadian teenagers (28 percent). As Bibby explains the results, "Canadian kids seem to be buying into American culture, primarily as a result of television. They're soaking up American life." In a 1993 article in the *Globe and Mail* analyzing Bibby's findings, Canadian basketball scout Pat Rutledge calls basketball "the perfect game for the fast-food generation."

A big part of the recognition of basketball players comes thanks to the sport's telegenic value. Simply, it makes much better television than hockey, where following the puck has proven difficult for neophytes, to the point where the International Hockey League experimented in the 1994–95 season with a neon puck. Basketball also works better on TV than baseball, which has been criticized for the length of its games and lack of airtime given to establishing individual players.

"Basketball is played in a closely confined space—you can get the whole floor in one camera shot," explained NBC Public Relations Director Ed Markie, in 1993. "The ball is big, so people can see it easily, unlike a hockey puck. It's played at a good pace, and the level of athletic performance is outstanding. The players don't have face masks, so you can see the expression on players' faces. In fact, the camera can literally get into their eyes—and that's just good television, period."

Writes Richard Sandomir in *The New York Times*: "Basketball is the sport of advertisers who prefer muscular, larger-than-life, semi-clothed athletic paragons, showcasing a game that reveals itself easily to a TV viewer. The moves, the joys, the frustrations of 10 men on a contained hardwood stage are easier to read than those of fully clothed, becapped ballplayers on huge diamonds."

Analysts even talk about the "sex appeal" and "intimacy" of basketball that is lacking in hockey and baseball. Baseball players in particular have struggled to attract endorsement contracts, even before the 1994 lockout. Part of the problem lies in the nature of the products themselves: basketball players can sell shoes that are wearable by a mass audience, whereas baseball spikes are not very marketable. Basketball clothing, and more recently oversize hockey jerseys, has a street appeal, even for urban street gangs. One of the few baseball players to attract an endorsement deal is the now-retired

Nolan Ryan, and his best-known commercial was for a pain medication. Deion Sanders and Bo Jackson had endorsement contracts but largely because they played two sports. Frank Thomas of the Chicago White Sox has a deal with Reebok, and Ken Griffey Jr. of the Seattle Mariners is featured in a Nintendo game (the company that also owns the team), but none of the baseball players is even in the same ballpark as their hoops counterparts. The NBA has played up this telegenicity by creating "personas" out of its players. A game is not marketed as "The Phoenix Suns versus the Orlando Magic," for example. It's "Sir" Charles Barkley against Shaq.

The league has also carefully cultivated a new generation of basketball fans by creating its "NBA Inside Stuff" TV show on Saturday mornings and its Stay in School program. While the latter has a virtuous goal, its primary target, nevertheless, is creating a future market for what the league is selling. And the strategy has paid off in spades. In the U.S., a survey by the National Sporting Goods Association shows that the kids from seven to 17, male and female alike, all name basketball as their favourite sport.

More kids call themselves fans of the NBA than of any other sport. A 1995 survey found that 72 percent of kids between 8 and 15 like the NBA, 66 percent are fans of the NFL and 65 percent are baseball fans. Teenagers, though only 10 percent of the population, buy 27 percent of the NBA gear, and three out of every four American kids between 12 and 15 owns an NBA-licensed product. It's a saturation level that is the envy of any corporation in the world.

The NBA works hard to nurture that support. In the 1995 season, the league is giving away trading cards in its magazines. Most other leagues want kids to dish out the allowance money for their sports cards. "Kids are our future season-ticket holders," NBA Marketing Communications Manager Jon Stern told *The Sporting News*. "Since David Stern has become commissioner, we have focused more and more on kids. It's at a young age when you connect with a sport. Therefore, kids have been one of our primary audiences."

The NBA's marketing strategy has been nothing short of brilliant, and it's modelled on some of the great success stories of American commerce. Stern compared the league's success to that of Disney:

"They have theme parks, and we have theme parks. Only we call them arenas. They have characters: Mickey Mouse, Goofy. Our characters are named Magic and Michael. Disney sells apparel; we sell apparel. They make home videos; we make home videos."

By 1994, 10 years after David Stern took over as commissioner, the NBA had become the marketing blueprint for other pro leagues. Some even say that it has overtaken baseball as the top sport in America, and the statistical evidence backs that up. In 1993, the NBA Finals commanded a larger television audience than the World Series (17.5 rating versus 17.3 for baseball). David Stern's reaction is typically savvy: "I really don't think you can say we're America's pastime. I think we really coexist. I've often said football is America's passion, baseball is America's pastime, and basketball is America's game."

Increasingly, basketball is also becoming North America's game, and to Stern's delight, an international success story. The turning point came with the Dream Team at the Barcelona Olympics in 1992. Since then, the NBA has put on the full-court press around the world, setting up business offices on six continents. Rick Welts, President of NBA Properties Inc., calls the Dream Team's success in Barcelona "the most important event in the history of the sport." And well he should, considering that sales of NBA merchandise jumped from $56 million in Europe in 1990 to $250 million after the '92 Olympics. The league has since projected worldwide retail sales in the billions of dollars.

The NBA has gone "international" with its move into the two Canadian markets and is considering expansion to Mexico City some time in the next 10 years. But league executives say they're not really interested in expanding to Europe or Asia, other than for exhibition games, and championship series like the annual McDonald's Open. Terry Lyons, the NBA's Vice-President of International Public Relations, is quoted as saying, "I don't think we'll see NBA expansion into Europe in our lifetime." However, the league will continue to push its product everywhere around the world because the sales of its television product and merchandise are integral to expanding league revenues. Currently, the NBA is seen in 140 countries, with more on the way, and that is what will continue to be the big growth industry for the league.

"What the NBA really wants to do is market the entire sport of pro basketball, run all the big events, sell all the licences and international sponsorships. The revenues from all those kinds of deals could, before the end of the century, dwarf what the NBA makes from its core business," speculates E.M. Swift of *Sports Illustrated*.

David Stern told *Forbes* in 1993: "There are 250 million potential NBA fans in the U.S. and there are 5 billion outside the U.S. We like those numbers."

Still, as the NBA's star has risen internationally, the league has also stumbled over the last two seasons. Ironically, these stumbles come just as the Canadian teams have dished out exorbitant expansion fees to join the prestigious circle of the NBA. It's hard to measure exactly how much the popularity of the NBA is waning. The league's regular season TV ratings were initially down in 1995. Up to the 1995 All-Star Break, ratings were 5.5, down from 7.9 two seasons ago. But with the return of Michael Jordan, ratings went up again. The playoff series featuring Jordan and the Chicago Bulls recorded the highest TV ratings in a decade. The game against Charlotte scored a 9.8 rating, and 20 share, making it the most-watched first-round game in history. (Each rating point represents 954,000 homes.) The overall ratings for the first round were also up from 1994, to 9.1 compared to 7.5 a year ago.

Still, the NBA is not immune to fickle fan disinterest. The ratings for the 1994 NBA Finals were 12.3, down from a record 17.9 the year before. The NBA's response is that the 17.9 rating in 1993 was a blip on the screen , because that final featured Michael Jordan and the Bulls against Charles Barkley and the Suns.

Still, the 1994 Final included the New York Knicks, in the largest American television market, and they still couldn't match the 1993 numbers. The league was undoubtedly disheartened to watch the 1995 Final which the Houston Rockets swept in four games. Only the sizable presence and popularity of Shaquille O'Neal of the Orlando Magic may have salvaged some ratings for an otherwise uneven matchup.

But more serious for the NBA is the proliferation of media reports about the demise in popularity of the league, and in particular, the image problems of some of its up-and-coming stars.

A January 1995 cover story of *Sports Illustrated* was headlined "WAAAAAAH: Petulant Prima Donnas like New Jersey's Derrick Coleman are Bad News for the NBA." The summer before, *SI* had done a similarly damning piece on why the NHL was "hot," and the NBA was "not." It's a theme that is being repeated more and more often by sports commentators across North America. Many of these articles include lists of so-called petulant behaviour from young superstars. For example:

- Scottie Pippen of the Chicago Bulls refused to play the last 1.8 seconds of a playoff game against the New York Knicks. He has also called Chicago fans racist, demanded to be traded and threw a chair when he didn't like a call.
- Chris Webber forced the Golden State Warriors to trade him because he didn't like coach Don Nelson. Nelson eventually quit his job and left coaching for a time.
- Isaiah Rider of the Minnesota Timberwolves called a news conference to criticize his coach, who had told him to "grow up."
- Derrick Coleman of the New Jersey Nets skipped a practice and refused to abide by the team's dress code. Coleman was fined for every offence, but he makes $7.5 million a year, so he eventually just handed his coach a blank cheque.

The most controversial of all have been the ongoing antics of Dennis Rodman, formerly of the San Antonio Spurs. In a much-publicized cover story in *Sports Illustrated*, Rodman poses in a shiny tank top, metallic hot pants and a dog collar. He talks in the article about his fantasies about gay sex, suicide and his relationship with Madonna. While Rodman is considered the best rebounding forward in recent NBA history, he has been an ongoing public relations nightmare for both the Spurs and the league brass. He was traded to Chicago before the start of the 1995 season. To some degree, advertisers seem willing to live with the tougher image of the NBA and are adapting their commercials to suit the up-and-coming stars. For example, Shaquille O'Neal shattered a glass backboard in a 1993 ad for Reebok and Charles Barkley battles Godzilla in one of his commercials.

But the action is also getting ugly on the basketball court. The number of ejections in 1994 had almost doubled since the 1980s, and the league handed out a record $156,250 in fines. While fines are up, scoring is down, and the 1994 season featured some of the lowest scoring games ever in NBA history. A large part of the problem is the astronomical salaries that many of these young players receive, often before they even set foot on the hardwood of the NBA. They make more money than their coaches, and unlike their predecessors, Magic Johnson and Larry Bird, these young players have never known the league's tough times. They've known nothing but the glory days of the NBA.

Some even blame the NBA for creating the young prima donnas through its own marketing genius. "The bottom line is that this is the greatest team game going, and we're doing everything in our power—from the rules, to the publicity, to the images we're creating—to make it an individual sport," Larry Brown, coach of the Indiana Pacers, said when asked about the young players in the NBA. "There's very little talk about team. We don't sell that. We try to establish stars, and this prima donna syndrome is what you get."

For its part, the league is trying to stay cool over the image problem. "It would be foolish to say we don't have any concern about it, " said Russ Granik, Deputy Commissioner of the NBA, in response to the charges in *Sports Illustrated*. "But it hasn't risen to any sort of crisis level. It hasn't diminished the fans' appreciation of our game."

The Toronto Raptors and the Vancouver Grizzlies hope that's true. They have bought more than a sports franchise. For their $125 million expansion fee, they're buying into one of the greatest entertainment packages around. The last thing the Canadian teams want is to see the league stumble, its popularity plateau, or worse, decline.

Chapter Three

CANADIAN ROOTS

Hockey and lacrosse may be Canada's national sports, but the game of hoops also has historical roots north of the border that will no doubt be evoked as the NBA finally makes its move into Canada.

On December 21, 1891, as a class assignment, a YMCA instructor from Almonte, Ontario came up with the fundamentals of the sport that would be called basketball. Dr. James Naismith was attending an international training school for the Y in Springfield, Massachusetts. He was asked during a psychology seminar to come up with a game that would provide physical exercise. He used a soccer ball and two peach baskets, wrote up a couple of simple rules, and the sport was born.

There were other Canadian connections: half of the 10 players on the original basketball team at Springfield College were Canucks. The Canadian connection continued when the NBA was established. The first game in the league's history was played in Toronto, on November 1, 1946, when the New York Knicks beat the hometown Huskies, 68–66, at Maple Leaf Gardens.

Ironically, while basketball has since overtaken hockey in popularity, the original league was conceived of as a way to fill big-market hockey arenas. Five owners of the original six hockey teams of the NHL met in New York on June 6, 1946 to form a professional basketball league, called the BAA—the Basketball Association of America. (Only the Montreal Canadiens opted not to join.) They were joined by five cities from the American Hockey League, and one from Washington.

The Toronto Huskies were described by John Strebig, writing for *The Toronto Star* in May 1994, as "a rag-tag bunch earning about $65 a game and decked out in rumpled green jerseys that were cast-off Boston Celtics uniforms, the shirts turned inside-out and relabelled."

There were two Canadians on the team: Hank Biasatti and Gino Sovran, both from Windsor, Ontario, but they didn't make it past the first couple of games.

Lew Hayman was the managing director of the Huskies. In 1946, he had helped to form the Montreal Alouettes, coached them, and then moved to Toronto when the football season ended. Decades later, Hayman reminisced about the inaugural year of the Huskies. "We started out with 10 or 12 owners, mostly Bay Street stockbrokers, and they put up $10,000 each. We ran out of money before the season was over and they wanted to fold the team. I insisted we finish out the season. We were down $40,000 at the end. Eric Craddock, who had been my partner with the Alouettes, came along and paid it off and we closed the team. We just bellied up and didn't operate again."

The Huskies had one "star" that year—a playing coach named Ed Sadowski, from Indiana, and almost every newspaper report from that time mentions the infamous Sadowski. He was 6'5" and reportedly weighed 249 pounds, and one man called him "the missing man mountain." It seems that Ed Sadowski ran off after the team's record reached a miserable three wins and 10 losses. Legend has it he walked into the locker room after the Huskies were badly beaten by Cleveland, took off his uniform and said, "I'm through."

John Strebig, a young fan in the early days of the Huskies, writes in *The Toronto Star*: "The Huskies had the thinnest playbook in the league—one play. That play was: throw it to Ed Sadowski. Now Big Ed was the Huskies' centre and he was big, about six-foot-one, whether you measured height or circumference. Big Ed hung around the offensive basket, wheezing a lot, and did his thing."

In other words, the Toronto Huskies were a fairly uninspiring team and were often outscored two to one in that first and only season.

They played at Maple Leaf Gardens, and prices were $2.50 for boxes, $2 for blues, $1.25 for greens and 75¢ for grays. Those were also the prices for the Leafs (a much better team) and were considered pricey for that time.

The Huskies finished that first season with a 22–38 record, tied with the Boston Celtics for last place in their division, and did not make the playoffs.

"They'd draw five to seven thousand," recalls sports writer Jim Coleman,"but basketball is a game of crowd heat. In a big rink like the Gardens those crowds were lost."

In the 1970s, Leafs owner Harold Ballard and entrepreneur Ruby Richman toyed with the idea of bringing the NBA to Toronto. They shipped in the Buffalo Braves for eight-game and 10-game packages, beginning in 1973, and considered buying the team. The Braves fared all right at the box office, averaging about 7,700 spectators per game.

Writer Trent Frayne reminisces about the Braves visits to Toronto: "Braves players complained that the arena [Maple Leaf Gardens] was cold, that the players tightened up sitting on the bench. That was because the basketball court lay on top of the ice surface over which a layer of styrofoam was placed."

Ballard apparently considered the players a bunch of whiners and suggested they could play harder. Perhaps then he would lay down a little more styrofoam. During the spring of 1974, it looked as if Maple Leaf Gardens Ltd. was going to buy the Braves. But the deal fell through, and Richman and Ballard decided to try for an expansion franchise instead. However, Ballard was not interested in being the sole investor in a new franchise and Richman was not able to secure a partner to put up the other 50 percent of the financing for the team. No one was willing to pitch in half of the estimated $6.5 million expansion fee, despite the fact that the league had already granted the franchise for the 1975–76 season. Richman blamed the economic turndown of the mid-1970s for his inability to find a partner for the deal. Ruby Richman tried several more times to get the NBA north of the border. Besides the Braves, Richman was also involved in discussions over the years about bringing the Detroit Pistons, the Houston Rockets, the San Diego Clippers and the Cleveland Cavaliers to Canada, but none of the bids ever came to fruition.

In 1982, the rumours of the NBA coming north of the border started again; this time the protagonists were three Toronto lawyers: Albert Strauss, Don Smith and Joe Bolla. Again, they were not able to attract enough investors to make the expansion dream a reality and the plans were put back on the shelf.

The Cleveland Cavaliers came the closest to moving north to Canada. In 1983, Cavs owner Ted Stepien announced it was "999 to one he'd be moving his Cavaliers to Toronto." He ended up selling the team to the Gund brothers, who also owned Richfield Coliseum in Cleveland. Ironically, Stepien was also the man behind another disastrous basketball experiment in Toronto.

The year was 1983, and instead of the NBA coming to Toronto, the Continental Basketball Association was going to try its luck in Hogtown. The CBA was started in 1946, just a few weeks before the NBA, under the name of the Eastern League. Later, it would be called the Eastern Basketball Association. In 1967, most of the best players in the Eastern League jumped to the American Basketball Association, which had been created to compete with the NBA. That lasted until 1975, when the two leagues merged to form a revitalized NBA. A few years later, the CBA picked up the competitive slack, and had gradually expanded to 12 teams by the time the Toronto Tornados appeared in 1983. (There had been another earlier Canadian franchise in the CBA in Lethbridge, Alberta.) Over the years, the Continental Basketball Association has developed into a kind of feeder system for the NBA and a league of last resort for older players on the decline.

The Toronto Tornados would avoid the earlier mistake of the NBA's Toronto Huskies, choosing to play at Varsity Arena, at the University of Toronto, rather than the chilly, cavernous Maple Leaf Gardens. That would be one of the only good decisions that the team would make. The Tornados would last only two seasons in Toronto, and the team's very public failure made many Torontonians wonder if pro basketball would ever fly north of the border.

The team was owned by Ted Stepien, whose track record as a franchise owner was suspect before he even came to Toronto. Stepien was also the owner of the Cleveland Cavaliers of the NBA, and reportedly lost millions on the team over three years.

Stepien had been a controversial figure in his home town of Cleveland, so it probably wasn't surprising that he caused quite a stir in Toronto as well. He had made his money from advertising: in the late 1940s, he started an ad agency with a loan of $500 from his father. The agency went on to become a national brokerage for want ads and by the late 1970s had $60 million in bookings and 35 offices, including six in Canada.

Stepien's first foray into basketball came in 1980 when he purchased a 37 percent stake in the Cleveland Cavaliers for $2 million. Eventually, he would own 82 percent, and that's when the trouble really started. When he took over the Cavs, Stepien decided to really put his mark on the team. He changed the team's fight song to a polka tune (Stepien is of Polish origin) and he hired the Super Fan, who sat in the stands during the games tearing apart aluminum cans with his teeth. He called the cheerleaders "the Teddy Bears." Soon, Stepien's colourful antics were being ridiculed by the media.

"He always wanted to be accepted into the sports community here," recalls sportswriter Bill Nichols. "He cried for acceptance. But he never made it."

The NBA didn't care as much about the polka music and the Super Fan as they did about some of Stepien's basketball decisions. In 1980, he started trading away draft choices for players and reportedly paying them hefty salaries, well above the current league norm. Finally, Stepien had made so many trades that the league Commissioner, Larry O'Brien, apparently put a one-month moratorium on any player movements by the Cavaliers. After that, Stepien reportedly had to get league permission for trades. Despite any sizable payroll, the Cavaliers were losers on the court. In two years, Stepien hired and fired five coaches. The team became known as "the Cadavers" and the fans stayed away en masse, with Cleveland constantly recording the lowest attendance figures in the league. In 1983, Stepien decided to sell out to the Gund brothers, who also owned the Minnesota North Stars of the NHL. The Toronto experiment was as great a fiasco as Stepien's experience with the Cavaliers.

When the season began, in the fall of 1983, the Tornados had only sold 162 season tickets, and the team had no community profile, to the point that few people even knew they were in Toronto. The front office staff was led by General Manager and Coach Gerald Oliver, who used to be an assistant NBA coach, and team Publicist Malcolm Kelly, whose only previous experience was as a reporter for a paper in Midland, Ontario.

The following story, recorded in *The Toronto Star* after the demise of the team, is vintage Toronto Tornados: "A radio station offers two weeks of publicity leading up to a contest to choose the team's cheerleaders. The contest is to be at the Heaven discotheque where pert young things would strut their stuff. But Stepien cancels it because he desperately wants to be on hand to judge and can't make it that night. By the time it's held, Stepien has decided he doesn't care any more. Only 16 girls show up, eight are chosen as Teddy Bears, none of whom will keep Karen Kain awake at nights.

"Game nights at Varsity Arena are choreographed by the Marx brothers. Everyone runs around like decapitated chickens.... One night, Stepien arrives, finds no heat in the building and no one to sing the national anthem. He rails at Kelly, walks over to the Teddy Bears and asks them to sing it. They refuse. He gets mad and fires them." (Wayne Parrish, *The Toronto Star*, January 31, 1985)

While there was a lot of mismanagement with the Toronto Tornados, their blatant failure to draw fans caused some speculation about the potential for basketball in the Toronto market. The team rarely drew more than 1,000, though the Tornados did draw 3,000 fans towards the end of its second season when they were fighting to make the playoffs. But at the opening game of the next season, the team only drew 700, and that number fell even more as the season wore on, averaging about 300 fans per game before the team pulled out. Then General Manager Keith Fowler told reporters, "There are some people here who like basketball but Toronto isn't a basketball town. Maybe people would like to come out to see guys like Larry Bird and Magic Johnson. Maybe then, you'd get a TV contract and the newspapers would give you regular coverage."

At the same time that the Tornados were faring so miserably, Ted Stepien was lobbying the Molson Brewery to bid for an NBA franchise for the 1985–86 season, with Stepien as a minority shareholder. Stepien apparently sent a "glowing" 34-page proposal on the bid, which would have cost $14–16 million at the time. Molson had its own report done, and as a Molson spokesperson put it, the report was less than promising on the potential for the NBA in Toronto: "We found the level of interest not as significant as Ted did."

In the end, Ted Stepien lost about $1 million on the Toronto Tornados. In December 1985, Stepien moved the team from Toronto to Pensacola, Florida. In their first home game, the team drew a franchise-record 3,611. It took them only a week to sell 169 season tickets, more than they had during their entire last season in Toronto. Said the team's assistant coach of the move: "The first night in Pensacola kind of reminded me of a basketball game. People were cheering, yelling at the ref, things like that." Toronto, it seemed, was not much of a basketball town.

Just a few months after the Tornados headed south, basketball was again big news in Toronto. The NBA was expanding, and despite the recent debacle with the Continental Basketball Association, a number of Toronto groups were hotly pursuing the idea of bringing big-league hoops to town.

The 1986 expansion of the NBA was an important development in the ongoing metamorphosis of the league. At the time, there were 23 teams in the NBA, and the original plan was to expand by two franchises. But the league's upswing in popularity was already catching a lot of attention and cities were eager to get on board. *Boston Globe* reporter Bob Ryan was at the expansion meetings in Phoenix in 1986 and called them "the most significant occurrence off the court in basketball history," an eye-opening experience as to the league's potential for the 23 existing teams.

The expansion committee received bids from Orlando, Charlotte, Miami, Minnesota, Anaheim, Vancouver and Toronto. The interest was so great that the league decided to expand by four teams, rather than the original two. Three of those four expansion teams turned into NBA success stories (Minnesota being the exception), and Vancouver and Toronto would be included in a later round of expansion.

Media from around the world gathered in Deerfield, Illinois as Michael Jordan announced his retirement from the Chicago Bulls. October 6, 1993.

NBA stars Manute Bol and Chris Mullen pose with the Eiffel Tower in October 1994 during a pre-season NBA promotional tour in Europe.

Canadian Dr. James Naismith, the inventor of basketball, poses with the ball and the peach basket that inspired the game.

Players from the Toronto Huskies, the city's entry in the original NBA in 1946. The team folded after one season.

Former NBA superstar Magic Johnson, left, and Michael Cohl talk to the New York media about the Cohl–Ballard–Johnson bid for an NBA franchise in Toronto. Earlier in the day, the group had made their presentation to the NBA expansion committee. September 20, 1993.

Ted Stepien, former owner of the Cleveland Cavaliers of the NBA, brought professional basketball back to Toronto in 1985 with the Toronto Tornados.

The World Basketball League was another short-lived effort to bring pro basketball to Canada. Dayton vs. Calgary, 1988.

The World Basketball League set a height limit of 6'5" for its players to differentiate itself from the NBA but the league never really caught on with fans.

All five of the Bitove children have held senior positions in the family business, under the chairmanship of their father, John Bitove Sr. From left to right: John Jr., Jordan, Tom, Nick and Vonna Bitove.

John Bitove Jr. celebrates winning the NBA franchise for Toronto with sons, Brett, 3, and J.J., 5. September 30, 1993.

Proposed arena for Bay–Dundas site. The arena design was later rejected as too small to accommodate both basketball and hockey.

Lenscape

A relieved John Bitove Jr. joins then Ontario Premier Bob Rae and NBA Commissioner David Stern in announcing that they have struck a deal to end the Pro-Line dispute. The deal was announced February 10, 1994, 98 days after the Bitove group had been granted the franchise.

The view from the 500 level at SkyDome.

The proposed Raptor stadium site, showing the properties owned by Canada Post and Marathon Realty.

Air Canada

The 1985 Toronto expansion bid was, as in the 1990s, a conglomerate of business and entertainment interests, including:
- David Fingold and his brother Paul, then major shareholders in Cineplex Odeon,
- Dusty Cohl, lawyer and founder of the Festival of Festivals,
- his son Robert Cohl, Vice-President of Fobasco, a private holding company owned by the Fingolds,
- Michael Cohl, President of Concert Productions Inc. (CPI),
- Bill Ballard, son of Harold and Vice-President of CPI, and
- Wilt Chamberlain, former NBA great.

The team would have played at Maple Leaf Gardens, owned by Harold Ballard, who had agreed to a long-term lease to fulfill the arena requirement of the bid application. There was, in fact, a second bidding group, though considerably lower profile than the Ballard–Cohl–Chamberlain contingent. It was led by Toronto lawyer Norman Freedman and backed by some unnamed corporations. What was different about Freedman's group was that they proposed splitting the prospective franchise's season between SkyDome and Copps Coliseum in Hamilton. Freedman actively promoted his concept by bringing an NBA exhibition game to Copps Coliseum on October 26, 1986, featuring the New York Knicks and Detroit Pistons. After the Toronto group lost its 1987 expansion bid, Freedman continued to promote the NBA in Canada, this time bringing in the Houston Rockets and the Pistons to Copps Coliseum on October 30, 1987. (One of the players in that exhibition game was John Salley, then with the Pistons, who would later be picked by Toronto in the 1995 expansion draft and would join former teammate Isiah Thomas on the Raptors. Salley said of the Canadian basketball fans: "I was really surprised at the size of the crowd and the enthusiasm. I always knew hockey was number one up here, and I thought maybe there was some kind of problem with basketball because there wasn't a team." And prophetically, Salley added he wouldn't mind some day playing for a Toronto entry in the NBA. "I took a drive through Forest Hill this morning and I wouldn't mind living there," said Salley.)

But it would take until 1995 for that expansion team to officially arrive in Toronto. One of the biggest problems in 1987 was money. The Toronto group originally expected the franchise to cost about $25 million, but the expansion fee was placed at $32.5 million, about $42 million Canadian, and the money had to be paid upfront. The most recent team to join the NBA as an expansion franchise had been the Dallas Mavericks in 1980. They had paid $15 million US to join the league. Unfortunately for the expansion hopefuls, the sale of a minority interest in the Boston Celtics the year before had inflated the value of the Boston club to about $90 million, which in turn inflated the expansion fee, particularly with so many strong bidders eager to join the league.

The $42 million Canadian ended up being a little steep for the Toronto group. "They're asking a very big price and an extremely tough arrangement on the payment of it. We're very interested in having an NBA team for Toronto and haven't given up on getting one in the future. But we're not in the business of financial hari-kari. We just can't commit that amount of money to a franchise, if we are offered one," said David Fingold at the time.

His comments echo some of the recent Canadian reactions to the $125 million US expansion fee paid by the Toronto and Vancouver franchises in the 1990s.

Still, the Toronto group did make its pitch on October 20, 1986, in Phoenix, Arizona. Each of the bidders had 30 minutes to convince the expansion committee of the merits of its application. Dusty Cohl explained his group's strategy in *The Toronto Star*: "Toronto itself is a big selling point because word of what a great city this is has spread in the past few years. We'll talk of the sound economy, the great record as a sports town, stressing, of course, the success of the Blue Jays and such events as Hulkamania and the Indy car race. One of our selling points is the way Toronto would fit into the Atlantic division, which is the only one in the NBA now with five teams [the others have six clubs]. We would be an easy road trip for those clubs."

The NBA expansion committee also wanted to know how many season tickets each franchise would be able to sell. The Toronto bid had about 2,000 sold, with $100 up front. In comparison, the Orlando group had 11,000 applications, also with $100 deposit, Miami had 7,300 and the Minnesota bid had 5,700. When the expansion announcement was made, there were a couple of surprises, but it was bad news for the Toronto group, which had realized by then that it was a long shot at best. The frontrunners were there: Minnesota and Miami. The two surprises were Orlando and Charlotte. Charlotte had been described as "a small city which isn't a major TV market." Orlando had pursued a franchise aggressively, and had plans underway for a new arena, if the bid was successful. The expansion committee had originally planned on granting two franchises, but had been so impressed that they granted four new teams. Charlotte and Miami would join the league for the 1988-89 season, with Minneapolis and Orlando joining the following year.

While not a surprise, the rejection was a disappointment to the Toronto group. The writing had been on the wall: Toronto and Anaheim were the only two cities that the expansion committee had not visited. There was reportedly some concern from the NBA governors about Toronto because it was perceived as a hockey city. Michael Cohl, of CPI, said later, "They were worried about the franchise failing. It would have been our money but it would have been their embarrassment. They really listened to us but they needed more proof." Cohl admitted to being surprised that the league had decided to take four expansion teams, including two in Florida, but acknowledged, "At $32 million each, they would have been crazy not to take four teams. When they set the price and people were agreeing to it, you knew they would admit more than one."

The most compelling argument in favour of the four winning franchises was an economic one. The Toronto market lacked one crucial ingredient that the NBA was looking for in the mid-1980s: a major television market. A high-ranking executive of an NBA team told *The Toronto Star*: "Toronto is an unknown as a basketball market and any projections of how a team might draw is just speculation. While Toronto adds nothing to the U.S. television market—and the Canadian TV market isn't likely to add anything to the NBA income—Miami is the largest market in the States without a team, Orlando isn't far behind and [the] Minnesota economy is one of the best in the country."

Meanwhile, the league felt that Charlotte was a basketball hotbed and was further convinced by the impressive number of deposits for season tickets that the Charlotte ownership group had collected.

However, all was not lost for Toronto. While expansion north of the border would be put on the back burner, there was no doubt that the league was interested. The Canadian city didn't fit into the current marketing plans of the NBA, but the groundwork had been laid for the next time around. One NBA executive even foreshadowed the NBA's eventual expansion to Canada: "Six years down the road if the NBA growth continues, and there's no reason to project that it won't when the awesome upswing in interest in college ball is considered, Toronto will be a leading candidate. There's a lot in the city's favour at the present time but there is just too much offered by the other applicants that Toronto doesn't have."

After losing the expansion bid, Bill Ballard said, "I still think you'll see basketball here in the next five years. I don't know of any cities left that would be better for basketball." It took slightly longer than five years, but Bill Ballard was right about the eventual arrival of the NBA in Canada. Interestingly, he would again be a losing bidder.

While basketball hoops are a staple of most American neighbourhoods, they have only recently become common in Canadian suburbs. The success of the NBA's marketing, seeping across the border on television, is also reflected in the number of Canadians playing organized basketball. The estimated number of Canadians playing basketball in 1980 was around 200,000. By 1995, that number had tripled, with more than half playing in structured leagues. But basketball participation has a long way to go to knock off hockey, which has 1.4 million participants, with almost 500,000 in organized leagues. Still, basketball has a simple advantage over other sports: it's inexpensive and easy to play. While the NFL may sell a lot of merchandise, and the NHL is increasingly following in the marketing footsteps of the NBA, basketball is the easiest sport for kids to pick up and emulate their heroes.

Says Canadian athlete recruiter Pat Rutledge, "It's a cheap game to play. All you need is a ball, running shoes and a hoop, whereas in football and hockey, the cost of equipment is seven,

BASKETBALL IN CANADA

Participation by province (1994)

Province	# Certified Coaches	# Players 10–14	15–19	20–35	TOTAL
Alberta	2,627	16,000	7,000	4,000	27,000
B.C.	1,559	30,000	19,000	7,000	56,000
Manitoba	1,127	18,000	6,500	1,200	25,700
N.B.	802	4,000	2,400	1,000	7,400
Nfld.	555	4,000	4,000	1,300	9,300
N.S.	574	2,500	4,000	1,000	7,500
Ontario	3,536	60,000	32,000	12,000	104,000
P.E.I.	86	2,000	500	400	2,900
Quebec	1,914	40,000	24,000	3,000	67,000
Sask.	1,459	20,000	8,000	2,000	30,000
TOTALS	**14,472**	**196,500**	**107,400**	**32,900**	**336,800**

Source: Basketball Canada

eight, nine hundred dollars and that automatically eliminates a third of the population from being able to participate in a sport because of social or economic abilities."

The proliferation of the game has also raised the quality of play in Canada. During the 1994–95 school year, there were 71 Canadian players, 43 men and 28 women, playing in the U.S. college system. Canadians are also playing in the European pro leagues and in the NBA—Rick Fox of the Boston Celtics and Bill Wennington of the Chicago Bulls are Canadians by birth.

Despite the sport's growing success at attracting players, the recent failure of two basketball leagues has raised some questions about Canadian fan support. The first failure was the World Basketball League, featuring small players under 6'5". The people behind the World Basketball League loved to describe their league as basketball the way James Naismith intended it to be when he first invented the game in 1891: a fast and aggressive contest not dominated by "genetic rarities," like the seven-footers who were then dominating the NBA. The league's Commissioner was Memphis lawyer Steven Erhart. He had been involved in the disastrous United States Football League, which tried to compete with the National Football League and was a bust.

In 1987, the height-restricted basketball league's founders, including Dennis Murphy and Ben Hatskin, tried to organize the basketball teams under the moniker "International Basketball Association." (Murphy had been one of the founders of the American Basketball Association, whose teams were now part of the NBA, and Hatskin was instrumental in starting the World Hockey Association.) Originally, the plans called for 12 teams, including a franchise in Vancouver and another somewhere in southern Ontario, either Toronto or Hamilton. The IBA was specifically designed NOT to compete with the NBA and would be a summer league, running from May to September. The franchise fees were $100,000 US and there would be a salary cap of $600,000 US per team.

A familiar name was behind the proposed southern Ontario franchise in the International Basketball Association: Ruby Richman, who years ago had tried to bring the NBA to Toronto and was now working as a "sports consultant." Richman was very aware of the previous basketball disasters in the city and was eager to avoid the mistakes of the ill-fated Toronto Tornados of the Continental Basketball Association. "The CBA was recognized as minor league and not, in my memory, has Toronto ever bought a minor league product. That's why I haven't even considered Varsity Arena. The stigma of the CBA's still attached."

Reporters wondered why, knowing Toronto fans as he did, Richman thought they'd be willing to come watch a league of short players. "What we've got here is a brand new product, the best six-foot-four league in the world. We've got to market it properly and, ultimately, profitably. And, if we can't influence that public perception...well, we're just not going to be around long," he explained.

They weren't. In February 1988, Richman announced that he was moving his planned IBA franchise from Toronto/Hamilton to Buffalo, saying it was for economic reasons. "The difference between the American and Canadian dollars, anywhere from 30 to

35 percent, is the difference between making and losing money. In Toronto, we would need to average about 4,000 in attendance; in Buffalo, we would need 3,000. The difference between those two figures is a monstrous hurdle for us."

Richman called Buffalo "basketball crazy," but seemed less convinced about Toronto fans. "I've really banged my head against the wall for 20 years to bring basketball here, and it's possible that Toronto is just not a basketball city. I think it is, but we see ourselves as the New York of Canada and we want the NBA in Toronto or nothing."

Richman's franchise in Buffalo never did get off the ground either.

In May 1988, the league changed its name to the World Basketball League and started its season with six teams: Calgary, Fresno, Chicago, Las Vegas, Vancouver and Youngstown (Ohio). It got off to a bumpy start in the spring of 1988. The owner of the Vancouver Nighthawks pulled out in June and the league was forced to sponsor the team for the rest of the season. The Calgary franchise, "the 88s," was one of the more successful teams, drawing an average of 3,300 spectators per game, the highest in the league. The team was owned by a consortium of Calgarians headed by Jon Havelock, a lawyer for Amoco Canada Petroleum Co. and a Calgary alderman.

By the second season, the WBL had lost the Vancouver franchise and the Fresno team, where owner Edd Becker had lost about $1 million and only had about 100 season tickets sold for the next season. The league added teams in Springfield, Illinois and Worcester, Massachusetts. In the third season, there was a second Canadian team in Saskatoon, dubbed the Saskatchewan Storm. The league had made some inroads by its third year. A major boost came with the signing of a three-year TV deal worth $3 million with SportsChannel America. League Commissioner Steven Erhart liked to point out that the WBL championship game, starting at 12:30 a.m., got better ratings on SportsChannel than some NHL games in prime time. The World Basketball League also became more international in 1989, adding a series of games against teams from Europe and the Soviet Union that would count in the league standings.

However, despite an average player's salary of between $15,000 and $20,000 for four months, none of the teams was able to make money. The league had the cable deal and it also had an agreement with Coca-Cola whereby the players would wear Coke advertising on the backs of their jerseys. Erhart said he was negotiating with other large multinational companies. He insisted that with some more marketing the World Basketball League would carve out its niche in professional sports. Because of the low team payrolls, he was optimistic that the owners wouldn't be losing too much money and could hang on until the league became profitable.

Canadian investors continued to back the WBL, adding franchises in Halifax in 1991 and Hamilton and Winnipeg in 1992. However, that was the season when the league began to unravel. Hamilton was never a hit. Saskatchewan drew reasonably well, as did Halifax. Although Winnipeg had some good crowds initially, reality set in after a few months. While the basketball was entertaining, and owner Sam Katz, a crafty concert promoter, had many promotions and enticements, it was tough to pull people in for semi-pro basketball on a summer evening. It was a confusing season, from a fan's perspective, because the schedule kept changing as teams folded and the league shrunk in size. It was difficult to get any sense of team rivalries or favourite players because the teams themselves were falling like flies.

In June 1992, the Jacksonville Stingrays and Florida Jades folded in mid-season, a first for the league, which had always managed to keep teams going until the end of the year. A month later, the Erie Wave packed it in, and on August 1, the World Basketball League suspended operations.

Jon Havelock of the Calgary 88s had been with the league since its inception but he admitted he was "fed up with the difficulties of trying to keep pro basketball alive in Canada." "I'm 37 going on 93," said Havelock.

Ironically, basketball season ticket holders were offered circus tickets in exchange for the games they were missing in the defunct league. "One good circus deserves another," quipped Geoff Pickering of GWE, the company left paying the bills in Calgary after the WBL went bust.

The rest of the Canadian teams showed remarkable optimism, and in the summer of 1993, the six-team National Basketball League rose from the ashes of the World League. In its first season, the NBL had a 40-game schedule over the summer months. There were teams in Halifax, Sydney, N.S., Winnipeg, Saskatoon, Hamilton and Montreal. As well, the Canadian national team committed to a 30-game schedule as part of the league.

Again, the league was plagued with problems early on. On June 10, National Basketball League President Sam Katz suspended the operations of the Montreal Dragons. The team had run into financial problems, but according to another general manager in the league, the Montreal owners were responsible for their own demise.

"They've expended about 70 percent of the budget in the first month," said Mike Doyle of the Halifax Windjammers. "The people that were involved with running the franchise had a different vision of what the league was and what the expenses were. All the other franchises were committed to the salary cap, but they were running it like an NBA franchise."

The Montreal team had apparently spent $28,000 in players' accommodations alone in its first month of operation, putting players up in hotel suites! When the Vancouver team went bust in the WBL, the league ran the team until the end of the season, but the NBL did not have the financial resources to carry the Dragons and the team was immediately disbanded.

Meanwhile, there were problems on another front. The owner of the Hamilton Skyhawks had taken out advertisements in newspapers across the country looking for investors and offering to move his franchise in return. The Hamilton team had only been drawing about 900 fans per game. The owner of the Skyhawks was none other than Ted Stepien, the man behind the Toronto Tornados debacle in the 1970s. Canadian basketball fans seemed reluctant to put their support behind the new league, concerned that it would go the way of its predecessor and leave unhappy creditors and fans. In fact, the Halifax Windjammers even went so far as to put their season ticket money into a trust fund. The team would draw a percentage of money from the fund after every game, putting the rest aside in case the league ran into financial difficulties.

By its second season, the NBL was struggling to draw fans. The Windjammers in Halifax were only drawing about 1,500 a game in May, about 2,000 less than what was needed to break even. The league's average attendance was around 1,000 fans a game, with the new Edmonton franchise really struggling financially. The Edmonton team was formerly the Hamilton Skyhawks, the Ted Stepien-owned franchise. He had sold that team and was now an investor in the Cape Breton franchise. Stepien was also blamed by many for the ultimate demise of the National Basketball League.

First, Stepien threatened to move his franchise from Sydney to Saint John, New Brunswick, where he hoped to get more local investors involved with the team. He says that the deal fell through because Sam Katz resigned as league president and the investors backed out. A source told a very different story to *The Daily News*. "Stepien, according to the source, changed the agreement so many times that the business group lost confidence in Stepien's integrity."

Stepien had been trying for years to bring winter basketball to Canada, including his cursed experiment with the Toronto Tornados. He decided to try to force the other owners in the NBL to agree to a winter season or he would pull the plug on his franchise. "I'm a firm believer that basketball should be played in the winter," said Stepien. "And for years, it's been played in Canada in the summer and it's never made a cent for any team."

The suggestion of a winter basketball season came to a vote of the owners in the National Basketball League, and no one supported Stepien's idea. Walter Newton, one of the co-owners of the Halifax Windjammers, describes what happened next. "So Stepien said he was out. Winnipeg said they simply wanted out. It was finally put to a vote."

There were six teams remaining in the league, and the vote was 3–1 in favour of disbanding, with two abstentions. In July 1994, the National Basketball League suspended operations, bringing another experiment with pro basketball in Canada to an unhappy and unprofitable close.

Those failures aside, the NBA has a couple of drawing cards that none of the previous basketball leagues had. Commissioner David

Stern is a cautious and shrewd investor who would never gamble with his league's success unless he was sure the concept would fly, and he will put all of the league's resources into ensuring the NBA flies in Canada.

The sport's popularity among teenagers will spread to the thirty-something crowd once the NBA marketing machine goes into full speed.

In 1991, former Canadian National Team Coach Jack Donahue was asked what it would take to make his favourite sport popular in Canada, and he said then that the key was having a Canadian team in the NBA. "That would change an awful lot of things. You'd have the sport in the news on TV every day, you'd have it in the papers every day. I think it would be just like what happened with baseball. Look what the Jays and Expos did for baseball's popularity in Canada."

There is also the peculiar Toronto mentality to love all things American. As *Toronto Star* sports columnist Dave Perkins describes it, "Basketball also is an American pastime and you know how this trendy city loves to be loved by Americans and tries to be like them."

In August 1994, Torontonians got to test-drive pro basketball, as the Raptors organization hosted the World Championship of Basketball. The final weekend of the tournament attracted over 32,000 to SkyDome, showcasing the growing support for basketball, at least on a one-time basis. The Raptors and Grizzlies hope the enthusiasm can translate into long-term support, even after the novelty of the new teams wears off.

CHAPTER FOUR

THE EXPANSION EXPERIENCE

The National Basketball Association doesn't like failure. That has made the league extraordinarily cautious when it comes to expansion. However, the NBA brass have found a formula for success when it comes to establishing new teams, and though the foray north of the border involves some new turf, the league is hoping that Toronto and Vancouver will join the list of previous expansion stories with happy endings. The teams in Orlando, Charlotte and Miami, despite some minor setbacks, have been triumphant both on and off the court. There is one exception to the expansion bliss and that is the woeful saga of the Minnesota Timberwolves, which can serve as a cautionary tale to the two new Canadian teams.

The 1986 expansion was a turning point in the history of the NBA and laid the groundwork for the eventual inclusion of the Canadian franchises. The Canadian teams have made pilgrimages to talk to management personnel with the Magic, the Hornets and the Heat, in order to garner their advice on preparing for the rookie experience as a new franchise in the NBA. There are some interesting lessons to be learned from each of the three successful teams.

The Miami Heat have been the "comeback kids" of the new expansion franchises. The Heat struggled through some pretty lean years before reaching the playoffs for the first time in 1992, the team's fourth season. (The Heat lost in the first round to the Chicago Bulls.)

EXPANSION FACTS

Toronto is the NBA's 15th expansion team and Vancouver is the 16th since 1966. Here are some facts and figures:

	1st SEASON	W.L.	1st .500 SEASON	W.L.
Chicago Bulls	1966–67	33–48	1970–71	51–31
San Diego Rockets	1967–68	15–67	1974–75	41–41
Seattle Supersonics	1967–68	23–59	1971–72	47–35
Milwaukee Bucks	1968–69	27–55	1969–70	56–26
Phoenix Suns	1968–69	16–66	1970–71	48–34
Buffalo Braves	1970–71	22–60	1973–74	42–40
Cleveland Cavaliers	1970–71	15–67	1975–76	49–33
Portland Trail Blazers	1970–71	29–53	1976–77	49–33
New Orleans Jazz	1974–75	22–44	1983–84	45–37
Dallas Mavericks	1980–81	15–67	1983–84	43–39
Charlotte Hornets	1988–89	20–62	1992–93	44–38
Miami Heat	1988–89	15–67	1983–84	42–40
Orlando Magic	1989–90	18–64	1992–93	41–41
Minnesota Timberwolves	1989–90	22–60	—	—

Source: The Vancouver Sun

Anything would have been better than that first season. There were plenty of Heat jokes at the time, including several told by Pat Williams, General Manager of the Orlando Magic, the Heat's rival team in Florida. Williams' line was: "The only difference between the launching of the Heat and the Titanic is that the Titanic had a band." Another Williams' quip noted that the Heat lost so frequently that "their mascot should be a Democrat." Yet another joke around the league went as follows: "May the wind be at your back and the Heat on your schedule."

The Miami Heat made their mark in NBA history in their first season taking until December 14 to record their first victory, an 89–88 win over the Los Angeles Clippers. Along the way the Heat surpassed the previous record for futility (0–15), which had been shared by the 1949–50 Nuggets, the 1970–71 expansion Cleveland

Cavaliers and the 1972–73 Philadelphia 76ers. However, the Heat did manage to avoid one nasty historical record: the Philadelphia 76ers still hold the record for worst season (9–73). That first year, the Heat ended up with 15 victories, and at one point, even went on a three-game winning streak!

These numbers are significant for the Toronto Raptors and Vancouver Grizzlies because traditionally, the first couple of seasons are rough for expansion franchises and the Canadian teams could find themselves challenging some of these records for futility. It's part of the expansion experience.

The Miami Heat were, ironically, a wild success off the court in those early years. The team was originally the idea of Billy Cunningham, a former player and coach with the Philadelphia 76ers, and Lewis Schaffel, an NBA player agent. They were joined by a syndicate of investors which included singer Julio Iglesias, producer Zev Bufman and Ted (Micky) Arison, founder of Carnival Cruise Lines. In 1994, Arison bought out Cunningham and Schaffel to acquire controlling interest in the team.

The Heat games reflected the entertainment backgrounds of the ownership group. In December 1988, *The Globe and Mail* put it this way: "A Heat game is an event, spiced with glitz and glamour—a live jazz band, scantily clad dancing girls, the occasional laser show and elegantly dressed cocktail waitresses who serve drinks to fans in their seats."

As with the teams in Los Angeles and New York, you could often spot celebrities at Heat games, including Don Johnson, Frank Sinatra, Liza Minnelli and Sammy Davis Jr. At the concession stands, Heat fans could buy Cuban coffee and a rum drink called "Frozen Miami Heat."

Initially, the Miami ownership group was concerned about ticket sales in the Florida market. Miami had a team in the former American Basketball Association—the Floridians—that had folded because of a lack of interest. The University of Miami Hurricanes football team was the national champion three times within a decade but they didn't always sell out their games. The city's sizable Latin American population was also considered to be more a potential baseball audience than basketball fans. Still, Miami reached the required season ticket total in late 1987 almost a year before the team's first regular season game. "I think we were lucky that our commissioner made it so tough, " said Pauline Winnick, Executive Vice-President of the Heat and one of the highest-placed women in the NBA.

The Heat had another advantage in their rookie years: the brand new $50 million Miami Arena, built specifically for basketball. The one early concern with the arena was its location in a less than desirable part of the city, but that did not discourage the fans. The average attendance over the team's first four years has been 14,982 in an arena that seats 15,008, with 13,000 season-ticket holders. It's also a very impressive group of fans and has been an upscale crowd since Day One. "The demographics of our season-ticket holders exceed the American Express profile, which is extraordinary," says Pauline Winnick. "I see all these people coming to the games, and I know we broke the code for downtown Miami."

The team has also made breakthroughs in marketing specifically to female basketball fans. The NBA has traditionally had the highest percentage of female spectators of the major pro sports and the Heat found ways to cultivate that. "We hold clinics specifically for the women; we want to educate the fan," said Billy Cunningham in 1993, while he was still part of the Heat ownership. "We've tried very hard to do that. We always have well over 1,000 women show up for the clinics. They ask great questions and they're perceptive."

"I suspected men would buy tickets," said Pauline Winnick. "I just think it's a different approach to the world. A woman will take care of her family. Not that a man doesn't love them, but a man will buy tickets for him and his son or his buddies. He won't necessarily think of his wife or his girl child—who might be a great basketball fan. And we have a lot of women who are big fans." (The specific marketing to female fans has also been successful in the Orlando market and is certainly a strategy that should be of interest to the two new Canadian franchises.)

Like the Orlando Magic, the Heat have also put a tremendous amount of effort into the "experience" side of the basketball game with the usual menu of live bands, taped music, giveaways and dancers. "I wasn't thrilled that we had to have dancers," said Winnick. "But I figured that if we were going to be in the T&A business, we were going to get good ones."

On the court, the Miami brain trust decided to take a risky approach to building a team, relying on rookies in its initial season rather than a mix of young players and veterans. "The first step was the decision not to go with older players, for the simple reason that we had to be bad before we could be good," explained Cunningham. "We knew we'd take our lumps early. And we'd have to have patience and live through some tough times and hopefully not make many mistakes when we got to the draft," he added.

Coach Ron Rothstein led a team of inexperienced players through the first season and the growing pains were obviously more painful than for some of the other teams. It was tough on players like Rony Seikaly, the team's number one draft choice from Syracuse University.

"This is very difficult for me," said Seikaly during the first major losing streak of that first season as the team tried desperately for its first victory. "When you're used to winning, it's tough to take losing so much. We used to lose eight or nine games a season in Syracuse and here, we've already lost more. We're probably going to lose more games in one season than in my four seasons with Syracuse."

That's what the players with the Raptors and the Grizzlies also have to look forward to.

At the end of the season, Rothstein looked back at the gamble of going with all rookies, and despite winning only 15 games, saw the experiment as a success. (As a means of comparison, the Heat's expansion rivals, the Charlotte Hornets, only won five games more than Miami.) "At the beginning, I could say it was nightmarish at times, simply because of the start. It took us so long to win our first game. But the fact is, we had such a good group of guys. We never lost our professionalism. We never let it get away from us. It never turned into the zoo-like, carnival-like situation a lot of people would have thought it would have turned into."

The stress of losing a lot of games aside, the Miami Heat did well at the box office that first season, with a profit of about $8 million in its rookie year. On the court, the team improved over the course of the next couple of seasons with the addition of a couple of marquee players in the draft like Glen Rice, Willie Burton and Steve Smith. The team improved to a 24–58 record in the 1990–91 season, followed by 38–44 in 1991–92. The next year, the gamble finally paid off as the Heat became the first of the four expansion teams to make the playoffs.

Recently, however, the Miami Heat have been wracked by internal turmoil in the ownership group. The owners have become increasingly unhappy with the Miami Arena as they realize that they had underestimated the popularity of the NBA. The ideal NBA arena seats 18,000 and the Miami Arena is now limiting the team's potential for further income. In addition, the luxury suites in Miami are high up in the rafters and the team is missing out on the lucrative corporate dollars that those boxes can bring in. The team is reportedly shopping around for a new home, possibly in a new arena that Wayne Huizenga, of the NHL's Florida Panthers and MLB's Florida Marlins, is talking about building. The problems have been exacerbated by some bad management decisions. The Heat have traded away some of their best young talent that they spent years developing, including Rony Seikaly, Grant Long and Steve Smith and spent much of the 1994–95 season below the .500 mark. The buy-out of Cunningham and Schaffel, and the hiring of Pat Riley as coach, apparently signals a new direction for the Heat.

There was another team that joined the NBA during the 1988–89 season when the Heat made its debut: the Hornets, based in Charlotte, North Carolina. Some observers had been surprised when the smallish city was selected as home to one of the new franchises. But the Charlotte fans soon proved to everyone that the NBA was going to be a hit in North Carolina.

For one thing, the team was moving into one of the most basketball-crazy states in the U.S., arguably second only to Indiana. Former NCAA champions, Duke, North Carolina State and the University of North Carolina, all have huge followings, with the biggest being UNC. That school is home to the Tar Heels and has a reputation as one of the top basketball schools in the nation, under perenially winning Coach Dean Smith. Generations of former Tar Heels, including the likes of Michael Jordan, James Worthy and

Sam Perkins, have gone on to become stars in the NBA. During basketball season, the Dean E. Smith Student Activities Center is jammed to the rafters, with all of the 21,444 seats filled with screaming, painted UNC supporters. It seemed like a logical market for professional basketball, but some nay-sayers predicted the Hornets would not be able to compete. They were absolutely wrong.

In their first season, the Charlotte Hornets became the first expansion city ever, in any professional sport, to lead the league in attendance. Despite a 20–62 record in that first year, the team drew 950,064 fans over the course of the season. The team played in the 23,388-seat Charlotte Coliseum (also known as the Hive), which is the biggest arena in the league, and sold out 37 of their 41 home games. For their second season, the team had 24,000 requests for season tickets, more than the capacity of the arena. They decided to limit themselves to 21,000 season tickets, and left the fans 2,388 tickets to compete for on a game-to-game basis. The team has been virtually sold out since then. What made the numbers all the more impressive was the price tag: at $50 for the best seat in the house, the Hornets' ticket prices were second in the league only to those of the Chicago Bulls, but still they sold like hotcakes.

The traditional fans of the Tar Heels continued to follow the fortunes of the NCAA team, but there were enough basketball fans in the Charlotte area market to go around. For example, during that first season, the Hornets were able to go head-to-head with North Carolina games and come out with a full house. The night of the Atlantic Coast Conference championship, featuring the Tar Heels, the Hornets sold out for a game against Sacramento. The university crowd seemed to take the arrival of the NBA in stride. George Felton, coach of the nearby University of South Carolina Gamecocks, said after the first Hornets season: "I think the Charlotte Hornets have definitely excited people in the area. I see a lot of students wearing Hornets shirts around campus. I've seen a lot of Hornets shirts at my basketball camp. I love it. To me, it's a great thing. We're less than two hours from Charlotte. It brings more pro scouts into this area, which will help our student athletes."

For owner George Shinn, that first year was surprising, even beyond his expectations, but gratifying. Shinn had been the impetus behind the Charlotte bid since the very beginning. He is a self-made multimillionaire who owns a number of auto dealerships, business and trade schools and has written several top-selling books on how to make it in business. He brought together several financial partners and choreographed the Charlotte campaign to win a franchise.

The Charlotte Coliseum probably sealed the deal for Shinn and his group. The Coliseum had been built with $47.4 million in public funds after a bond referendum was approved by voters in 1982. The Coliseum Authority didn't have a major tenant at the time, so the arena was a gamble. When the possibility of an NBA franchise came along, the Coliseum Authority was willing to work out a sweetheart deal for the team. It offered the group a $1 per game, five-year lease on the facility. When Shinn and his co-investors explained that to the NBA expansion committee in Phoenix, the committee members reportedly sat up in their chairs when they heard those figures. (The agreement with the Coliseum also said that the team would pay a graduating four to eight percent of the franchise's revenues in the second five years of the deal, still below the 10 to 12 percent of revenues that was the norm in the league.)

Before the Phoenix presentation, one newspaper commentator had said that the only franchise that Charlotte had a chance of getting was "one with golden arches." Suddenly, with the juicy arena deal in hand and several key investors, including a local bank, on board, the Charlotte group had credibility, and soon afterwards, a franchise.

In that first season, Shinn made sure the team lived up to some of the lessons preached in his motivational books. His general manager, Carl Scheer, had a series of cards printed and distributed to every front-office employee with five rules about how to treat season ticket holders, such as: "A season-ticket holder is the most important person ever in this office in person or by mail." Like many of the other expansion teams, the Hornets put the emphasis on "class entertainment," featuring "Hugo the Hornet" and elaborate half-time shows.

"We borrowed the philosophy from Disney that the small things count," said General Manager Scheer in 1990. "To us, taking fans for granted is the ultimate sin. So we concentrate on the things that more established teams sometimes forget about, like parking-lot ambience, restroom cleanliness, half-time shows."

The team was also very careful to reflect its roots in the community. The team started every game with a non-denominational prayer despite some hints of displeasure from the NBA office in New York. "We live here in the Bible Belt," said Shinn. "The objective is not to offend anyone, even if it's three old ladies. So I have some requirements. I require the team's head coach to wear white shirts and conservative sports coats. I require the team to wear ties when travelling. And I require control. I've told the coach that if he ever embarrasses the club or community, throwing a chair like Bobby Knight, his job ends when the chair stops sliding."

The same rules applied to the players. Each player's contract included a provision for community service. "When I meet players, I tell them to give something back to the community for their big salaries," explained Shinn. "The kind of stuff that plays in New York or Los Angeles doesn't always play here. Charlotte is a very different kind of town."

However corny it may sound, Shinn knew his market and the team made an estimated profit of $11 million in that first season. Shinn said the turning point was a December 23 last-second victory, 103–101, over the Chicago Bulls, which was shown nationally on cable television. "I think everybody was afraid they might miss something," he told *The Sporting News*. "Players on the opponents' benches are seeing this and think they would love to play in this atmosphere if they become free agents. The fan support will help us build for the future."

In fact, the Charlotte Hornets fans quickly made a reputation for themselves as the noisiest crowd in the NBA, giving their team a real home-court advantage, like a playoff atmosphere every night of the year. Said the late Jack McMahon, a longtime player and coach in the NBA, after a visit to the Hive: "In all my years of pro basketball, I never experienced anything like they have at Charlotte. The crowd was unlike anything I have ever seen. They have 60-year-old men doing 'The Twist' to music, just like they were 18 again."

The Hornets were obviously quick learners at the feet of the master marketers of the NBA. An interesting historical note is that the team's original name was not the Hornets but the "Spirit," as selected by the Charlotte NBA Executive Advisory Committee from a name-the-team contest. That was in November 1986. The team wisely held another contest and in June 1987 announced the "Hornets" as the name for the franchise. But the real marketing coup came with the unveiling of the logo: a teal and purple bee. The colours and uniform design came from fashion designer Alexander Julian and would go on to make millions for the team's coffers. By 1994, the Hornets were on their way to displacing the Chicago Bulls as the NBA's most popular team in worldwide merchandise sales.

On the court, the team was also successful beyond owner George Shinn's modest expectations. He had predicted that the Hornets would take five years to reach the playoffs. But in the 1992–93 season, the team finished with a 44–38 record and made it to the second round of the playoffs.

A large part of the success of the Charlotte Hornets, and even more so the Orlando Magic, has come through the "luck of the draw," or more correctly, a happy bounce of the ping-pong ball. In 1985, David Stern devised the famous lottery draft in the NBA. Under the new system, the league's worst teams are given a certain number of ping-pong balls. The worse your team's record, the more balls you will get. Then the balls are placed in a popper machine and an NBA official draws one ball at a time to determine the drafting order for the teams. That way, a team can not benefit from deliberately losing late in the season in an attempt to get the first pick.

The Charlotte Hornets and Orlando Magic, in particular, have been well served by the ping-pong balls. In 1991, the Charlotte Hornets received the first ping-pong ball, and therefore the first choice overall, and ended up with a marquee player in Larry Johnson. In 1992, the Hornets drew the second choice and took another future star, Alonzo Mourning. (According to the odds and how many ping-pong balls the Hornets had, they should have picked no higher than fifth in 1991 and eighth in 1992, so they have been incredibly fortunate.)

In 1992, the Orlando Magic were the benefactors of the bouncing balls. Orlando General Manager Pat Williams still calls it a "miracle," the events which eventually left them with budding superstar Shaquille O'Neal and Anfernee Hardaway in successive years. "After getting Shaq, we only had a 1.5 percent chance to have our ping-pong ball chosen first again in 1993. And it was chosen. That is a miracle. A miracle. It changed our franchise's future."

In 1993, the Magic used the top pick to choose Chris Webber, then immediately traded him to Golden State, which had chosen Anfernee Hardaway out of Memphis State. Suddenly, they had the foundation of a team that would lead them, just two short years later, to the NBA final. But if he has any advice for the Raptors and the Grizzlies, Pat Williams of Orlando is clear about the vagaries of the NBA lottery system: "It's a very fragile way to live your life...to have your next 10 or 20 years be determined by just one ping-pong ball."

The management of the two Canadian teams don't have to worry about getting the first ping-pong ball, though, for a few years. Some owners, including Harold Katz of the Philadelphia 76ers and Donald Sterling of the Los Angeles Clippers, have reportedly decided they're tired of watching expansion teams get first-round college picks and then go on to whip the shorts off their teams (which, frankly, is as much a comment on the state of those other franchises as it is a reflection of the good fortune of the expansion teams). Therefore, under the expansion agreement that brings Toronto and Vancouver into the league, the two new teams are denied the first pick until the summer of 1999. If the number one ping-pong ball bounces their way, they will be placed second and another team will get the first pick. Commissioner David Stern was quick to explain the motivation of the owners behind the measure: "The feeling among owners is that there are some NBA teams who have struggled for a long time. They feel we shouldn't use expansion to deprive them of a pick they need and deserve."

Deputy Commissioner Russ Granik was even more specific in his explanation: "I think the good fortune of Orlando and Charlotte probably had something to do with it. The owners think that's a lot to give up to a team right away."

So, they paid their $125 million US, but the Canadian teams are still not quite in there with the rest of the teams. There is no doubt that the Canadian franchises will be among the worst nine teams in the league, for a couple of seasons at least. After all, their teams are made up of players that the rest of the franchises didn't want any more. One can only imagine their frustration should one of the Canadian teams have the misfortune of drawing the number one pick some time before 1999. But the Raptors and Grizzlies were putting a brave face on the whole situation. (The teams did try to keep the draft rules quiet when the expansion deal was announced. It was not until February 1995 that anyone in the media made a big fuss about the second-class treatment of the Canadian franchises.)

Vancouver General Manager Stu Jackson was philosophical about the restriction. "Even if we were eligible for the number one pick, there's no guarantee we would get it. And the number two pick is not that bad." Jackson also points out that for the near future at least "there's no Shaquille O'Neal on the horizon" that the teams would pine for.

However, the draft picks have certainly made Orlando, Charlotte and Miami the teams of the future. For example, Shaquille O'Neal of Orlando, Larry Johnson and Alonzo Mourning of Charlotte, and Steve Smith of Miami made up 25 percent of Dream Team II at the World Basketball Championship. (Smith has since been traded to Atlanta.)

If Pat Williams of the Orlando Magic calls his team's success at the draft lottery a "miracle," it is a miracle that has made the team millions of dollars. By 1994, the Magic were third on the list of merchandise sales, according to NBA Properties. The league had also realized that it had a hot product in its three successful expansion teams. In the 1994–95 season, the Heat, Hornets and the Magic were scheduled to appear in 37 percent of the league's nationally televised games.

However successful the Hornets have become on the court and with their merchandise sales, there have been some bumpy points along the road. The ticker-tape parade honouring George Shinn in 1987 for winning the NBA franchise was soon forgotten when he said in a television interview in 1990 that he was considering moving the team from Charlotte to Fort Mill, South Carolina. At issue was the $1 per game lease arrangement with the Charlotte Coliseum, which didn't turn out to be as advantageous as it first appeared. The lease allowed the Coliseum to keep the $3 parking fees and concession revenues, which added up to $5.3 million over the first 18 months of the deal. Shinn now wanted a cut of those revenues. There was an enormous public outcry and Shin quickly denied that he was threatening to move. He called a news conference to read a two-page statement saying that he was keeping the team in Charlotte. But the damage was done.

There were other public relations disasters as well. Shinn fired Coach Dick Harter after saying he wouldn't and happened to do it on the same day that Harter's brother died. Shinn switched banks after he discovered that his banker was involved in a bid to bring the NFL to Charlotte, which Shinn saw as direct competition to the Hornets. Then, in a messy buy-out, Shinn took over the ownership of the club and ended up in court, being sued by minority owner Cy Bahakel, owner of the local independent TV station that carried the Hornets games. The North Carolina Supreme Court ruled in Shinn's favour in 1991 but again, it was a public feud that tainted the team's image.

By the spring of 1991, *The Charlotte Observer* was detailing the team's slide in popularity. Scalpers outside the Coliseum were having trouble getting face value for their tickets and fans were even starting to boo the team. However, it's hard to quibble with the team's attendance record which at that point had reached its 110th straight sell-out. The sell-outs have continued and the team is currently in the second five-year term of its lease at the Charlotte Coliseum. The two sides were able to work out a deal where the Hornets will pay about 12 percent of their net ticket sales in rent and get to keep the revenue from courtside advertising, while the Coliseum continues to keep the parking and concession revenues. However, the Coliseum and the sell-outs have turned into one of the team's biggest problems.

In February 1995, the Hornets offered $65 million to buy the Charlotte Coliseum from the city. The team has argued for the last couple of years that it needs a better arena and there has been talk about building another one, though the $150 million price-tag makes it unlikely. The team blames escalating operating costs (like the $84 million contract for Larry Johnson) and the paucity of luxury boxes at the Coliseum. The Hive has only 12 corporate suites compared to 88 in Phoenix. Now the Hornets are looking at renovating to cash in on the corporate audience, which is the only new potential source of income for the team. (The team may also want to follow in the footsteps of the Grizzlies and Raptors who have significant corporate sponsorship of their arenas—GM Place and Air Canada Centre.)

On the court, the Hornets have blossomed under the leadership of stars Larry Johnson and Alonzo Mourning, making it the second most successful of the 1980s expansion teams, after the impressive Orlando Magic.

In 1989, the future of the Orlando Magic on the court could have gone either way, to success or failure. The Magic employed a gutsy strategy in the way they built their team in its first year. For one thing, they aggressively pursued the free-agent market. They didn't want to go the all-rookies route of the Heat, but wanted players with more experience. Helped by their voluminous season ticket sales, the Magic had between $500,000 and $1 million to lure a free agent to the beginner team. The Magic then traded two second-round draft picks to Chicago for aging centre Dave Corzine. That left their starting lineup with Corzine at centre, Terry Catledge at power forward, Jerry Reynolds at small forward, Sam Vincent at point guard and Reggie Theus at shooting guard. Many observers were impressed by the Magic's philosophy in pulling together their starting lineup, calling it "perhaps the best first-year NBA team since Chicago finished 33–48 in 1967."

Those are lofty words of praise, and the plan worked. In 1989, Pat Williams explained his strategy. "The Charlotte theory and the Miami theory—that's what everybody is honing in on. The Miami theory, long-range, may work, but it is wrought with peril. There are lots of risks. You go through a lot of heartache early, and then what happens if these young players you've gambled on don't come through? Then you're right back where you started. Charlotte has gone with a more proven team and is bringing one youngster along rather than six or seven. Actually, I'd like for us to be somewhere in the middle of those two theories, with not too many rookies and not too many of the veterans, either."

Their success on the court was not all that surprising, considering the Orlando Magic had basically done everything right from minute one of their expansion bid. Pat Williams left his job as general manager of the Philadelphia 76ers to join Orlando businessman Jim Hewitt in the expansion bid. On July 2, 1986, they presented a cheque for the application fee of $100,000 and a set of Mickey Mouse ears to Commissioner David Stern. By late July, the team had its name, again selected from a name-the-team contest. Perhaps the most compelling part of the Orlando bid was the $100 million Orlando arena. After the team partnership started construction on the arena, they sent a jar of dirt to David Stern solidifying their place in the expansion sweepstakes. On April 22, 1987, Orlando was awarded a much-coveted NBA franchise.

While the Magic did well putting together their team for that first season, they actually struggled to meet the season ticket requirement imposed by the NBA. "With a month to go, we needed to sell something like 1,500 season tickets," Pat Williams recalled. "Our lives flashed in front of our eyes. Can you imagine the pain and struggle and euphoria that we went through and experienced getting the team and then have the thought that it might all go down the drain?" While they had over 14,000 deposits on file for season tickets, the Magic did struggle until December 24 to sell 10,000 seats. Those times are now just memories for the Orlando team, which, like Charlotte, has been sold out for the last three seasons and has a waiting list for season tickets.

Again, like their counterparts in Miami and Charlotte, the Magic are cursed with an arena that doesn't fulfill the financial needs of a franchise in the 1990s. (Unlike some of the older franchises, like Boston, Portland and Seattle who have recently built new arenas, the expansion franchises of the 1980s are saddled with fairly new buildings that fall short of what they need in today's marketplace but would be too costly to replace.) While the number of Orlando sell-outs is impressive, the arena is obviously too small. "The arenas were built with the '80s in mind, and our buildings [Miami's and Orlando's] are dated in some respects," says Magic General Manager, Pat Williams.

The Magic could easily sell another 5,000 seats per game, beyond the 15,291 that they currently have. That translates into a lot of lost dollars. The team has been studying ways to add to the current seating capacity. But even more costly for the team is the absence of mid-level corporate suites. "Our skyboxes are at the top of the arena," said Magic Director of Publicity and Media Relations Alex Martens in 1993. "It's difficult to see the game and you have to rely on TV monitors. In the future, we want to move some of the luxury boxes down to the lower level."

The other option that the Magic will eventually have to face is to raise ticket prices. Initially, the team aimed at making the tickets affordable and set the prices around the middle of the league average. Then, the Magic froze those prices for three years. Since then, however, they've had to raise them significantly to cope with the increased payroll and are now in the top 10 in the league in ticket prices. They'll have to stay high in order for the team to continue to make a profit because there are not any more seats to sell.

Still, the Orlando Magic have turned into the big success story of the 1980s round of expansion. However, it would be a very different team had the ping-pong balls bounced differently and not landed them the highly marketable Shaquille O'Neal. Many observers of the NBA predict that Shaq will become the league's best player as he matures. His inexperience showed against Hakeem Olajuwon in the NBA Final, but that was more a tribute to the underrated skills of Olajuwon who has finally earned his place as one of the best centres in the history of the NBA. In April 1994, O'Neal was modest when he talked of his team's ambitions. After all, the Magic were, in 1994, only five years into the league. "We don't have a deadline to win a championship," Shaq told *Sport*. "We don't have to win it in 1994. It took Michael Jordan seven years to win his first championship, so I don't think we need to put a timetable on these types of things." The Magic moved one step closer in 1995, making it to the championship series.

The Miami Heat similarly have great potential, with none of their stars even close to age 30. As their players age, the expansion teams of the late-1980s will play an even more dominant role in the league. That is, except for the Minnesota Timberwolves.

The history of the Timberwolves is like a litany of "don'ts" for an expansion franchise. The team has been unlucky in the draft lottery, but most of the troubles the "T-Wolves" have had have been of their own making. In six seasons in the NBA, the Minnesota Timberwolves have never made the playoffs. They have had financial problems. They have lost so many fans that the team almost moved to New Orleans. The team's petulant superstars have made a name for themselves as whiners rather than players, and seem incapable of turning around the fortunes of this team.

Minnesota hasn't had a tremendous track record when it comes to its NBA franchises, or any sports franchise, for that matter. The city of Minneapolis lost the Lakers in 1960, when the team moved to Los Angeles. In January 1984, Minnesota Governor Rudy Perpick appointed a 30-member task force to bring an NBA franchise back to the Minneapolis–St. Paul area. Two local entrepreneurs, Harvey Ratner and Marv Wolfenson, quickly stepped up to take on the job of wooing the NBA back to the Twin Cities. The two were boyhood friends, business partners in the Northwest Health and Racquetball Clubs chain and had other real estate holdings around Minneapolis–St. Paul.

As with Miami, Orlando and Charlotte, the Minnesota group was able to draw a lot of interest during the bidding process for an NBA franchise. The team-to-be attracted close to 9,000 deposits for season tickets, and that would work to their favour as they appeared before the NBA officials to press their case. That was in October, and by December, the ownership group had held a name-the-team contest, which attracted over 6,000 responses, from which Timberwolves was selected by a 2-to-1 margin. By February 1987, the group also had approval from Minneapolis City Council for a new arena to be built in downtown Minneapolis. The arena would be owned by Timberwolves investors Ratner and Wolfenson and was scheduled to open for the 1990–91 season. That sealed the deal and by April 1987, the city had its franchise back, this time under the moniker "Timberwolves." As with the other three expansion teams, the purchase price would be $32.5 million.

It wasn't long before things started to go wrong for the new Minnesota Timberwolves. The owners, Harvey Ratner and Marv Wolfenson, came under fire in June of 1987 when they named

Bob Stein, a Minneapolis lawyer, as the new team's president. Stein was the son-in-law of Wolfenson. Kevin Harlan, the team's play-by-play announcer, says that decision would cause a lot of problems for the team. "They made him president because his father-in-law was one of the owners. So he was making important basketball decisions—and the two owners, just old men who had made some money, they were interfering, too."

Stein did have some sports connections. He had played for the University of Minnesota football team and then as an NFL linebacker for eight years. While he was playing for the Kansas City Chiefs, Stein obtained a law degree from the University of Missouri. Shortly after he took up his new post, Bob Stein talked to *Twin Cities* magazine about his aspirations for the team: "We know we're not going to be the Boston Celtics the first year, but we're going to be hustling. Our commitment is to do everything first class, to the limits of our abilities, to be an addition to the community above and beyond a real nice sport/entertainment opportunity."

In the same article, Stein talked about what the new team and new arena would offer, including theatre-style seats and restroom capacity more than double that of any other indoor arena in the world. The emphasis, he said, would be on customer service. While it's arguable how well he did on that front, what Stein was clearly lacking in his vision was a strategy for the product on the court.

Stein's first major decision on the basketball side of the operation was to hire Bill Musselman as the team's new head coach. Musselman appeared to have impeccable credentials. He was coach of one of the most successful teams in pro basketball history. His team in the Continental Basketball Association, the Albany Patroons, had won four consecutive CBA championships. In 1987–88, the Patroons had finished with a 48–6 record. The final year he coached there, the Albany team was even better, finishing a remarkable 50–6.

However, the winning record had come at some cost. Musselman had a reputation for a fiery temper, exploding one time at his team that had won 11 straight games and then lost by two points. "I was just beside myself," Musselman recalled. "I went into the locker room and took off my coat and threw it down. I took a chair and threw it against the wall. I looked at the guys and said, 'How could you blow a chance to go 54–0?'"

Musselman had also been the coach of the University of Minnesota basketball team that was put on probation because of an infamous brawl in 1972 against Ohio State.

The strategy that Musselman took in the first season with the Minnesota Timberwolves was part of what has destined this team for mediocrity in the foreseeable future. At the urging of Stein and the two owners, Musselman was of the opinion that the team had to win as many games as possible, as quickly as possible. Doug West was one of the starters during the first year with the Timberwolves. "The first two years, Bill Musselman brought in all his people, players from the Continental Basketball Association teams he'd coached. My first two years, we'd have six or seven veteran guys playing 35 to 40 minutes a night," recalled West. Musselman would sometimes use the older CBA veterans as much as 40 minutes per game and even played Tyrone Corbin for 121 consecutive minutes at one point in that first season.

The playing time of the older "retreads," as they were called, came at the expense of the development of the younger potential stars. West, the 38th pick overall in the 1989 draft, and Jerome "Pooh" Richardson, the 10th pick overall, were the youngsters on the team. Richardson, who now plays for the Los Angeles Clippers, has some good memories of that first season. "I remember my first year, playing the Celtics and the Lakers at home in front of 60,000 in the Metrodome. The fans were crazy. It was the best feeling I ever felt in my life."

However, by his second season, Richardson became increasingly frustrated with the coach's bizarre substitutions, which often came at the expense of the younger players, and he was soon openly critical of the coaching.

Meanwhile, the Timberwolves were running into other problems. While they were waiting for their own arena to be built, a situation that the Raptors will become all too familiar with in their first few years of operation, the Timberwolves had to compete with other teams for time at the Metrodome. So in their inaugural season, the Timberwolves were not able to have a big opening weekend because the Gophers football team and the Minnesota Vikings were already booked into the Metrodome.

"This just shows why you have to have your own building," Timberwolves president Bob Stein said. "Last year, Charlotte opened at home Friday night, Miami opened at home Saturday night and the commissioner was at both games and it was a big deal. We lose the impact of one of the biggest games in the franchise's history because we can't get into the building."

Overall, though, things went well for the Timberwolves that first season. Under Coach Musselman, they had a respectable 22 wins, and the fans in the Twin Cities seemed to like what they saw. On April 17, 1990, 49,551 fans came out to the Metrodome for Fan Appreciation Night. It was the third-largest crowd in NBA history and made the Timberwolves the NBA's all-time single season attendance champions, with a season total of 1,072,572.

For their second season, the Timberwolves moved into their new home, the Target Center. While a milestone in the team's history, the arena had already proven to be a financial millstone around the owners' necks. The problems with the Target Center started in February 1989 when the Midwest Federal Savings and Loan Association was declared insolvent. The Timberwolves owners, Wolfenson and Ratner, bought $15 million in subordinated debt from Midwest in late 1987 or early 1988. Subordinated debt is basically unsecured corporate IOUs. Wolfenson and Ratner had dealt almost exclusively with Midwest in securing mortgages for their projects, which included health clubs and apartments. But the subordinated debt was not insured and so the Timberwolves owners basically lost the $15 million. Midwest had also been the main source of the loans to build the new arena, to the tune of $50 million, and had also committed some money towards the team's franchise payments. The bankruptcy of Midwest forced Wolfenson and Ratner to pay for the construction of the Target Center out of their own pockets because the building was already under way when the Savings and Loan Association went belly up. The financial struggles of this time period would ultimately put the Timberwolves ownership in trouble and eventually force them to turn to the state government for a bail out.

The 1990–1991 season was fraught with turmoil for the team as the novelty of the first year wore off. While the attendance remained strong and the team won 29 games, including six of their last eight, the owners weren't happy. In April 1991, the Timberwolves announced that Head Coach Bill Musselman and Assistant Coach Tom Thibodeau would not be returning for the next season. In May 1991, Tim Leiweke, Executive Vice-President of Marketing and Sales, left to work with the Denver Nuggets.

It was an ominous sign when the Timberwolves opened their third season to a crowd of only 6,973. The attendance could be excused because the game was played during the largest snowfall in Minnesota history (24 inches in 24 hours). But it was a sign of things to come.

Players like Pooh Richardson admitted that the first couple of seasons started to take their toll on everyone. "Losing is not easy. Some of your friends are playing for established teams and they're winning. You're not winning but you're developing and you're having fun," said Richardson. He was traded at the end of the third season, and now plays for another perenially losing team, the Los Angeles Clippers.

It wasn't the younger players, however, who struggled in that third season so much as the veterans. "When it got to the point that the older guys couldn't keep up at the same rate, we didn't have young people who had been developed on the bench to take their place," recalled Doug West, who was one of those younger players in the third season of the Timberwolves. The team only won 15 games in the third season, as the collection of Continental Basketball Association players assembled by Bill Musselman collapsed against younger, more talented lineups. The Timberwolves would win 20 games in their fourth season and just 21 games in their fifth. In contrast, the Orlando Magic, who entered the league the same year, had its first 50-win season in its third year of existence and made it to the NBA Final two years later.

The Timberwolves suffered for a couple of reasons. Bill Musselman didn't develop a core of talented young players like his counterparts in Miami, Orlando and Charlotte did. Miami may not have won as many games in the first two seasons, but they have now surpassed the pathetic Timberwolves. Secondly, the other teams drafted much more wisely than the team from the Twin Cities. In the 1991 draft, the Timberwolves made two choices that baffled onlookers: centres Felton Spencer and Luc Longley (the first Australian to play in the NBA!) were described as marginally talented at best, and made little or no impact on the team. The Minnesota team was also perenially unlucky when it came to the bounce of the ping-pong balls. For example, in 1992–93, they had the league's second worst record but they ended up picking fifth.

In 1992, the Timberwolves appeared to make a better choice, selecting Christian Laettner, a forward from Duke. Laettner played for the Dream Team in Barcelona and in 1993 was named "College Basketball Player of the Year." He impressed everyone with a buzzer-beating shot against Kentucky that put Duke into the Final Four. In his first season in the NBA, Laettner was named to the NBA All-Rookie First Team.

Laettner should have become the star player that the Timberwolves needed to turn their fortunes around, but he has struggled with the mantle of being the leader of losers. In 1992, he made *People*'s annual 50 Most Beautiful People list but it is his ugly behaviour that is usually captured in the media. In February 1994, Laettner received a one-game suspension without pay for screaming at Assistant Coach Bob Weinhauer. There is also no love lost between Laettner and the Minnesota media.

"Christian reeks of hostility," said Rachel Blount of the *Minneapolis Star Tribune*, the beat writer who covers the Timberwolves, in a 1994 profile of Laettner in *Sports Illustrated*. "His problem is, he thinks it's a waste of time to speak with people like us whom he considers not his intellectual equals."

Despite leading the team statistically in many areas of play, Laettner has also become the subject of criticism by many fans in the Twin Cities who have continued to fill the Target Center to an amazing 98 percent capacity despite the team's record. "I've been losing a lot since I've been here," he said in response to the criticism. "If we're winning, they're not going to be asking, 'Why all the turnovers? What're you doing? You're a jerk. You're selfish.'"

However, Laettner doesn't help his own cause when he continually chooses to criticize his fellow players publicly. In a typically Laettneresque move, he launched into a 30-minute critique of his team after the final game of the 1993–94 season. "I'm not worried about my game," said Laettner. "I'm more worried about the team getting some players around me. I'm 200 rebounds ahead of anyone on this team. I want someone to compete with me."

Some of Laettner's vitriol can be justified, because as Pooh Richardson observed, it's hard for players who are used to winning when they have to adjust to losing all the time, which is the reality of an expansion team. But Laettner's tantrums seem particularly spiteful considering his paycheque. As a rookie in 1992, he signed a six-year, $21.6 million contract.

In 1993, not learning from their experience with Laettner, the Timberwolves used their first pick to draft another brilliantly talented young player who came with an attitude. Isaiah (J.R.) Rider, a guard from UNLV, is a superb scorer and is exciting to watch. (He won the 1994 NBA Slamdunk contest with an unforgettable leap-in-the-air ball between-the-legs dunk. It was one of the few highlights for Timberwolves fans all year.) Last season, in his second year in the league, Rider called a news conference to respond to the suggestion from Minnesota Coach Bill Blair that he needs to grow up. In December 1994, Rider was facing jail time if he didn't complete 28 hours of community service, after being convicted on an assault charge. In August 1995, he was ordered to go to jail for a few days for non-compliance. The only response from management was that they'd use a staff car to drive him to his community work if that was the only way to get him to do it. Rider currently makes $3.5 million a year.

Both Christian Laettner and Isaiah Rider made the 1995 *Sports Illustrated* list of petulant prima donnas. But in the same article, some players in the league, including Danny Ainge, recently retired from the Phoenix Suns, expressed sympathy for the young stars of expansion teams. "A Christian Laettner and Isaiah Rider, for example, come to Minnesota and they're expected to turn that franchise around. When they lose, the perception is that it's their fault. If there had not been expansion, those players would be going to teams that were already established, and you could give them a chance to mature," said Ainge.

But not all talented young players on expansion teams choose to behave the way that Laettner and Rider do. Certainly, a star like Shaquille O'Neal has a team of handlers around all the time to make sure he doesn't behave like a prima donna. But other young stars like Anfernee Hardaway of the Orlando Magic and Larry Johnson and Alonzo Mourning of the Charlotte Hornets have not exhibited the same personality problems as have Rider and Laettner.

As the Timberwolves have continued to struggle on the court, so too have they been in constant turmoil financially. In 1993, the Target Center's other tenant, the Minnesota North Stars of the NHL, packed up and left town after owner Norm Green was offered a better lease arrangement in Dallas. That left the Target Center financially unviable with only the basketball team to chip in money towards the arena's hefty mortgage. (The Target Center cost $104 million to build.) The arena was losing an estimated $6 million per year despite the Timberwolves drawing near-capacity crowds.

In early 1994, Harvey Ratner and Marv Wolfenson went to the Minnesota legislature to ask for a bail out to the tune of $42 million. Ratner and Wolfenson then said they couldn't afford the other $76 million to pay off the mortgage so they wanted to put the team up for sale. After three months of debate, the state government agreed to pay the $42 million, but only on the condition that the team be sold to local investors.

On May 23, Ratner and Wolfenson announced that the Timberwolves had been sold for $152.5 million to a group led by Houston attorney John O'Quinn and boxing promoter Bob Arum. The surprise was that the team would be moving to New Orleans. There was a tremendous outcry in Minnesota over the prospect of losing another professional franchise and then the New Orleans group fell apart. The Timberwolves remain in financial trouble but, for now, they remain in Minnesota.

Despite the ongoing problems of the Minnesota Timberwolves, the NBA's expansion in the 1980s was, overall, an overwhelming success and has set the standard for expansion into Canada. There was, in fact, no way that the expansion could be anything other than a success for the four new teams, barring such unlikely disasters as the bankruptcy of the Midwest Savings and Loan, which damaged the fortunes of the team in Minnesota. The league guaranteed that the new teams would do well by demanding the $32.5 million fee up front, proving that the owners had financial means. Then, the NBA enforced a strict minimum to season-ticket sales, and as in the case of Toronto and Vancouver, threatened to revoke any franchise that didn't meet the required numbers. Those season ticket sales instantly catapulted Orlando, Miami, Charlotte and even Minnesota, for a while, into the upper echelon of the league's top performers financially.

Michael Megna is a sports consultant in Milwaukee. He says the NBA's franchise requirements help the expansion teams remain financially viable during the early years when they won't fare too well on the court. "In the first year, there's the glow of success and the team benefits highly. It's the second and third year when the reality sets in."

The Orlando Magic, for example, made more than $12 million in ticket sales in their first season, and over $800,000 a year in luxury box sales. That gave them the financial wherewithal to be able to pay their budding superstars and therefore build the basis for a successful team on and off the court.

The Raptors and the Grizzlies would be well advised to have deep pockets in those early years if they want to avoid the kind of struggle that beset the Minnesota Timberwolves. They should also prepare carefully for the let-down in their second and third seasons when the novelty will have worn off and the teams will still be struggling to do well on the court. Neither Toronto nor Vancouver has the ready-made audience for basketball of a place like Charlotte, and the Canadian teams will have to nurture that interest until their teams start to win, particularly in the Toronto marketplace where fickle baseball fans, at least, seem only to want to support a winner.

The NBA doesn't want to see another Minnesota Timberwolves experience and the league hopes it has done everything necessary to prevent any other similar expansion experiences.

Chapter Five

THE GAMBLE ON GAMBLING

The initial delight over the NBA's arrival in Canada was tarnished by an ominous comment from Commissioner David Stern as he welcomed the Canadian teams into the league. "We don't like to see people encouraged to bet the grocery money on sport, particularly our own," said Stern, at a news conference announcing the two new franchises. Stern was referring to the Pro-Line lottery in which Ontario bettors could lay wagers on pro basketball games, as well as hockey, baseball, Canadian and American football.

At the time, John Bitove Jr., the triumphant leader of Professional Basketball Franchise, Inc., stated confidently that the Pro-Line issue would be dealt with simply and swiftly. "I did receive a call of congratulations from Premier Bob Rae. He understands the seriousness of the issue." What Bitove didn't bargain on was the high-stakes poker game over Pro-Line that would erupt and even, at one point, appear to jeopardize the future of the Toronto franchise.

Pro-Line had been a tremendous hit in Canada since it was introduced in October 1992. In its first year, ending October 1993, Pro-Line recorded revenues of $200.7 million, $50 million more than had been originally projected. About 25 percent of that money ended up going to community groups and hospitals across the province of Ontario.

There are basically two ways to win with the Pro-Line game. The object of Pro-Line itself is to correctly predict the outcome of a sports game: visitor win, tie or home win. The rules vary slightly depending upon the sport and whether or not it's the regular season or playoffs. For example, during the 1995 NBA Finals, which were still included on Pro-Line, any game decided by five points or less was considered a tie. The amount of money the bettor wins for a correct prediction varies depending upon the odds. They're calculated by the Ontario Lottery Commission and are available by the day of the game.

There is also a game called Over/Under where the bettor needs to predict if the total score of a game will be over or under what the Ontario Lottery Commission has predicted. Again, there are odds set by game day, which determine how much each correct wager is worth. The maxiumum wager per Pro-Line selection slip is $100, and the maximum payout for a single wager is $2 million.

The game has proven very popular since it was introduced in Ontario, and by the time of the NBA controversy it was the second-most-played game after Lotto 6/49. The Lottery Commission also found that Pro-Line attracted new bettors, not just people playing the other lottery games.

Of the five sports, hockey was easily the most popular ($119.3 million), followed by baseball ($36.7 million), NFL football ($21.6 million), NBA basketball ($19.4 million) and CFL football ($3.7 million). Still, basketball was ranked number three on a per-game basis, and with the arrival of an NBA franchise in Toronto, that number was projected to balloon dramatically.

The two sides in the Pro-Line debate—the Ontario government and the NBA—soon dug in their heels, and the rhetoric and the threats began to fly. The NBA commissioner was unwavering in his refusal to allow betting on basketball in Ontario. A league source told *The Toronto Star*, "This is religion to David Stern." In part, Stern's opposition to gambling is rooted in his overall philosophy of marketing the squeaky-clean image of his sport, and that philosophy has obviously been tremendously successful. But the roots of his aversion to gambling go much deeper.

Gambling scandals hit college basketball and even the pro game in the 1950s and '60s. While they have been largely forgotten, and happened on a much smaller scale than the Black Sox and Pete Rose scandals in baseball, they remain a black mark on the sport's history. During Stern's tenure, there have also been some serious gambling allegations, which are perhaps closer to the root of the commissioner's angst over sports betting. The ongoing rumours over Michael Jordan's betting activities finally prompted the league to investigate the star player on several occasions, including shortly before his retirement.

A 1991 book detailing Jordan's gambling problems, entitled *Michael and Me: Our Gambling Addiction...My Cry for Help*, alleged that Jordan owed the author Richard Esquinas a golf debt of $300,000. The debt was reported to have gone as high as $1.25 million, including putts worth $100,000 or even as much as $250,000. At the same time as the book was published, Jordan was reported to have travelled to Atlantic City for late-night, early-morning gambling sprees between Games One and Two of the Bulls–Knicks series, charges that Jordan vehemently denied. In an interview aired during Game One of the NBA Finals, Jordan told NBC's Ahmad Rashad that he did not have a gambling problem and that his golfing debt to Esquinas was not in the seven digits, as alleged.

Commenting on the allegations at the time, the NBA commissioner said he was convinced that Jordan was not a compulsive gambler. A league investigation had also excused Jordan after cheques totalling $165,000 to pay off golf and poker debts were found and made public.

At the time of Jordan's retirement in October 1993, the league was about to release a report on the ongoing allegations over the star's gambling. Jordan saved them the trouble by leaving the sport voluntarily. Obviously, if the league had actually discovered any wrongdoing by its greatest celebrity, it would have been loathe to disclose it. Still, the risk of tarnishing Jordan's image, and that of the NBA, was too great, and Jordan's retirement was the perfect convenience. The league struggled by without him until his triumphant return in March 1995. No one but David Stern and Michael Jordan will ever really know whether Jordan was urged to leave for a time, but the brush with Jordan's gambling problems obviously touched a deep-seated fear in the commissioner.

The battle over sports gambling in Ontario was not the first time that the commissioner had laid down the law, literally, on the subject. In 1990, a similar sports lottery in Oregon dropped NBA games, saying publicly that poor sales were to blame. In actual fact, league sources say the NBA threatened to move the Portland Trail Blazers from the state if the sports lottery didn't comply. David Stern personally travelled to the state legislature in Salem, Oregon, to make his case. The NBA eventually sued the state to stop betting on basketball. The state settled out of court, agreeing to take basketball out of the lottery for a five-year period ending in 1995.

The league's next anti-gambling crusade came in New Jersey, where casino operators wanted to legalize sports betting, particularly in Atlantic City gambling casinos. Again, the NBA put on the full-court press to lobby the state's Casino Control Commission. The Commission voted four to one against the proposal, saying that the New Jersey legislature had already rejected sports betting through its gaming statutes, and had refused to put a sports betting referendum on the ballot. The casino operators filed a lawsuit appealing the ruling, arguing they needed the sports gambling to stay in business.

An even bigger victory for Stern came in the form of a long-coveted federal law passed in 1992 banning sports betting in any state where it was not already legal. That shut out all states except New Jersey, Oregon, Delaware and, of course, Nevada. Las Vegas is currently the only place in the United States with legalized gambling on the NBA.

Michael Roxborough—or Roxy Roxborough as he answers the phone—is the president of Las Vegas Sports Consultants, the largest independent odds-making company in North America. He makes the line for many betting shops in Vegas and also writes a syndicated column, which is carried in 128 newspapers in the U.S. and Canada. Roxborough estimates that about $300 million is bet on the NBA in Vegas every year. While football is the most prominent of the pro sports, pro basketball, he says, would be number two.

That is legal gambling. Then there's illegal wagering, which Roxborough figures is worth between $50 and $75 billion a year in the United States. "I think it's safe to say that betting on the NBA makes up about 15 percent of that," says Roxborough from his office in Vegas. "And that's probably rather conservative."

There is no love lost between Roxborough and the NBA. He calls the league's hard line on gambling a "righteous stance" and wonders about the NBA's obsession with the issue. "It's obviously a game of high integrity if there are billions of illegal dollars bet on it every year," he says. He adds that any kind of "game-fixing" scandal would be "pretty improbable considering the salaries of today's players."

"They're marketers," says Roxborough. "The gambling issue to them is just an image problem. They feel they have the right to coerce people into doing what they want."

Roxborough admits that he sympathizes with the Ontario and B.C. lotteries, which were squeezed out of pro basketball betting even though the millions of dollars bet legally on the Canadian lotteries was a tiny fraction of what's bet illegally on the league every year. "They were blackmailed by the NBA," he says.

The gambling community in Las Vegas got a first-hand look at how the NBA works a couple of years ago. The Utah Jazz decided to play a handful of home games in Vegas and the league insisted that there be no betting on those games. Several of the bookmakers took the issue to the state gaming commission, which ruled in their favour, against the league. The NBA has not played any games in Nevada since then.

In Ontario, however, the NBA's threat to withdraw over the Pro-Line issue caused a division of loyalties in the province. For its part, the Ontario NDP government's argument in favour of betting was based, it argued, purely on economics. Some observers found it ironic that a government based on socialist philosophies was promoting gambling, turning it from "a vice into a virtue," as one editorial put it.

"As bookies," wrote Stephen Brunt, "the government can hardly claim the moral high ground in this one." (Though Brunt also added that he doubted the veracity of the NBA's ethics, claiming that the league was really more interested in making sure that someone else was not profiting from their sport without cutting them in!) The province launched a public relations campaign in favour of Pro-Line, describing all the wonderful things that Ontario had been able to afford, thanks to the sports lottery, including medical equipment.

As the stalemate continued, both sides began to throw around a lot of numbers, detailing the consequences of ending the betting on basketball, or conversely, losing the NBA franchise. Conveniently enough, the Metro Toronto Convention and Visitors Association had recently done a study for the owners of the new Toronto franchise. The study estimated that the team will support the equivalent of 6,803 full-year jobs in Ontario, with 5,640 of those in Toronto. The total activities related to the team, and the construction of an arena, would total $418.8 million in Toronto and $550.8 million in all of Ontario.

These calculations were widely bandied around and used for many purposes. For example, Lyn McLeod, then the Ontario Liberal leader called her own press conference urging the NDP government to agree to the league's conditions. Her argument was that the benefits from the NBA team would outweigh the revenue from the basketball portion of Pro-Line. She used a figure of $6 million a year from basketball betting, compared with $81 million in revenues from the first year of the actual Toronto franchise.

David Reville, a special adviser to Premier Bob Rae, replied to McLeod's comments by pointing out that if the province ended basketball betting, it would also have to stop all sports betting because a precedent would be set and the other leagues would protest the special treatment for the NBA. Losing sports betting entirely would end up costing the province $100 million a year by 1995–96.

The survey by the Metro Toronto Convention and Visitors Association was also challenged on the basis of its calculations. University of Toronto professor Bruce Kidd argued in the *Globe and Mail* that the mathematics in the report represented nothing more than what he calls "booster economics"—used by promoters of sports franchises to "justify their optimism and to make the pitch to politicians."

Kidd pointed out that a team's net benefit is very difficult to really calculate, particularly when the highly paid athletes often don't live year-round in the city. Also, the money paid by fans to attend the games is often just redirected from other parts of the economy, or even of the province, if they come to basketball games from out of Toronto. While the team will bring in a share of the NBA's radio and TV contracts, as well as revenues from NBA merchandise, it has also paid $125 million US out of the province's economy. Basically, these figures can be manipulated to make whatever argument one chooses.

As the deadline of February 14, 1994 drew closer, the standoff continued, and the Professional Basketball Franchise (Canada) Inc. floundered, putting all development on hold until the gambling issue could be resolved. In mid-January, John Bitove Jr. took his case behind closed doors to a meeting with Premier Bob Rae. In late January, the province made a compromise offer to the NBA, which was not revealed. The league turned it down and did not make a counter offer. There seemed no solution in sight.

"The situation was overblown, and so were the reports of the franchise just being yanked," Professional Basketball Franchise's David Peterson would say later.

What appeared to be people taking tough stances, with threats and deadlines being thrown around, was, according to Peterson, just a normal process that involved some posturing. "It was really just negotiation. It was never a problem."

"The NBA was not particularly angry with us," says John Bitove Jr. "Yes, we had assured them that the Pro-Line thing would not be a problem, but so did the other two bidding groups say that. Russ Granik told me if we had been the only ones to make that assurance, he'd have been pissed off at the Rae government's obstinance, but he said, 'John, everybody in the bidding process said the same thing.' Really, I think it was just a situation of people wanting to save face—the Rae people not wanting to appear to have a bunch of Americans come in and tell them how to run the province, and the NBA wanting to stick to a much-publicized position on gambling."

The settlement of the dispute came down to the wire, with the league's Board of Governors meeting just days away. NBA Deputy Commissioner Russ Granik reiterated, in making the announcement of a deal, that the franchise was in jeopardy. "There was a time a few weeks ago where I felt that maybe it wasn't do-able. We were prepared to meet with the owners this Monday and recommend they pull the franchise."

The turning point came almost a week earlier, in a meeting at the home of Allan Slaight, owner of Standard Broadcasting and a majority owner in the franchise. It involved then-Premier Bob Rae and John Bitove Jr. "We just got together and said, 'Enough of this, let's get a deal done on this,' and we did," said Bitove.

The settlement took 98 days, but in the end, both the NBA and the Ontario government claimed victory. The Ontario government agreed to take basketball off the Pro-Line game as of October 1, 1995. In return, the NBA would contribute $1.5 million to medical research programs across the province. The league would provide $2 million in television time and advertising space over the next four years to the Ontario government to promote tourism. The league also agreed to stage the 1995 NBA Draft in Toronto, ensuring an immediate injection of several million dollars to the tourism and hospitality business. In addition, the Toronto franchise and the league would create a charitable foundation, starting with a $5 million donation from the club. The Toronto team also agreed to add at least $1 million a year after that to contribute to the foundation. The team also committed to supporting stay-in-school campaigns and to appearing in television campaigns against drug abuse, child abuse and domestic violence. Those campaigns would cost about half a million a year. Finally, the club committed to having the foundation poured for its new arena by October 1, 1995, or it would pay another $1 million to the province as a penalty.

Premier Bob Rae said the deal was worth in total about $12–13 million over the next five years. Said Rae at a press conference with John Bitove Jr. and NBA Commissioner David Stern: "As far as I'm concerned, this was a big win for us but it was a big win for everybody."

The NBA also claimed a successful outcome, though Stern agreed that the league had never had to meet such an extensive list of conditions before granting a franchise. "This is unprecedented, but we think that the opportunities and the circumstances here are unprecedented," Stern told the Toronto media about the league's willingness to pay money to prevent gambling on basketball. "It's the principle, and we're prepared to pay the money to support the principle."

The deal with the NBA did open up some tricky territory for the Ontario government because the National Hockey League, in particular, had been lobbying to have its games removed from Pro-Line and now a precedent had been set. Both Major League Baseball and the NHL had said that if the NBA was dropped, they wanted a similar concession. But Premier Bob Rae quickly deflected that possibility by pointing out that the basketball league had compensated the province for the privilege, and that the other sports would have to follow suit. "I think what we've done is very fair and we're prepared to say to other sports, on a comparable economic basis, if you want to talk to us about what your concerns are, we're happy to have those discussions," said Rae.

In response, the Commissioner of the National Hockey League, Gary Bettman, released a statement to the media saying that he looked forward to meeting Rae to talk about the issue. But, with annual revenues from betting on hockey games close to $120 million a year, the NHL would be unlikely to want to pursue a similar compensation deal with the province of Ontario.

The Pro-Line decision also had implications for the prospective Vancouver franchise which, at that point, had not been formally confirmed. British Columbia has a similar sports betting game called Sports Action, but its revenues from the game were traditionally much smaller than those in Ontario. The B.C. game brought in $26 million in sales in 1992, compared to $210 million in Ontario. After the NBA made its deal with Ontario, the B.C. government quickly followed suit. At a news conference following the Ontario announcement, B.C. Premier Mike Harcourt and Arthur Griffiths, President of Northwest Sports, announced that B.C. would also pull NBA games from its sports lottery. The games would be taken off the lottery listings as soon as the franchise was granted and all the expansion fees were paid. In return, the B.C. government asked for a $500,000 annual payment from the Vancouver franchise.

With the Pro-Line dispute settled, the Toronto team could finally get down to business after 98 days in limbo. While the Ontario government and the NBA had come out winners, the big losers were the group trying to organize the Toronto franchise. "We're at least four months behind right now because it literally brought everything to a halt," said team President John Bitove Jr.

What he didn't anticipate at the time were some of the other obstacles, similarly troublesome and time-consuming, that lay just around the corner.

Chapter Six

THERE'S NO PLACE LIKE HOME: THE SEARCH FOR AN ARENA

The Pro-Line standoff and the rush to meet the season-ticket sales deadline caused some stress for the Raptors organization. But the struggle to build a new arena has been by far the greatest challenge for the team. The original concept for an arena at Bay and Dundas in downtown Toronto was one of the selling points of the Bitove group's bid for the NBA franchise. The Ballard and Cohl group did have a specific facility, a proposed arena/theatre at Exhibition Place. However, the Palestra group, the original bidder and considered by many the front-runner during the bidding process, always remained non-committal about where its team was going to play. There were plans for a downtown site, and Palestra had even named a specific piece of property in its presentation to the NBA, but it was never made public.

In contrast, the Professional Basketball Franchise people had always been very upfront in their commitment to the Eaton Centre site. The group had a written agreement with Cadillac Fairview, the developer that owned the land adjacent to the Eaton Centre, and had designed an arena specifically for that site. Peter McAlister, Vice-President of Development for Cadillac Fairview, says he was contacted in April 1993 by John Bitove Jr. to work with him on developing a site for the potential basketball franchise. (Cadillac Fairview had previously worked with Bitove Jr. on other projects.) While they discussed various venues, McAlister says Cadillac Fairview proposed the Bay–Dundas site, home of the Eaton Centre, which they co-owned along with Eaton's and the TD Bank.

The PBF group hired architect Murray Beynon, of the firm Brisbin Brook Beynon, to come up with a specific building design. Beynon had impressive credentials: he was the supervising architect for SkyDome and a managing partner for the Northwest Group's new arena in Vancouver.

As described earlier, John Bitove Jr. and his partners dazzled the NBA expansion committee with a presentation at the Eaton Centre site, complete with free hot dogs and kids and guys in suits shooting hoops right where the new arena was to be built. Peter McAlister took the NBA group on a tour of the Eaton Centre, and he said they asked questions about various elements of the bid and about the Centre and the number of people who passed through it on an annual basis. McAlister also accompanied the Bitove group to New York for the final presentation before the expansion committee.

In October, the Professional Basketball Franchise group won the bid. By June of the following year, the Eaton Centre site was dead. By September 1995, the Raptors had still not started construction of their new arena. The proposal that the Bitove group presented to the NBA expansion committee was for a "basketball-dedicated arena." It was the Palestra group that proposed a facility that the NBA team would have shared with the Toronto Maple Leafs. When Larry Tanenbaum and his group lost, Leaf president Cliff Fletcher said the team would perhaps look at building its own arena. This would become a factor in later equivocations by the Bitove group, as they tried to decide whether to go with a basketball-only facility, or a basketball/hockey arena that they would share with the Maple Leafs.

However, the Raptors had to fight other fires before they could concentrate their attention on the arena issue. When the Pro-Line dispute was resolved, John Bitove Jr. announced that the team was four months behind schedule, but they would be proceeding with plans to build the 20,000 seat facility, called the Centre Court project. But sources say that the enthusiasm had already started to wane for the Eaton Centre site, and by March 1994, the Professional Basketball Franchise group was actively searching for another downtown site.

By summer 1994, Bitove was still publicly denying that the group was thinking of giving up on the Bay and Dundas location. "We love the Eaton Centre site," he told the *Globe and Mail* in July 1994. "For a basketball-only building it works extremely well. A lot of people have called us and made noises that they want us to go elsewhere. And we listen, that's all, like any other group of businessmen would."

One of the noisiest proponents of moving the Raptors arena was the mayor of North York, Mel Lastman. He ardently pursued the team, hoping to persuade the group to move the arena to his neck of the woods, and minced no words when analyzing the proposed site at the Eaton Centre: "There's no way Bitove can build it there. It doesn't make any sense with all the extra costs it will take to build there. Plus, Cadillac Fairview has no money. So the site is out. There's no way he can go on that site."

Lastman did have a point. The finances of Cadillac Fairview had been shaky, to say the least. The real estate developer had gone through a major restructuring as commercial property values crashed during the recession. The proposed arena project at Bay and Dundas called for Cadillac Fairview and the other co-owners of the Eaton Centre, Eaton's and the TD Bank, to absorb the cost of moving the Cineplex Odeon multiplex theatres to another location to make room for the arena, and also the cost of demolishing the parking garage. Still, as late as July 1994, Peter McAlister, Cadillac Fairview's Vice-President of Development, said that negotiations were continuing to make the Eaton Centre arena possible.

But Mayor Mel Lastman wasn't giving up. He could offer the Raptors a 24-acre site in North York, a piece of land owned by the Weston family, at Yonge Street and Highway 401. Lastman continued his sales pitch: "It's the best site anywhere in Metropolitan Toronto," he said. "There's nothing to touch it. The visibility is phenomenal. There's over 350,000 cars that pass that spot every single day. It will stand out like a sore thumb."

What Lastman didn't mention was the amount of road construction it would take to improve access to the site in North York. One city official estimated the road upgrading would cost as much as $30 million, which North York hoped would be paid for through the federal government's infrastructure program.

Peter McAlister of Cadillac Fairview dismissed the pitch from North York, saying it could not even compare with a downtown location, particularly the Eaton Centre site. "This site is so much better than anything else that anyone's talked about," he said. "I laughed when they talked about North York. This is a winter sport. Can you imagine being able to walk underground...from your office, leave at 6:30 and watch a game at 7?"

McAlister was right. The Bitove group was definitely sold on a downtown site. However, it would not be the Eaton Centre location.

As late as September 21, 1994, the parties involved in building an arena at Bay and Dundas were still talking optimistically about the start of construction. Pat Howe, spokesperson for Cadillac Fairview, said that the deal was almost complete with Cineplex Odeon to move the multiplex theatre. Howe said Cadillac Fairview was waiting for the Raptors to finish their design for the arena, and that was expected by November 1. That is what was being said publicly. In the meantime, however, sources say that the team was not only looking at other downtown properties, it had even placed a sealed bid on a location at Bay and Wellesley, which was put up for public auction. The property, including a vacant lot near the downtown YMCA, was, however, awarded to another bidder. The Raptors had obviously decided by that point that the Eaton Centre was not going to be their final location.

On October 14, 1994, the first media report linked the Raptors with the old Postal Delivery Building at 40 Bay Street, just off Lakeshore Boulevard. The *Globe and Mail* reported that the franchise was in negotiations with Canada Post for the building and an area of about 12 hectares (six acres) near Union Station. The limestone building was designated historically significant, which would have to be factored into the Raptors design concept. But otherwise, the location seemed ideal, with access to major thoroughfares and high visibility. Above all, it was right downtown in the heart of the corporate district.

The property had a troubled history. During the 1990 real estate boom, it was reportedly sold for $200 million to Bramalea and Trizec for use as an office, retail and residential space. But the deal didn't go through. Canada Post was still trying to sell it when the Raptors came calling. It was valued by Canada Post at $65 million. Apparently the first offer from the Raptors was $14 million, described by one reporter as "a lowball bid."

In only a matter of months, the Raptors had dropped their corporate cousins at Cadillac Fairview and were about to sign a deal with Canada Post. Peter McAlister of Cadillac Fairview says there were several reasons why his company eventually shook hands and parted company with the Raptors. For one thing, the team had originally contracted with Cadillac Fairview to provide development services for a new arena. Since then, however, the Raptors had hired Jay Cross as the full-time manager of the stadium project. Cross had extensive experience in real estate and made the services of Cadillac Fairview redundant. McAlister says it was obvious that the Raptors preferred "to do the development on their own." He does, however, clarify that at no time was Cadillac Fairview or anyone working for Cadillac Fairview a shareholder in the team or the arena. McAlister says that was incorrectly reported and was never true.

McAlister says there were also problems with the Eaton Centre site that, in the end, could not be resolved. It was, as he calls it, a "difficult site" and the economics and the logistics were too much for the team. Even though the owners of the Eaton Centre were going to pay to move the movie theatres and demolish the parking garage, an arena at Bay and Dundas would be "very expensive," says Peter McAlister, though he declines to name an exact amount. But the size of the site was even more of a problem. As the plans evolved into a basketball and hockey complex, it became clear that the space at Bay and Dundas just wasn't big enough. McAlister says that Cadillac Fairview and the Raptors came to a business agreement to sever their relationship and the Eaton Centre arena was dead.

Officially, the franchise told the media that they'd given up on the Bay and Dundas site at the Eaton Centre because it was too small to accommodate a hockey surface. As Peter McAlister confirms, somewhere along the way the plan had gone from the basketball-only building of the original proposal made to the NBA, to a joint hockey/basketball facility. Yet there was still no formalized deal with the Maple Leafs, with whom there was some bad blood, both business-wise and family-wise. The Maple Leafs had been aligned earlier in the history of the NBA team with the losing bidders from the Palestra group. So they were off to a bad start with the Bitove bunch. Then, to complicate matters, Maple Leaf Gardens Ltd. was taken over by grocery magnate Steve Stavro in a controversial buy-out involving the shares of the Harold Ballard estate. Stavro is a blood relative of the Bitoves but there is reportedly some competition between the two branches of the family, though this has been denied by John Bitove Jr.

Instead of pursuing a deal with Stavro and the Maple Leafs, the Raptors were now talking about obtaining a franchise in the International Hockey League, a flashy pro league with teams in several large American cities like Las Vegas, Cleveland, Houston, Denver, Detroit and Chicago. It was a brash move, in some ways, thumbing their noses at the Maple Leafs. In a December 1994 advertising supplement about the team, John Bitove Jr. admitted that there had been some preliminary discussions with the IHL and that he had attended a league meeting as an observer a few weeks earlier in Detroit. "We're pleased with the interest from the league with respect to locating in Toronto, but our ownership group has yet to even formally consider the merits of a franchise application at this time," said Bitove.

Still, the team had considered the merits enough to design an arena that could accommodate both basketball and hockey. The truth was, whether it was the NHL or the IHL, the Raptors needed another major tenant in the building. The NBA team would only provide 40 guaranteed dates for the new facility and the owners needed to fill at least twice that many to survive financially. "We're at the exploratory stages for a host of other potential sports entertainment properties and tenants for our new stadium," explained Bitove in December 1994.

First, however, the team had to definitively decide where that new stadium would be. As usual, the team left the location of the arena to leak out in media reports, rather than through any direct confirmation by the team. In fact, the team had already sent a memo to Toronto City Council asking it to fast-track the site, citing a similar consideration given for the expansion of the Metro Convention Centre. All John Bitove would say was that "we're not working hard on any of the other proposed sites. We're negotiating on what we believe is the best site."

In December 1994, Canada Post and the Raptors announced that they had reached a deal. The Toronto franchise would pay a reported $60 million, with payments spread over many years. There was some public concern about the historical nature of the building, and the team agreed to maintain two of the building's decorated facades and build behind them. So far, so good. But then things got a little complicated. The site where the Raptors wanted to build their arena also included a piece of land owned by Marathon Realty. This turned the entire land deal into a gigantic game of "let's make a deal" involving the City of Toronto, Canada Post, Marathon Realty and the Raptors.

The Raptors and Canada Post had made a side deal. The arena wouldn't take up all the Canada Post land, and the crown corporation wanted to transfer the density not used by the arena to its land. That would apparently allow Canada Post to build an office tower as tall as 58 storeys on its remaining land. That angered the people at Marathon Realty, who said that the tower would crowd out its buildings. It too asked to have its density rules transferred as part of the fast-track proposal submitted by the Raptors.

Marathon's proposed buildings, three residential apartment buildings, would contain 1,500 units and would rise to a height of 137 metres, even though the area was only zoned for 76 metres. So suddenly, Toronto City Council found itself considering a deal that included a lot more than just a basketball facility. Because the proposal was being fast-tracked, some city councillors thought they were being rushed into making a decision that, in the long term, they'd regret. Toronto City Councillor Michael Walker was a fierce opponent to the Raptors deal from day one. "I saw the warning signals from early in the new year [1995]. I anticipated being stung. Whenever professional sports are involved, we're supposed to drop to our knees before the new holy grail," said Walker.

He contends that the deal proposed by the Raptors was nothing more than a business transaction: a big land transfer among some high-powered corporate pals. To make things even more complicated, the Raptors were now proposing a three-way swap so that Canada Post and Marathon would end up with continuous land on either side of the arena. That way, the Raptors would end up paying less for the Canada Post land because part of it would be involved in the swap. One of the first concerns of City Council was the sheer magnitude of the buildings being proposed by Canada Post and Marathon Realty. The council had spent many years designing a development model for the Railway Lands East, as the area is known. At the time the plan was designed, developers, including Marathon Realty, agreed that there would be no more density transfers that would compromise the area's design. That concept was already in jeopardy. Council was also very aware that there was a glut of office towers in Toronto and that there had been a community backlash against big, tall buildings in that area, having suffered through the adverse reaction to the Harbourfront development in the late 1980s. That development provided part of the impetus for coming up with rules such as the ones that would be broken by the Canada Post–Marathon Realty–Raptors density swaps. As urban affairs columnist John Barber wrote in the *Globe and Mail*: "This is the Wild West poker game that led to so much bad building in Toronto a decade ago."

By May 1995, the shovels were still not in the ground, and as the wrangling with Toronto City Hall continued, the Raptors actually went so far as to threaten to scrap the $110 million project. The team was particularly frustrated after a city land-use committee suggested that the development was too big. Councillor Kyle Rae proposed that the Raptors should split the application into two parts—the arena and the highrise proposals. That was later rejected by City Council. But there was a definite animosity growing between certain councillors and the franchise. Councillor Kyle Rae described the entire proposal as "gun-at-your-head planning." Michael Walker, referred to the deal as a "scam attack," and said the deal "puts the city in the position where the city has to waive all its rules." At a meeting in early May, Council voted to support a motion from Councillor Rae asking the team to come back in three weeks to explain why the city should make the proposed amendments.

The Raptors wasted little time, sending an avalanche of paper back to Toronto City Council. Jay Cross, the stadium projects manager for the franchise, defended the development request: "This is very solid land-use planning at work. It's a great plan. We've been working with the city planning staff since last October–November. This is not shotgun planning by any extent of the imagination."

About a week later, there was another crisis, again involving the proposed arena. *The Toronto Sun* obtained a confidential letter written by Jay Cross asking City Hall to give the Raptors a piece of city property for free. The land in question is a one-foot reserve along the property owned by the Raptors and their partners Marathon Realty. Neither party wanted to pay for the land, which the team valued in the letter at $1.6 million. The city had the land appraised for $4 million. The letter was addressed to Barry Gutteridge, the City of Toronto's Acting Commissioner of Property. In it, Cross argued that the Raptors would be contributing more than $6 million over the next 10 years towards community and youth outreach programs at the arena, so that the team should not also be expected to provide community services or facilities. Cross said that the arena development would push the value of the land over $17 million, and so, in exchange, the city should "accept these items as full and complete compensation to the city for the transfer by the city of the municipal land and the one-foot reserve."

The leaked letter didn't go over very well with some members of Toronto City Council, especially Michael Walker. "As far as I'm concerned, they're not getting a nickel from the taxpayers. I'm not being party to us being taken to the cleaners. What do they think we are, brain dead? They just want a free ride and as far as I'm concerned they're not going to get it," said Walker.

All sparring aside, the delay was beginning to cause problems for Jay Cross and the rest of the Raptors' organization. The cost had already ballooned for the 22,500-seat arena. While it had started around the $100 million mark, now Bitove himself was estimating it could go as high as $175 million, and the delays weren't helping.

Still, the Raptors had taken a huge step forward in financing the new facility earlier in 1995 when they signed Air Canada as the name sponsor for the arena. Air Canada paid an estimated $20 million to have its name and logo on the outside of the building. And Bitove managed to get an unprecedented $15 million of that as "up-front money," with the rest coming in lower payments over the years. The deal also includes prime advertising space inside, which will give the airline good exposure on Canadian and American broadcasts, though it doesn't necessarily guarantee the airline will serve as the team's exclusive carrier.

The Air Canada deal sounded like an earlier deal between General Motors of Canada and the Northwest Entertainment group, the parent organization of the Vancouver Canucks and the Vancouver Grizzlies. General Motors also paid an estimated $20 million to have its name on the new home of the Vancouver hockey and basketball clubs. But only $6 million came "up-front."

While GM will be very visible for the Vancouver basketball fans, the car-maker didn't get in on the Raptors action. The Ford Motor Co. of Canada, a major sponsor of "Hockey Night in Canada," signed on as a major marketing partner with the Raptors. That deal will give the company advertising and sponsorship rights for several years and is reported to have cost about $35 million. The move foiled any plan by GM to tie up the pro basketball scene in Canada but does continue the sports theme in Ford's advertising. As well, Ford had recently paid $10 million to have its name put on the Ford Centre for the Performing Arts in Toronto, with a similar deal in Vancouver. (GM Place and Air Canada Centre join a growing trend among professional sports franchises. In the United States, most of the major new arenas and stadia have been named for large corporate sponsors. For example, the new Cleveland basketball arena is called Gund Arena, after a $14 million US contribution from industrialist Gordon Gund. The Chicago Bulls and Chicago Blackhawks play at the United Center, while there is the CoreStates Spectrum in Philadelphia and the US Air Arena in Washington. There are some exceptions, like Camden Yards in Baltimore, where arenas and ballparks still have regionally or historically significant monikers rather than names purchased by large corporations.)

Over the summer of 1995, the wrangling continued between the Raptors and Toronto City Council and the rhetoric flew, with councillors arguing for or against the basketball franchise. Ironically, the councillors who were against the Raptors development became so obsessed with the deal for the piece of land that the bigger picture seemed to be forgotten. By mid-July, the Raptors had proposed a deal whereby they would compensate the city for the triangle of land at the corner of Bremner Boulevard and York Street with a package of goodies: $80,000 in cash, 450 season tickets and six days of stadium use annually for 20 years—a total value between $400,000 and $600,000 annually. The Raptors felt that the land was really only worth $1.6 million.

Toronto City Councillor Kay Gardner was outraged, calling for the Raptors to pay "cash, not trinkets. I think they're treating us like a bunch of hicks, throwing a bunch of tickets at us." Gardner received 200 calls, faxes and letters from taxpayers complaining about the proposed Raptors deal. "People are mad," she said, adding that many considered the proposed swap "a major giveaway." She added: "I'm prepared to welcome the Raptors with open arms, but not open pockets. They're not a charity. They're in this to make money."

The open-line shows on Toronto radio stations were filled with debates about the merits of the proposed deal between the city and the Raptors. The Raptors primary argument was that they were "at their limit in terms of what they were willing to pay" and would not pay the $4 million that an independent assessment had said that land strip was worth.

"It's like a negotiation for a car or a house. You dicker back and forth and at some point you say, 'Enough, we're not paying any more'." said John Bitove. "We're paying $20 million already in this city for development and infrastructure surrounding a privately funded arena. So the city is getting plenty from us. No need for us to fork out any more money."

But it was another public relations nightmare for the Raptors because the way it was presented and covered by the media was that the Raptors were "crying poor." Callers to phone-in shows and writers of letters to the editor wondered how the Raptors had been able to afford the $125 million US expansion fee and how they were going to pay their million-dollar-a-year players if they were in fact so cash poor.

Still, the Raptors had several key players on Toronto City Council on their side, including Mayor Barbara Hall. Hall had once voted against taxpayer subsidies for SkyDome but was now fully in favour of the Raptors project. (The timing worked in the Raptors favour as many real estate projects had recently ground to a halt in Toronto because of the election of the Conservative government, which had cancelled many public building projects.)

Councillor Tom Jakobek argued on behalf of the Raptors, saying that the piece of land was "a dump. If the Raptors stadium wasn't going there, what would? Nothing."

So on July 24, 1995, Toronto City Council voted approval of a deal that gave the Raptors the land they wanted in exchange for the tickets, the stadium use and the cash. The vote was 13–3, with the three votes against the deal coming from Kay Gardner, Michael Walker and Chris Korwin-Kuczynski. Said Korwin-Kuczynski after the vote: "It leaves a bad taste not only in my mouth, but in the mouths of a lot of citizens who don't think this is the best deal for the taxpayers of the city."

Several days after the vote, Michael Walker was still fuming, calling the deal "the biggest municipal giveaway ever." From Walker's perspective, the Raptors had fronted what was basically a major land swap to get around the city's Official Plan for that part of downtown. He says it's particularly ironic that Marathon Realty was one of the groups that agreed to the new Official Plan that limited development on the so-called Railway Lands East. "The ink is barely dry, and we've spent millions in staff time coming up with this Official Plan," said Walker.

Walker had tried to question Marathon Realty and the Raptors about their business relationship, but had gotten nowhere. He says that Marathon, in particular, has done well by the deal because the land it will receive from the Raptors has changed from commercial, which has no value in Toronto's current stale marketplace, to residential, which is a potential area for growth. Walker says that another piece of land near the Metro Toronto Convention Centre that

Marathon now owns was re-zoned for a hotel, which could also prove to be potentially very valuable. Walker says that he was especially struck by the arrogance of the Raptors who "held City Council to ransom." Asked if he was going to take advantage of any of the 450 season tickets that the city now owns, Walker could only snicker: "Absolutely not."

The supporters of the Raptors on City Council were thrilled by the deal. "It's a good night for the city of Toronto, a good night for the citizens of Toronto and, finally, a good night for basketball," said Mayor Barbara Hall. Councillor Steve Ellis added: "We need to get Toronto moving again. Let's get a shovel in the ground before the snow flies."

The Raptors got what they wanted, as did their corporate partners at Canada Post and Marathon Realty. Everyone, with the exception of a few councillors and a few hundred grumpy taxpayers, was happy. But once again, the Raptors had attracted a lot of negative publicity. The deal with Metro Toronto attracted some disparaging editiorials in Toronto newspapers. The editorial in *The Toronto Sun* read: "...the Raptors' attitude, which has often seemed to be that the entire city should bow down to them over the fact they've deigned to set up shop here, is wearing thin. Toronto is now accustomed to having major league sports franchises and to serving as a host for prestigious sporting events. This isn't some hick town any more ready to play dead for sports entrepreneurs waving around the promise of dollar bills."

A few days later, the *Globe and Mail* had similar scathing comments for the Toronto basketball franchise: "The political arm-twisting and cap-in-hand poor-mouthing that characterized this deal was sad enough to watch. But as a portent of a business/political relationship that is unfolding it is positively scary."

So the Raptors now have a name for their new arena—Air Canada Centre—and a place to build it. They opted to wait until October 1, 1995 to start construction. That, of course, was the date on which they had agreed to break ground or pay a $1 million penalty. When the day passed with no arena foundation begun, the Raptors paid the $1 million to the Raptors Foundation, established to disperse help to charities.

The unclear NBA labour picture over the summer also caused added stress for the new team, which paid the $125 million US expansion fee with no guarantee that there would be labour peace by the time the season was scheduled to begin.

The Raptors have also expressed official interest in buying Maple Leaf Gardens Ltd., but with no intention, according to PBF Chairman and part-owner David Peterson, of playing in that old building. "We would be interested in purchasing that company with a view to owning the hockey team and having a second team playing in the Air Canada Centre. Maple Leaf Gardens we would then sell, or develop, or whatever. It's not suitable for our needs. Too small... too old. We're interested in the hockey team as a co-tenant for our new place."

The Raptors ownership people do admit, though, that their plan is to have many other events in the Air Canada Centre. While reluctant to admit it in the summer, Bitove and company have a deal with the guru of performing arts promotion in Canada, Garth Drabinksy, to stage some musical theatre events at the new building.

David Peterson admits that they want the place booked as much as possible. "Oh, of course.... We plan to have tennis, wrestling, ice shows, theatre, all kinds of things. Basketball only guarantees us 40-some home dates. That leaves a lot of nights that would otherwise be dark."

The Raptors Vice-President of Business Development, Brian Cooper, is not only confident about sales revenues, he thinks the building can work even without NHL hockey. "I do believe the forces of sports economics in the city will eventually drive the Leafs to our building. They can't get another dollar out of that old place they play in. Every seat, every box is sold, tickets are priced awfully high already. They've got to join us in the new place," said Cooper. "And if not, we can make IHL hockey work here. It works in NHL cities like Detroit and Chicago. They're averaging 12–14,000 thousand fans a game for IHL hockey. People love it because it's affordable at 13 bucks a ticket. We'll also stage all kinds of shows and acts in the new place. I've already talked with the tennis people about a major indoor stop in the winter with a

$2 million purse and a week-long tournament. Figure skating competitions like the World Juniors and the Nationals and ice shows that refuse to go into Maple Leaf Gardens will come to us."

Cooper says Maple Leaf Gardens had 45 nights of hockey in 1993 and a handful of other events that brought the total use up to about 51 nights total during the year. "We expect to do about 150–200 nights in our first year. We'll take concert business away from SkyDome too. Most of these shows have staging specs that are for arenas. So are their cost projections. The move-in and move-out fee for SkyDome is $17,000. Ours will be $3,000."

CHAPTER SEVEN

THE NAME GAME

Comedian Jerry Seinfeld has a great line about watching pro sports. He says that when we don't know who the players are, basically, we're just cheering for "a bunch of laundry." In the NBA though, that "laundry" is worth over $3 billion a year in sales.

Choosing a marketable name and logo is big business, and the two new Canadian franchises presented a bonanza of opportunities for the league.

The Toronto franchise decided to make a big event out of choosing a name for the new team and came up with a cross-Canada contest early in 1994. Tom Mayenknecht, the spokesman at the time for the still-nameless team, travelled across the country asking groups for suggestions, eventually compiling a list of 10 finalists. Meanwhile, behind the scenes, the people at the NBA head office in New York were doing their own research and would definitely influence the final outcome of the "democratic" process of the name selection.

There were, originally, over 2,000 different suggestions collected from some 100,000 Canadians in the name-the-team contest. The suggested names included Sturgeons, Killer Whales, Tomcats, Hoops, Swish, Sneakers, Dribblers, Blue Basketballs, Canadian Eh's, Snowbirds, Blizzard, Northern Lights, Kool Kats, Metro Maroons, Mosaics, Pro Liners, Trilliums and John Candy. Obviously some of the suggestions were more likely choices than others. The top 10 were selected by a panel of celebrities, including athletes Myriam Bedard and Josée Chouinard, and headed by Lincoln Alexander, former lieutenant-governor of Ontario.

But what was really important about the contest was the publicity that the team drummed up during the national travels leading up to the actual unveiling of the final choice. It was the kind of hype and coverage that the NBA likes to see. For that very reason, most modern-day NBA teams went through a similar process when they were in their formative stages.

At the same time, however, the team, it appears, was leaving nothing to chance. On February 10, 1994, the day the name-the-team contest was kicked off by President John Bitove Jr., team lawyers registered the winning name in the so-called contest. A report in the *Toronto Star* said that the lawyers only registered two names: The Raptors and Toronto Raptors, as well as the name Raptorwear.

In its defence, the team points out that this wasn't the first time that the franchise had protected certain names. A batch of names was also listed with the Canadian trademark office in October 1993. The team's response, through public relations spokesman Tom Mayenknecht, was that the team was concerned about other groups registering the name Raptors.

"We registered every name we came up with," says John Bitove Jr. "We registered about 17 or 18 in all I think.... I could show you the legal letters."

Needless to say, the name Raptors was the final choice in the fan vote, getting 24 percent of the 152,000 votes, followed by Bobcats with 15 percent, and Dragons at 14 percent. Unfortunately for the team, the final choice did leak out and was mentioned on TSN, and then in the local newspapers a few days before the planned unveiling on a Sunday. It's not surprising the secret did leak out, considering some retailers were told in advance so they could stock up on Raptors gear for Monday, the day after the unveiling. Eight new Canadian firms had been licensed by NBA Properties in New York, the league division that maintains strict control over all use of the NBA name and logo.

In choosing the name Raptors, the franchise owners and the NBA were counting on the continuing appeal of the dinosaur craze, which was propelled largely by the hugely successful movie *Jurassic Park*. The Raptors were, in fact, made famous in that movie. Anyone who saw the film would need no introduction to what a raptor is, but the team's promotional material does describe the characteristics of the raptor for those who aren't up on dinosaur lore. (The raptors in the film were a nasty bunch of creatures that Steven Spielberg portrayed eating a lawyer and chasing small children...just what you want in a sports logo?) In the team's promotional material, raptors are described as fast-moving, jumping predators, standing six to seven feet in height. The velociraptor had particularly sharp teeth, were fast runners and were quite fierce. The oviraptors preyed on the eggs of other dinosaurs, while the deinoychus had a leaping attack, with a large, spur-like claw, that again will be memorable from *Jurassic Park*. The claw ends up as a key part of the future editions of the Raptors team logo, which is called the globoraptor.

In fact, the Toronto Raptors of the NBA are not the first professional team to use the dinosaur logo and name, but they are the first big-league team to do so. The Ogden Raptors are a minor-league baseball team, and the Rockford Raptors are an American semi-pro soccer team. Still, the NBA was very keen on the dinosaur concept. John Bitove Jr. preferred the name T-Rex, but sources say the NBA nixed that idea, saying the image was too fierce. The league pushed for the Raptors image instead, and Bitove confirms that the artwork for the Raptors name and logo was clearly the best of the final choices. Bill Marshall, Vice-President and General Manager of NBA Properties, the group that helped design the logo, said at the time of its unveiling: "We think the kids are really going to fall in love with the Raptor and the colours." And on the dinosaur image, Marshall added: "I frankly find it amazing no one has thought of it before."

The Toronto team had also definitely done its research on the current hot colours in team merchandise. The logo incorporates most of the most popular colours in 1990s marketing. There's a snarling red dinosaur on a deep purple background, with features and lettering in black and "Naismith silver" (a sentimental nod in the direction of Dr. James Naismith, the Canadian inventor of basketball).

Within hours of the logo's unveiling on May 16, 1994, there were about 100,000 T-shirts in production, and 120,000 baseball caps went on sale the next day. Kellogg's even planned a commemorative box of cereal for June.

The league reaction was predictably positive, seeing as it had been involved in approving the team's name and logo. NBA Properties handles all the licensing of NBA merchandise and does extensive marketing on what's hot and what's not in the sports retail business. Bill Marshall said in May 1994 that he thought the Raptors merchandise would likely double the Canadian sales of NBA gear: "Right now, retailers in the U.S. are buying Raptors material just as heavily as they are up here in Canada," said Marshall.

In 1988, the sales figure of NBA gear in Canada was around $2 million. Incredibly, the forecasts from the league suggested that figure would be up to $75 million by the time the Raptors and the Grizzlies hit the court. The teams get to keep between seven and nine percent, with the rest going into the NBA pot. (The percentage of merchandise sales was another negotiating point in the expansion agreement. It's believed the Raptors asked for a higher cut to balance the hefty expansion fee.) The overall sales of NBA merchandise should hit $3 billion in 1995, and the 29 teams in the league all share in that wealth. One of the actual buyers of the merchandise, Larry DeFlorio of the Cole Sports Agency, had already presold 15,000 T-shirts to Canadian retailers. At the time, he told the *Toronto Star*: "I think it'll be as big as the Hornets."

The Charlotte Hornets, with a logo in the very popular colours of teal, purple and black, were then number two in NBA merchandise sales. The Hornets were an expansion team that joined the league in 1987, and they're also part of the new wave in sports marketing that is growing ever more sophisticated, as demonstrated by the strategic design of the Raptors name and logo. NBA Deputy Commissioner Russ Granik reflected on this trend at the unveiling of the Raptors' design: "In terms of marketing, we're a little more sophisticated than we were six or seven years ago during our last expansion. I don't think we were able then to develop as co-ordinated an approach with the team as this one has been."

Still, some of those expansion teams from the 1980s have been among the most successful ever in the league's history, giving the Raptors quite a benchmark to surpass. In fact, of the top 15 teams in merchandise sales in hockey, basketball and baseball, seven are expansion franchises that have done extensive research and gone for

Air Canada Centre, the proposed home for the Raptors, situated on the Toronto skyine.

Isiah Thomas, General Manager of the Toronto Raptors, and John Bitove Jr., club President, unveil the proposed stadium design for the old Postal Delivery Building. December 21, 1994.

Everol Bennett, a 12-year-old Toronto student, wears the new Raptors jersey at the team's official uniform unveiling. February 1, 1995.

Tom Mayenknecht, then Communications Director of the Raptors, poses with Raptors paraphernalia. By February 3, 1995, the team had already moved to seventh place out of 29 NBA teams in product sales.

Isiah Thomas, with the Detroit Pistons, makes the cover of *Forbes* magazine. December 19, 1994.

Wearing a leather Raptors jacket, Isiah Thomas talks to the media after it is announced that he has signed on as the team's first general manager. May 24, 1994.

Arthur Griffiths, right, introduces Stu Jackson as the Grizzlies' general manager. July 22, 1994.

Isiah Thomas led the Indiana Hoosiers to the NCAA championship in 1981. (John Bitove Jr. was at Indiana University during Thomas' glory years.)

Paul Beeston of the Toronto Blue Jays is brought in to help the ailing Argonauts of the Canadian Football League. May 5, 1994.

Cazabon/Canada Wide

Steve Stavro, the troubled owner of the Toronto Maple Leafs and Maple Leaf Gardens, is a cousin of John Bitove Jr.

McKenna/Canada Wide

The Blue Jays opener in Exhibition Stadium, 1977.

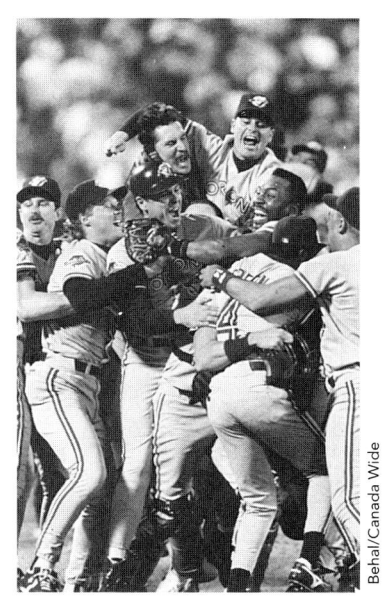

The Toronto Blue Jays pile onto the field at SkyDome after winning the World Series.

Since the death of Harold Ballard in 1990, several groups have expressed interest in buying the storied Maple Leafs franchise, including the Raptors.

John Candy and Raghib "Rocket" Ishmail hold the Grey Cup after the Argos' victory in November 1991.

heavily marketable logos when their teams started up. Other examples beyond basketball include the San Jose Sharks and the Anaheim Mighty Ducks who have propelled merchandise sales in hockey to an all-time high.

The company that designed the logo for the Raptors has extensive involvement with other professional sports franchises. The Sean Michael Edward Design company of New York has also redesigned the uniforms for the St. Louis Blues of the NHL, the Denver Nuggets of the NBA and the Seattle Mariners and California Angels of Major League Baseball. The company originated the designs for several other teams, including the Florida Panthers of the NHL, the NFL's expansion Jacksonville Jaguars, the new Tampa Bay Devil Rays, who will join MLB, and the Ottawa Lynx, the triple-A farm club of the Montreal Expos. The company has just become involved with the Canadian Football League, including work with the Toronto Argonauts, the Memphis Mad Dogs and the Birmingham Barracudas.

The Raptors' uniforms were unveiled in February 1995, again with a splashy party, and again, the team was trying to push all the right marketing buttons to ensure big sales. Besides the now-familiar globoraptor, the shorts have a claw-print logo on one side, and there are two layers, including a pair of spandex shorts trimmed in globoraptor print. The Raptor bites into a large TR, the team's initials. The player numbers are jagged in outline, as are the players' names, like a sawtooth border, the kind of effect you'd get with pinking shears. At the unveiling, David Strickland, the team's Director of Consumer Products, modestly called the new uniforms "the freshest look in the NBA."

So far, the dino-look appears to be a hit. Since the logo was unveiled, the Raptors have taken a giant globoraptor leap into seventh place, out of the 29 teams in the NBA, in merchandise sales, generating an estimated $20 million for the Toronto franchise.

While the consumers are the ones who really count, the dinosaur logo has not been universally popular. *Globe and Mail* columnist Stephen Brunt questions the wisdom of naming a team based on a fad that could easily fade in five years, rather than on a more geographical or historical concept. "Raptors is so obviously a concept, a package, one with no conceivable link to the city other than one floor of the Royal Ontario Museum. There aren't a lot of lakes around Los Angeles and Utah isn't know for its great jazz heritage, but those names are flukes of franchise shifting. As a rule, it's nice to have some sort of local association. Blue Jays might not have been an inspired choice (unless you're trying to peddle a brand of beer commonly referred to by that same colour), but at least you can see them pilfering peanuts from your backyard feeder in the winter."

While the dinosaurs themselves may have become extinct, the NBA research has shown that the dino concept has legs and will continue to sell over the next 10 years, even taking into account the fickle aspect of fads. That being said, the Raptors management obviously has longer-term confidence in the dinosaur name. John Bitove Jr. told a media conference when the logo was unveiled: "At our board meeting, when everyone saw the logo for the first time, we did get a bit choked up. We realized we were putting the stamp on a part of the Toronto scene for the next 100 years."

One of the potential team names that didn't make the final list did have some geographical roots in Toronto. The name "Towers" was suggested over and over again in the cross-Canada name-the-team contest, in honour of the CN Tower, which dominates the Toronto skyline. There were a couple of problems with the name. One of the criteria for the winning name selection was that it couldn't be challenged legally. A tower logo would have been difficult to design without it looking like the CN Tower and could have potentially caused a legal infringement. There was also a Towers department store, which still had some legal protection of the name. But the greatest complication was that one of the rival bidders for the Toronto franchise, the Palestra group, had registered the name Toronto Towers during the bidding process. Relations were strained between the Palestra group and the Bitove-led organization, making it doubtful that the two could have come to any sort of a deal.

Like the Toronto group, the Vancouver organization had run into some legal pitfalls in its quest for a name. Originally, the West Coast expansion team had been very keen on the very Canadian nickname Mounties, and had been introduced as such. But the

Royal Canadian Mounted Police had just launched a crackdown on businesses using the name and likeness of the RCMP and, of course, the Mounties. The RCMP has since made a deal with the Disney Corporation that might have cleared the way for Vancouver's NBA team to use "Mountie" but, at the time, despite some negotiations, it appeared it wouldn't be usable. Also, the NBA wasn't wild about the idea. It had done some market research as had the Vancouver people and found that "Mounties"wasn't going to be a hit with the young, hip, cap-wearing basketball fans in the U.S. or Canada. So, with gentle urging from the league, with trademarking and licensing wrangles looming with the RCMP, and with the B.C. public hating the name Mounties for their team (a Vancouver TV station polled viewers and found that 83 percent of the respondents favoured changing the name, and one retailer said simply: "If they don't change the name, they won't sell a single T-shirt.") the Vancouver team had to select another name and logo. A local newspaper held a name-the-team contest and got suggestions and artwork from all over the lower mainland, urging names like Vancouver Reign, Dragons, Stealth, Quakes, Vipers, Thunderbirds and Force. The Griffiths people toyed briefly with the Force but, in the end, they decided in August 1994 that it would be the Grizzlies.

Interestingly, in May 1994, Raptors President John Bitove Jr. was talking about the choice of a dinosaur for his team's name and logo, and was reported in *The Financial Post* as saying that a name like Grizzlies would have been a problem. "How do you have a big, fat bear as a mascot? Kids in the focus groups said, 'We don't like bears. Bears are big dumb things.'"

Bitove's comments aside, the Vancouver franchise liked the name, and it did well in market research and it became the choice. However, the Vancouver people did have one more obstacle to deal with. Like the name "Towers", the Grizzlies name had also been protected by the Palestra group during its bidding for a team in Toronto. This time, however, Larry Tanenbaum of the Palestra group was willing to make a deal. In exchange for courtside seats whenever he travels to Vancouver, he was willing to transfer the Grizzlies trademark to the Vancouver franchise.

As with the Raptors uniform, the designers for the Grizzlies also made use of the hottest, hippest colours in sports marketing. The home uniforms are white, with the team colours being red, bronze, turquoise and black. The away uniforms feature the same colours on a turquoise background. They also have a West Coast taste to them, as the trim on the uniforms features a pattern reminiscent of the traditional Haida art. The shorts feature a large grizzly bear gripping a basketball with its claws, not unlike the claws of the globoraptor. The unveiling of the Grizzlies' uniform in Vancouver in May 1995 was also a splashy affair, and the Grizzlies brought in beach volleyball star and Nike model Gabrielle Reese to show off the new outfit. The uniforms were being manufactured by Champion, which is licensed by the NBA to have exclusive rights for official game uniforms, another way in which the league maintains strict control over the way its logo and products are manufactured and sold.

While the Raptors may have overshadowed the Grizzlies somewhat with their radical choice of name and logo, the Grizzlies have made some large and quick strides in their merchandising. At the start of 1995, they were ninth on the list of NBA merchandise sales, out of 29 teams.

With the names and logos in place and the all-important merchandise sales underway, the marketing departments could turn their attention to preparing for the team's debuts. The Canadian teams would receive a crash course in the entertainment side of the NBA, a formula that has been duplicated in cities throughout the league and would now be introduced north of the 49th parallel.

CHAPTER EIGHT

THE TELEVISION DEAL

There was another condition that the two new Canadian franchises had to meet as part of the expansion agreement with the NBA. Besides the $125 million US expansion fee and the guaranteed 12,500 season tickets, the Raptors and the Grizzlies promised to have a television deal in place by December 31, 1994.

Television has played an integral role in the success of the NBA over the last decade. The sport of basketball works on TV for a variety of reasons. The games are shorter and faster than baseball; a basketball game is over in two hours, compared to an average of more than three hours for a ballgame. (Major League Baseball has recognized the snail-like pace of its games as a problem and is experimenting, during the 1995 season, with ways of shortening the games through a variety of rule changes.) The basketball itself is easier to follow on the television screen than a hockey puck, and there is more non-stop action than, for example, in an NFL game. One of the biggest advantages that the NBA has had in its television coverage is the very nature of the game itself. There are fewer players on the screen at any one time, as compared to the other pro leagues, and they don't wear a lot of protective gear, as in hockey and football. So fans at home get to see lots of tight facial shots of their basketball heroes, which makes the players more identifiable and builds their popularity.

As part of its deal with the American, and now Canadian, networks, the NBA maintains very tight contol over the way its games are produced, to the point of dictating a certain number of cameras, with very specific placement of each one. Similarly, the NBA was the first professional league to have not only its own broadcast division, but also its own television studio. The league's entertainment division, NBA Entertainment, produces its "NBA Inside Stuff" program, which is aired on Saturday mornings throughout North America, and has been instrumental in building the NBA's strong fan support in the younger demographics. The program got a widespread audience after Commissioner David Stern asked NBC to guarantee a free half hour of airtime, between 11 a.m. and 1 p.m. Saturdays, right after cartoons. The show is fast-paced, with many of the same entertainment values that the league tries to promote at its games, and provides even more visibility for its players.

The league has also been able to capitalize on basketball's popularity in its latest television deal with NBC and Turner Sports. The four-year deal, beginning in the fall of 1993, was worth $750 million, about a 25 percent increase over the previous package. More importantly for the Raptors and the Grizzlies, that then breaks down to about $10 million US per team, one of the reasons the NBA gave for the dramatic increase in expansion fees for the two new Canadian teams.

The NBA's TV deal also shows how far the league has come since its darkest days in the early 1980s, when none of the networks wanted to show the championship series live and it was actually aired on tape delay. In the first decade since David Stern took over the league, network television fees have gone from $22 million per year to $150 million, with cable TV monies also rising dramatically from $5.5 million in 1983 to $68.75 million 10 years later.

The NBA TV deal is the envy of several other pro leagues. The NHL, under the leadership of former NBA executive Gary Bettman, is still struggling to get a big-time deal with American television. The league does have a deal, though a minor one, with the Fox Network, which it is constantly trying to upgrade. The NHL bent over backwards during the 1995 hockey playoffs to try to please the Americans and convince them to broadcast even more games during the 1995–96 season. The league even went so far as to schedule back-to-back games during the semifinals, much to the chagrin of the teams and Canadian hockey fans, just so that the NHL could accommodate the Fox Network.

Major League Baseball also saw its television deal fall apart, after CBS lost millions on the previous controversial $1.06 billion agreement. (The deal was controversial because it was so lucrative, to the point that it was unlikely the network could possibly make money with such an agreement. It was also predicted at the time that the CBS deal would drive up the price of television contracts throughout pro sports.) Baseball's current deal, with NBC and ABC, is worth 54 percent less, which translates into about $6.5 million a year per team, about $3.5 million less per franchise than the basketball deal.

David Stern also has other ideas in mind for the league's television coverage in the future. In 1991, Stern had the All-Star Game taped for high-definition TV, so it could be aired that way in Japan where HDTV is already available. He has also talked in the past about the possibility of regional pay-per-view packages available to bars and private homes as another way for the league to generate more television revenues and expand its fan base and, therefore, merchandise sales.

The Canadian television market won't generate the kind of dramatic revenues that the NBA will eventually obtain through its programming in places like Europe and Asia. But the league considered the television deal an important enough part of the NBA's modus operandi to insist that the Canadian teams search out as lucrative a package as possible in their local markets.

The Toronto Raptors have had mixed success in selling themselves as a television commodity. The broadcast deal, along with the corporate sponsorships, were two areas in which John Bitove Jr. insisted on maintaining hands-on control through all stages of the negotiations. He didn't endear himself with certain Canadian broadcasters throughout the process.

The Raptors were, however, the first to sign a local broadcast deal, one month before the December 31, 1994 deadline. The team surprised some with its choice of a local broadcaster, deciding to sign a deal with CITY-TV in Toronto and CKVR in Barrie, Ontario, about an hour north of Toronto. The two stations, both owned by CHUM Ltd. of Toronto, cover most of southern and central Ontario. CKVR reaches as far south as Niagara Falls, east to Peterborough, north to Parry Sound and west to Wingham, with CITY reaching further southwest to Windsor.

CITY founder Moses Znaimer is also President and Executive Producer of both CITY and CKVR. At a news conference to announce the deal, Znaimer talked about his station's first foray into covering professional sport. "Basketball is the only pro sport with soul. It's young, it's street, it's hip. Our viewers will love this game. We're going to work hard with the Raptors to make basketball the talk of T.O. in sports entertainment and to make our T.O. sports entertainment coverage the talk of the NBA," said Znaimer.

Raptors President John Bitove Jr. was equally exuberant over the deal with CITY/CKVR, again because of the station's youthful demographics. "It was the young, hip channel. There was almost a complete overlap in demographics between them and us."

Added Znaimer: "The Raptors approach is to be unique, edgy and entertaining. That's exactly the approach on which we've built CITY-TV." Under the deal, CITY and CKVR will cover 41 Raptors games, the maximum allowed in the team's local market, with 25 on CITY and 16 on CKVR, which, since the Znaimer takeover, is being marketed as "The New VR." All of the CITY games would also be simulcast on CKVR. The Raptors paid in the neighbourhood of $2 million for the deal.

The two stations lost no time in working the Raptors into their promotional material. CITY now bills itself as "CITY-TV: News, Movies, Music, Raptors," while its sibling station is using the slogan: "The New VR: Very Rugged, Very Raptors."

The Raptors deal was particularly significant for CKVR, which has just ended its ties as a CBC affiliate as of September 1995. That means the station will no longer be showing "Hockey Night in Canada," a staple on the channel for years. CKVR marketing spokesperson, Marlene Lone-Studley, said the basketball deal offered not only good demographics, but also a chance to fill the void left by hockey. "Advertisers and people who were used to watching hockey or CFL football were thinking there would be no sports after we break with the CBC. That's not the case." However, Lone-Studley did set the record straight after John Bitove Jr. described CKVR as turning into "almost a 24-hour Raptor channel." (He also talked about the possibilities for NBA promotions on MuchMusic and Fashion Television, obviously seeing all sorts of extra bonuses in the deal for his team.) Lone-Studley didn't like the 24-hour Raptors channel concept, telling the *Globe and Mail* that it overstated CKVR's coverage of basketball. "It is a major acquisition...but there's more to our programming than that."

Besides the games, the two stations also committed to several other chunks of Raptors programming, including a regular Raptors Report, a weekly coach's show and up to six 30-minute specials, spread out over the season.

Like many of the NBA teams south of the border, the Raptors opted to maintain creative control over the game telecasts. The team's Director of Broadcasting, Chris McCracken, will be in charge of the producers, directors, on-air talent and broadcasting crew. ESPN's John Saunders, once a CITY-TV sportscaster and a Canadian, has signed to call some of the Raptors games on CITY/CKVR.

Many of the NBA teams also produce their own games and then sell them, as packaged, to a local station or network. This way the team maintains control over the "look" of the broadcast and over the editorial content of what is being said about the franchise; more importantly, this approach maximizes the profit potential for the team. While this practice is becoming more common in other areas of professional sports, particularly with the increasing degree of cross-ownership between broadcasters and pro franchises, the NBA teams are far ahead of those in other leagues in their hands-on approach to television coverage.

The Orlando Magic have produced their television broadcasts since the team tipped off in 1989. In that first season, gate receipts were estimated at about half of the franchise's revenue while TV and radio broadcasts accounted for about 40 percent of the team's income, worth about $5–8 million in that first year. The team signed a five-year deal with the Sunshine Network, a regional cable network that would pay a flat fee for the broadcast rights to 40 games a season. Then, the team purchased two half-hour blocks of time on a local independent station in Orlando to air 25 away games during the season. (The other Florida team, the Miami Heat, took a similar strategy, signing a 5-year, $12.5 million deal with SportsChannel Florida.)

John Cook is the Director of Broadcasting for the Orlando Magic. He says that some teams may not want to broadcast so many home games in that first season, but the strategy certainly worked out for the Magic. "There are some philosophies that too many home games being available on free TV would take away from the gate. We had a strong season-ticket base so we went ahead and did most of our games on local television and made them available," recalls Cook. "On our over-the-air network, the first three or four years, we carried 25 games and this past season we raised it to 30 because of our recent success and popularity. That means 30 over-the-air games and 40 cable games for a total of 70 games that are available on free TV."

The Orlando Magic have an obvious advantage that the Raptors will not have: superstar Shaquille O'Neal. "Shaquille has made a large impact on our sponsors," says Cook. "We're able to bring on more sponsors, it's easier to get them and they're spending a little bit more with us."

Still, Cook would recommend to the new Canadian teams that they pursue the production of their own television broadcasts. "The advantages of going in-house with all our television is that we control everything. We can control what sponsorships are sold, we can control our prices. Same thing with radio. It just allows us to be in total control of everything.

"Mostly you're controlling your bottom line. You have total say over your costs and your revenues. The quality of the broadcast has something to do with it as well. You want to be on top of it. There are some teams who have sold the rights to their broadcasts and have not been happy because they don't have the say in what goes on the air," Cook explains.

"It can be more lucrative but it's also a risk. It's easy to take a rights fee of 'x' number of dollars and not have to do anything for it. You just know that you're guaranteed that income. But if a team plays its cards right, or if it knows the game, they can go out and make more money by selling its own advertising and setting its own rates and marketing themselves," says Cook.

The Magic don't like to reveal their financial figures for the broadcasting operation, but a Florida newspaper estimated that, in that first year, the Magic charged advertisers an estimated $2,000 to $3,000 for a 30-second spot. It was a hefty fee, but the market could support it, particularly with the appealing demographics of the basketball audience. By 1989, when the Magic joined the NBA, Cook estimates that "about half the teams were in-house. So we had seen track records, and we had seen that if you do it right, you can benefit."

The Toronto Raptors have bought wholeheartedly into the concept of producing their own broadcasts. John Bitove Jr. talked enthusiastically about the new broadcast arrangement: "Let's say we're doing a game and we're going to a commercial break. We'll be able to say to the director before we go "There's a cute picture of a kid with a Coke cup. And Coke's our sponsor. Pick up that shot.'"

An incident during the 1995 baseball season emphasized the importance of that kind of control of the broadcast. The Blue Jays and SkyDome sold a billboard behind home plate to Coca-Cola. It was a great commercial buy for the soft-drink company because it was perfectly framed within a commonly used camera shot of the pitcher and batter. However, The Sports Network refused to use that camera angle in its next broadcast because Coke's rival, Pepsi-Cola, is one of TSN's primary sponsors. A meeting among the network brass, the Jays and SkyDome people worked out the problem. The end result? The Coke sign was gone by the next week.

John Bitove Jr. agrees that advertisers are better served when the team controls the content of the broadcast. "As advertisers get more sophisticated in their buying, they want more. They don't want a situation where Chevrolet buys the rinkboards, Ford is on the television broadcast, Toyota's on the radio broadcast, Pontiac's the official sponsor of the team. It's so cluttered that are they really leaving an impression on the fan? The reality is that if you took the sum of all those parts and sold them to one car company, they'd pay a lot more of a premium for exclusivity."

The Raptors have already made a lot of money off two very exclusive deals: the arena sponsorship from Air Canada, which has generated $15 million right away for the team coffers, and a 10-year deal with Ford that is worth $3.5 million a year.

There never was a dollar figure revealed for the deal with CITY and CKVR, though with a shared owner, they obviously got a package deal. Sources say that there was actually very little money changing hands in the deal, as the team would be responsible for selling most of the commercial air time, and it would be up to them to command whatever the advertisers were willing to pay. One estimate put the price of the annual cost of the air time at $2 million. The Raptors already have a guaranteed $1.75 million in commercials from Ford and will probably be able to sell another $8–10 million, after the expenses of salaries and production costs for the broadcasts. John Bitove Jr. is certain that advertisers will be lining up to be part of the team's broadcasts. "Corporate-wise, this thing is huge and it's because basketball delivers the demographic that is the hardest to reach—a teenager to 27 years of age. It's the age group where they're young and you can influence them on a brand and you've got them for life. Advertisers all know that, they've all seen the research done in the U.S," said Bitove to Neil A. Campbell of the *Globe and Mail.*

That "youthful" approach is already evident in the coverage of the Raptors over the summer of 1995. The draft was carried in Canada on YTV, which programs exclusively for children and teenagers. (TSN and CTV would have been more obvious choices, but both networks had previous obligations.) Though the YTV coverage was lambasted by some of the local media for its uninformed commentators and gosh-gee-whiz enthusiasm—"I don't know who's gonna be next, but I'll bet he'll be tall...COOL!"— the NBA and YTV are a perfect demographic fit, and the network is already pursuing more broadcast opportunities with the league, which could be on the air as early as the fall of 1995. Similarly, the CITY-TV coverage of the Toronto franchise has targeted young people in its approach. The station has hired a reporter/cameraperson named Lisa Gray and is calling her a "Raptor Specialist." She's a former fashion model, and the station's news release says: "Lisa is the logical choice for Raptors Specialist because she shoots video as well as hoops and will bring her beauty, brawn and high-tech gear to bear on the task of getting the access and the stories the other guys can't."

The Raptors also have a radio deal in place. Not surprisingly, the radio rights have been purchased by CFRB, which is part of the Standard Broadcasting company. The president of Standard Broadcasting is Allan Slaight, who was instrumental in bringing the team to Toronto and who owns 40 percent of the Raptors.

However, the Raptors have had mixed success selling their games on the national level. Sources say that the NBA was extremely pushy while negotiating with the national cable all-sports channel, The Sports Network (TSN), and after a time, network executives were so frustrated with the league and with the Raptors that they opted out of the negotiations for now. Over the last year or so, TSN has been experimenting with split signals, which gives them the capability of broadcasting two different programs to two different parts of the country. For example, they were able, during the 1995 CFL season, to offer a western game and an eastern game through the split signal. The concept is being evaluated further, with a possible view to cutting a deal with the Vancouver Grizzlies to show some of their games regionally in B.C. while giving the rest of the country something else.

Considering some of the past history of the two groups, TSN may have been disinclined to be too chummy with the Raptors even before the personality clash with John Bitove Jr. Until recently, TSN was owned by John Labatt Limited (JLL), which was involved in one of the competing bids for the Toronto NBA franchise. Conversely, when TSN went up on the trading block after Labatt was purchased by a Belgian company, the Northwest Entertainment Group, which owns the Grizzlies, was part of a conglomerate brought together to try to purchase TSN. Another member of this congomerate was Western International Communications Ltd., controlled by Frank Griffiths, the brother of Arthur Griffiths, which further strengthened the ties between the Grizzlies and TSN. In the end, neither group was ultimately part of the new TSN ownership but it is evident there are friendly corporate relations between the Vancouver team and The Sports Network.

The Grizzlies, however, did struggle to get a local broadcast deal in the Vancouver market and had to ask the NBA for an extension when they couldn't meet the December 31, 1994 deadline.

Some West Coast broadcasters were apparently a little uncertain about the appeal of basketball and were hesitant to make a deal. So the Northwest Entertainment group decided that the best way to sell the Grizzlies' games was to put them as a package with the Vancouver Canucks, whose deal with BCTV was expiring at the end of the 1994–95 NHL season.

The strategy worked, as BCTV agreed to the joint package. The station will broadcast 25 Grizzlies games and 25 Canucks games, and the deal is estimated to be worth about $3 million per season, with about 60 percent of that going to the hockey team. The radio rights to the Grizzlies were sold to CKNW radio, which has for many years been the home of the Canucks as well. Ironically, both BCTV and CKNW are owned by Western International Communications Ltd., which in turn is owned by the Griffiths family, though Arthur Griffiths of Northwest Entertainment has always stated that family connections would not be a factor in any deal, however convenient they may be.

With both the local television deals in place, the NBA was also able to secure a national television package. (The league maintained control over the national network and cable sales in Canada.) In May 1995, NBA Commissioner David Stern appeared at a slick news conference at CTV headquarters in downtown Toronto to announce a three-year broadcast agreement with the network. CTV already had extensive connections with the NBA, having simulcast the league finals for several years. The network had also worked with the Raptors and the league during August 1994 as the broadcaster of the World Basketball Championship in Toronto.

The audience numbers for basketball on CTV are still much lower than for hockey, but again, the network is pitching advertisers on the sport's ability to reach a younger demographic group. For example, *Marketing* reported that the top-rated game of the 1994 NBA Finals drew 510,000 viewers compared to an average Saturday night audience of about 1.5 million for "Hockey Night in Canada," with even higher numbers during the playoffs. But the breakdown of the basketball audience is significant: 40 percent of those viewers (205,000) were female, and 15 percent (79,000) were between the ages of 12 and 17. Similarly, for the 1994 All-Star

Game, over 50 percent of CTV's audience was between 12 and 34 years old. In *Marketing,* Tom Bathos of the McKim Media Group of Toronto points out the significance of these numbers: "If advertisers want to tap into the young-adult market, basketball will indeed be a hot buy. It will provide an avenue to reach them effectively. Currently, there are not a lot of avenues that allow us to reach the younger market, so basketball will open that group to us."

The Raptors and the NBA were also very eager to convince Canadian broadcasters that they not only offer a young audience, but also guarantee advertiser exclusivity. Again, this harkens back to the league's strategy of controlling the broadcast and, therefore, the commercial airtime, something fairly new in the Canadian market. Steve Weber, the Raptors' Director of Corporate Sponsorships, told *Marketing* that this kind of control means that advertisers don't have to worry about ambush marketing from competitors once they've purchased time during an NBA broadcast. But Weber admitted that the policy also benefits the team: "It gives you the ability to channel how you are imaged, how you are presented to the market. That is especially important in Canada, a new market, where we are very concerned with making people aware of what the NBA is."

The NBA deal with the CTV network guarantees that the league will get a lot more of that kind of exposure in the Canadian market. Though CTV will produce the games involving the Raptors and the Grizzlies from Canada, the network will pick up the feed provided by NBC, the NBA's national broadcaster in the U.S. for the rest of the games. The deal, which runs to the end of the 1998 season, includes about 30 games. Of those, the network has agreed to provide prime-time coverage of the home openers for both the Raptors and the Grizzlies, as well as two games between the two Canadian franchises. There will also be 15 Sunday afternoon games, five Raptors, five Grizzlies and five other NBA games, as well as the NBA All-Star Game, six playoff games and the NBA Finals, which have to be shown in prime time. (The league was very strategic in negotiating the deal to guarantee good audiences for its games, as well as an equal balance of games from both franchises. CTV would likely have preferred more Raptors coverage, considering the market size for the Toronto team.)

CTV President John Cassady said his network recognized the potential of the NBA as it moved north of the 49th parallel. "We are sure that basketball will become the dominant sport of the '90s."

His network also plans to develop a kids' sports program for Saturday morning that he promises will include the NBA as a centrepiece, and Cassady said that basketball would now figure more prominently on "Canada AM."

The arrival of the Raptors and the Grizzlies has already increased the amount of column space and airtime that the NBA, as a league, receives in Canada. The ratings for basketball will probably never rival those of hockey but each increase in market share translates into more merchandise, ticket sales and eventually more lucrative broadcast deals, and those factors will ensure the long-term viability of professional basketball north of the 49th parallel.

CHAPTER NINE

IT'S SHOWTIME!

In June 1994, Arthur Griffiths, then President of the Vancouver Canucks, the new West Coast NBA franchise, and boss of a brand new arena said: "I'm not in the hockey business, I'm not in the basketball business, I'm probably not even in the arena business. I like to think that the business I'm in is the entertainment business."

Griffiths' philosophy reflects perfectly the attitude of the NBA when selling its product.

It's showbiz.

That has been part of what has made the NBA so successful over the past decade. The "entertainment" part of the NBA has given the league an appeal beyond the traditional audience of mostly male sports fans and has widened the audience to include more women, children and families.

"We view ourselves as being in the entertainment business," said NBA Deputy Commissioner Russ Granik in an interview with *The Financial Post*. "You want to keep the customers entertained from the time they set foot in the building until the time they leave."

These same principles are applied by all the teams around the league under the watchful eye of the people at the league's Team Services office in New York. Team Services makes sure that the teams have all the latest information on "what's hot" and what's not working as entertainment around the league.

There are certain standard features you can expect at NBA games across the United States and now in Canada: loud music, flashy scoreboards, wild mascots and attractive dance teams. Many of the NBA games start with the arena darkened for team introductions, highlighted by a laser show, and even indoor fireworks, as at the Orlando Magic games. While the intros are wildly popular with the younger fans, they haven't impressed some of the more traditional basketball types. As Phil Taylor writes in *Sports Illustrated:* "Player introductions used to be a P.A. announcer reading a list of names. Now the intros are more like a Stones concert, what with the laser-light shows, scoreboard videos and music louder than a runway at La Guardia, and guys taking longer to say 'Shaaaaaaaquiiiiiiiiiillle O'ooooNeeeeeeeal' than it takes to play the first quarter."

The snazzy openings may be for the younger crowd, but it also may not suit every team, according to Taylor, as he talks about the introduction of the New York Knicks at Madison Square Garden during the 1994 NBA Finals. "It's safer to try plucking Charles Barkley's chest hairs than to sit among a crowd of 19,000 New Yorkers with the lights off."

Still, the flashy intros are definitely here to stay. They're part of the NBA package.

For a Canadian, some of the hype surrounding the NBA games seems a little overdone, especially compared to the low-key simplicity of a Canadian-based NHL game. (Although the NHL has changed too with the recent arrival of Anaheim and San Jose and their marketing and showbiz gimmickry.) In fact, some of that may have been shown at the 1995 NBA Draft at SkyDome in Toronto. The Canadian crowd seemed relatively unmoved by the indoor fireworks and hardly reacted to the dance team. The audience seemed to fall within the right demographics for the league, and the setting was right, but the entertainment tricks, that evening at least, seemed to miss the mark.

Entertainment, however, will be the name of the game in the early years of the two Canadian teams. They will definitely have to concentrate on making the non-playing time entertaining for fans. That was the key philosophy of the Orlando Magic when they started out. "We had to bring them a full entertainment package right away, knowing we weren't going to be very competitive," recalls Alex Martens, Director of Publicity and Media Affairs for the Magic. "So our idea was that we'd provide an entertainment package that when they came to the building, they had an outstanding evening. So even if the team lost, the fans went home saying, 'Wow, that was a great night!' We built a full package around exciting half-time shows. We have a glittery opening with lights out, indoor fireworks, spotlights, lasers et cetera. We have a lot of entertainment things during time-outs, whether it's our mascot, 'Stuff', or our Sports Magic dance team or music or promotional contests. We felt that every minute of our fan's night while here at the arena needed to be filled with entertainment."

The Magic, incidentally, have sold out all but two games in their franchise history.

Greg von Schottenstein is the Director of Game Presentations and Special Events for the Vancouver Grizzlies, a post similar to the one he held for nine years with the NBA's Golden State Warriors. He's fully aware of the challenges he'll face when the new season starts in Vancouver. "It's a new sport, in a new country, and I think for the first couple of years the entertainment part will be extremely important," says von Schottenstein.

Not only will he be selling a game and a league that has not been closely followed by a lot of Canadians over the age of 20, but, traditionally, expansion teams don't win many games for the first few years. That will be the case with the Grizzlies and the Raptors. The teams will have to rely on something other than what is happening on the court to keep fans interested, particularly after the novelty wears off.

"How were we going to get people to come to the games, once the newness wore off, and when we weren't going to win much?" recalls Orlando's Director of Marketing Cari Coats of those first seasons. "I mean, that is traditionally why people go to sporting events—to see their teams win. So it was important for us to build a foundation of loyalty among the fans before we ever had a team."

As the Grizzlies and the Raptors will have to do, the Orlando marketing people had to deal with the difficulty of selling the game to people who traditionally follow other sports. In Central Florida, the hot sport was football. So the team did lots of promotions and clinics about the sport of basketball, something the Toronto and the Vancouver teams will do as well. But at least the Magic had no other pro sports competition in the city, something that gave them the instant profile the Raptors and Grizzlies will have to work for. But working strictly on the level of competing for the entertainment dollar, the marketers of the Magic had the daunting task of providing this great, enticing entertainment package in a city that is home to some of the biggest draws in family entertainment: Disneyworld, SeaWorld and Universal Studios.

"We assumed there was a certain level of sophistication among our fans towards the entertainment element. If we were going to get into the entertainment business as we discussed, we were going to have to get into it in a big way and at a level of quality that was going to be acceptable to our fans," says Coats.

There were, therefore, two other main elements to the Orlando strategy, according to Coats. "The second one was community relations. We wanted to be engrained in the community so that if we won or lost, people would still be loyal to the Magic. The third strategy, in my opinion, should always be to have a competitive team. To survive in the long term, you've got to have that element."

While most expansion franchises can count on five years of losing before becoming competitive, Orlando turned it around quickly. The Magic had their first .500 season in 1992–93, only their fourth year in the league, and by 1994–95, they made the NBA Final.

"What I would suggest to any new franchise is to teach the same thing we taught ourselves in the early years, and that is patience," counsels Alex Martens. "It takes five years to build a team on the court, and that needs to be preached from day one. Fans and media must realize that a new team will go through growing pains and success is not going to come immediately."

The two Canadian franchises are also dedicating some time to educating the Vancouver and Toronto media about the way things are done in the NBA. For example, the Grizzlies took a group of B.C. reporters to a Seattle Supersonics game during the 1994–95 season to give the uninitiated a taste of what an NBA game is like. Rob Martin is the Director of Game Operations for the Sonics, and that night he had programmed a jazz pianist, a long-distance shootout and a tricycle race, as well as the regular staples of dance teams, a hairy bigfoot mascot named Squatch and all sorts of prize giveaways. Said Martin: "The NBA is more than just tipping a ball off and playing four quarters. The people in the crowd want to feel they're really part of the game. The NBA has gone from being just about basketball to being an overall entertainment package. It's more of a complete show than a sport."

Over the 48 minutes of playing time, the average NBA game may have as many as 20 timeouts, between TV commercials and breaks called by the teams or by the officials. Add to that the fact that NBA games are infamous for taking an extraordinarily long time to play out the final few minutes as coaches use the timeouts to try to engineer victory, and you have a lot of "down-time" or, as the marketers read it, "entertainment opportunities," so the home team's game presentation staff will have something prepared for each and every break.

This represents a far cry from what Canadian hockey fans grew up with. Remember when the organist was the only form of entertainment during the breaks at NHL games? And those who didn't want to sit and listen and look over the ads in their programs had the option of filing out to the mezzanine for a smoke, some bad concession food and drinks and a lot of analysis of the period they had just seen. Not in the NBA . In fact, at some arenas, there is actually sometimes greater fan applause for the timeout entertainment than for the play on the hardwood.

As regards the music, you won't hear any Stompin' Tom during an NBA game. The music selections are very contemporary and change constantly from game to game. Rob Martin of the Seattle staff told Canadian reporters on their visit that a lot of planning goes into the music played at an NBA game. "Music is something that's well thought out and we aim for a certain demographic, the 18–35 crowd. As a city, Seattle is kind of an innovator in the new rock sound and we play a lot of alternative Seattle-based music. We mix that in with some oldies and some Top 40 rhythm and blues."

Greg von Schottenstein of the Vancouver Grizzlies says he'll be applying a lot of his experience from his days at the Golden State Warriors games when he draws up his program for the Grizzlies home games. "I'd liken the Vancouver market in some ways to the Bay area. It's cosmopolitan, progressive and multicultural."

When he's doing his "package" for the Grizzlies, von Schottenstein says he'll start with the anthems, which will feature local talent as well as artists who are touring on the West Coast. He looks at the anthems as a way to "set the tone" for the fans, particularly those who have never been to a live NBA game.

In his 10 years in the league, von Schottenstein has witnessed first hand the evolution of the NBA into the high-powered entertainment machine of today. "When I started out, all that was available were a couple of audio speakers, with a little music coming out, and a simple scoreboard. Now there's state-of-the-art audio and huge scoreboards with varied video replays."

The scoreboard at the Vancouver Grizzlies game at GM Place is being touted by Orca Bay Entertainment as the most advanced in North America. It will include giant video replay screens, which are now turning into a staple in most of the newer arenas, including the Seattle Center Coliseum. Rob Martin of the Sonics described the screens as a way to share the intimacy of the game of basketball, which has already made the game so successful on TV. "With video, you have an opportunity to give fans a different angle on the game. Other than the first five rows, you don't see the facial expressions the players make when they go up for a basket. Video gives it back to the people who make up a majority of your house."

Greg von Schottenstein of the Grizzlies suggests that the eight-sided scoreboard at GM Place, when combined with the sound system, gives the fans the feeling of being "in your living room."

Both teams will also be working hard at drumming up the best contests to run during breaks and timeouts, and both plan to have their own dance teams, something which has always done well in NBA cities in the U.S.

In preparation for the debut of the Grizzlies, the team took a page out of the PR handbook of the Raptors and decided to hold a contest—not national but regional in this case—with the aim of finding a mascot. It was called the "Be the Bear" contest, and travelled around to 11 high schools across Alberta and B.C. The schools were chosen because they were considered hotbeds of basketball, and of course, the high-school audience is the perfect demographic for the NBA. The contests were usually held at noon hour, in front of the student body, and anybody from the community was invited to try out to become the Grizzlies mascot. At stake was a full-time job with the team, including lots of appearances at community events as well as at home games. The winners from each contest then went on to the final selection, by fan vote, the week of the draft.

"We want creativity, spontaneity, interaction with the crowd and tremendous acrobatic skills," said von Schottenstein before the competition began in early May.

The entire "Be the Bear" competition was choreographed to try to whip up some hype and support and to increase visibility in the communities the team hopes to draw from. It was certainly successful to some degree, as the events were covered by several local television stations, and at the final competition at Richmond Secondary, the team actually had to turn away prospective mascots. While the students seemed to enjoy the event itself, there were only a few young people in the audience sporting Grizzlies merchandise, showing that the team still needs more marketing to break into the big leagues of NBA merchandising.

That's one of the challenges for Greg von Schottenstein, as he tries to describe a night's entertainment that will bring fans, like those Richmond teenagers, back for more. He is certain that the NBA's great success in the U.S. will translate into success in Canada, and likens it to his own education, as an American, to the sport of hockey. "I hadn't seen a lot of hockey before I came here, and in the last couple of months, I've seen more than in my life. Both sports are better live," says von Schottenstein. "It's the same with basketball. I think people will come and see a game or two and enjoy the experience."

Canadian fans may take a while to get used to all the hype and glamour of the NBA games but in fact, the same entertainment principles are coming soon to many Canadian NHL franchises as well. The National Hockey League is now run by a former NBA-er in Gary Bettman, and he is encouraging hockey teams to use the success models of the NBA entertainers. The Calgary Flames have hired a Winnipeg consultant, Deb Belinsky of DCB Productions, to jazz up its games for the 1995–96 season. Belinsky choreographed the game presentation for the Anaheim Mighty Ducks of the NHL, featuring the Duck lowered down from the crane, and a dance troupe.

While hockey traditionalists may scoff, the high attendance figures for a team like the Mighty Ducks speak for themselves. Many NHL teams are slowly edging in the direction of an NBA-like emphasis on presentation. Tod Leiweke is involved in the front-office operations of both the Vancouver Grizzlies and the Canucks, and he directed an extensive survey of Canucks fans during the 1994–95 season about what they wanted to see at the rink, besides the hockey game. "One of the questions there is related to hiring a mascot," Leiweke told the *Globe and Mail.* The playing surface is obviously different from basketball, but as you see teams push the envelope on this, the old excuse about the dasherboards [rink boards that separate the crowd from the playing surface] doesn't hold up as much. The Anaheim Mighty Ducks presentation is as good as any NBA game."

As the NBA's cultural influence extends north of the border, the glitz and glamour elements of an NBA game will likely become de rigueur for Canadian sporting events. Fans are paying more and more to watch professional sports teams and it makes sense that they want more for that entertainment dollar. The NBA turned the league's fortunes around by learning to market itself better. Those lessons will be invaluable when it brings its products here and sets up shop in Canada.

Chapter Ten

THE DUCATS DILEMMA

Considering the popularity of the NBA, selling tickets was supposed to be the easy part. By February, 1994, the Toronto franchise had been chomping at the bit for 98 days, waiting for a chance to get on with the sales pitch. There was already some urgency: one of the NBA conditions for granting the two Canadian franchises was that they had to sell 15,000 season tickets by December 31, 1994.

"No problem," said the two new owners.

They were wrong.

To begin with, the NBA condition of 15,000 in season-ticket sales (later scaled back to 12,500), like the inflated expansion fee, asked more of the Canadian franchises than had ever been asked of any other American team just joining the league. For example, during the last expansion in 1986, the four new teams had to guarantee 10,000 season-ticket holders. The number had jumped dramatically by the time the Canadians came on board. As well, the season-ticket requirement seemed steep compared to the level of ticket sales in some current NBA cities. For example, traditionally, the Los Angeles Lakers are at just under 11,000 season-ticket holders. The number is even lower for the Seattle Supersonics: close to 10,000. The embarrassment of the NBA is the Los Angeles Clippers sales figure of only 3,500 per year, with the Philadelphia 76ers at around 4,000.

Of course, the NBA has little leverage when it comes to forcing those teams to up the ante and increase their season-ticket sales. The league looks far more favourably upon teams like the Orlando Magic and Utah Jazz, with 13,000 season-ticket holders, the Houston

Rockets at 14,000 and the Phoenix Suns at 15,000. Other successful teams include the Chicago Bulls, the New York Knicks and the Charlotte Hornets. The only expansion team not on the list is the Minnesota Timberwolves, who have struggled since their inception and epitomize everything the NBA doesn't want the Canadian teams to become.

The Canadian teams had no choice but to meet the NBA target, and with the threat of having the franchise revoked, the teams got right to work. But each adopted a very different strategy when it came to selling season tickets. True to their early motto of "the hungriest team in the NBA," the Raptors decided to go for a licensing fee to maximize their revenues. The Grizzlies did not. The licensing fee would be charged to season-ticket holders for the privilege of paying for season tickets. The licences ranged from $5,750 plus tax to $1,750 plus tax. The licence was not transferable during the first three years of the franchise without the approval of Raptors management. The ticket holder then paid the price of season tickets on top of the licensing fee. (This practice was likened to the initiation fee at a country club; you pay for the privilege of joining, then you pay your annual golf fees as well.)

"This is done all over the place with pro sports teams in the U.S.," said John Bitove Jr. in defence of the licensing fee. "Unfortunately, we look like the bad guys, because were the first ones to introduce it here, and it was unpopular, and the media made a big deal out of it. Believe me, this is the way of the future in pro sports economics."

Majority investor Allan Slaight considers the licensing fee fuss to have been the one major mistake the ownership group made. "I admit it. We messed up there. We should have had a big, well-staged, well-planned press conference before introducing the licensing-fee concept. We should have had media people there, and members of the public, and explained it all to them, that this is the wave of the future, that we are not getting any public money for our building and, therefore, have to raise money where we can.... That would have been the way to do it. Instead, we just tried to slide it through, and the press jumped all over it, and there was a huge outcry."

Still, corporate clients didn't seem to balk at the fee, although some average fans did. One such fan, Mike Ford, decided not to buy Raptors' tickets because the licence was not transferable. He was already upset because he had paid $2,000 for tickets to the World Basketball Championships so he would be on a priority list for tickets for the Toronto team. The trouble was, he found out when he got to the World Championship that none of the promises included in his "gold" ticket package had been met. He got worse seats than he had paid for and had to "watch" the final from behind the press section. But as Ford told *Globe and Mail* columnist Stephen Brunt, the final straw was the licensing fee and its non-transferability. "Given how accommodating, ethical and fair-minded management had been so far, excuse me for assuming that in a financial crisis, if you lost your job or your kid got sick, management would deny their approval."

Still, the Raptors didn't have much trouble selling the high-priced tickets, licensing fee or not. However, once those tickets were sold, the sales seemed to stall. By November 8, 1994, the team had only sold 6,500 tickets overall, and the panic started. The Raptors announced they were dropping the so-called mandatory fee for those seats located behind the basket, which were moving slowly. The team had only sold about one-fifth of the number it expected to sell behind the basket. In part, this can be attributed to the inexperience of Canadian fans who have traditionally been told that the only place to watch a game is between the baskets. The teams had to work hard at convincing prospective ticket buyers that the seats behind the basket were also desirable. The Raptors Communications Director at the time, Tom Mayenknecht, told the media: "I think that some people are still looking at basketball from the perspective of hockey fans. Prospective buyers were concerned they might not be able to see the action at the far end if they're located behind the basket."

On November 8, when the licensing fee was lifted, 92 percent of the seats sold were between the baskets. So the "mandatory" fee became optional on lower-bowl seats, which were priced at $75 and $55 a game.

The dropping of the fee drew some criticism and caused some confusion. It was estimated that dropping the fee would cost the Raptors $11 million in much-needed revenue, but desperation was certainly motivating the team at this point. While John Bitove Jr. had always spoken glowingly about the 20,000 names that the team had collected in prospective season-ticket holders after the World Basketball Championship in August 1994, fewer than 7,000 of those alleged basketball fans had agreed to commit to season tickets with the Raptors. Bitove expressed surprise at the lack of interest: "At the high end, we came up aces. The low end, I thought we'd do better. When I was a kid I just wanted to be in the building."

Apparently, Toronto basketball fans weren't quite that eager.

On the West Coast, sales weren't going much better. By early October 1994, the Vancouver Grizzlies had only generated 8,200 season ticket sales. Team chairman Arthur Griffiths admitted he was "a wee bit disappointed and a tad worried." The stagnant ticket sales were big news, especially after the *Vancouver Sun* put together a full-page feature on the ticket crisis. While the Grizzlies sales were disappointing, the numbers were not far off those of the team's hockey cousins, the Vancouver Canucks, who had sold around 9,000 in season tickets, and that was after an appearance in the 1994 Stanley Cup final.

As the deadline approached, the panic continued at both ends of the country. The teams became more and more desperate and it began to show. In Toronto, the Raptors came up with a new category of season tickets that they cleverly labelled "Basketball 101." With no licensing fee, of course, a season ticket would retail for $101 annually. Unfortunately, when the team held a big, splashy open house to showcase the SkyDome for prospective season-ticket buyers, the "Basketball 101" tickets were found to be less than desirable. They were in the 500-level seats of SkyDome. As one Toronto writer joked, someone standing in the 500 section looked down during the open house and asked, "Which one's Bitove and which one is Thomas?"

In other words, they weren't great seats, but what really mattered to the Raptors was moving towards that elusive number of 12,500 in total sales.

The Raptors asked the NBA if they could put 5,000 of these "nosebleed" seats on sale, which, if sold, would put them close to the targeted number of 12,500. The NBA refused, at least on the matter of counting them as part of the season-ticket sales. For one thing, the seats would disappear after the two (or three) seasons at SkyDome. Secondly, the NBA was far more interested in the cold, hard cash that 12,500 season tickets would generate—a cool $13.5 million—to ensure the financial stability of its Canadian franchises. The NBA didn't want any more Minnesota Timberwolves or Los Angeles Clippers experiences. They wanted to make sure that the Canadian teams would be successful before the league put its lucrative reputation on the line. The *Globe*'s Stephen Brunt wrote in late November 1994 that again, the future of the Toronto franchise could be in jeopardy: "It had been conventional wisdom that the league would never let the Toronto market slip away, no matter what happened with the Raptors. But in his dealings with the province over the Pro-Line lottery, NBA Commissioner David Stern showed himself willing to go to the wall over something that in the end was more a matter of principle than of bottom line. Since then, he has been unequivocal: deadlines are deadlines, minimums are minimums. The NBA is cutting the new franchises in for a share of television and properties revenues. And for that, Stern says, the league wants something solid in return."

With less than a week to go before the New Year's Eve deadline, the Toronto Raptors and Vancouver Grizzlies received an unexpected Christmas present: a bail out from the Shoppers Drug Mart chain. The drugstore chain had purchased blocks of tickets in both of the new NBA cities. (The chain has about 700 stores across the country.) Though the deal had been in the works for several weeks, it was announced on December 21, just before Christmas.

The size of the Toronto purchase was particularly surprising: a block of 4,250 seats, worth a reported $4.7 million. The seats are in the upper reaches of the SkyDome—the same tickets that the Raptors wanted to sell through the "Basketball 101" program. This time, however, the NBA agreed to the sale, saying that the drugstore ticket sales would allow people to come see the Raptors who otherwise wouldn't be able to afford it. It was an interesting spin, considering that a month earlier the NBA had been unwilling to accept the "Basketball 101" numbers towards a final season-ticket count. The following day, though, the Raptors held a celebration at the Royal York Hotel, throwing a cocktail party for 4,000. The team announced that its season-ticket count had set a new league record at 15,127, surpassing the 13,536 in ticket sales set by the Charlotte Hornets before their inaugural season. The Toronto figure, of course, included the 4,250 Shoppers Drug Mart seats. Without them, the Raptors number would not only have been under the Hornets record, but also below the number required by the league. But again, the Raptors were ultimately able to put a positive spin on what could have been a huge embarrassment.

On the West Coast, Shoppers Drug Mart West purchased fewer tickets than in Toronto, but in a higher price range. Shoppers bought 2,500 Grizzlies tickets in the $21 and $28 range, to put the Vancouver season ticket total at 12,624, just over the league-required number of 12,500. The drugstore chain did receive a 10 percent discount on the tickets, but the down payment on the tickets put about $1.4 million immediately into the Grizzlies' bank account. That was the most important part for the league, which wanted 50 percent of the season-ticket sales on deposit by December 31, to prove the financial viability of the two Canadian teams.

Shoppers Drug Mart will be selling the tickets to Raptors and Grizzlies games on a per-game basis. However, once the NBA requirement for season ticket sales was met, the teams had another important sales pitch to make. The selling of corporate boxes is an important source of revenue to any franchise, and both the Canadian teams needed the money.

The Vancouver Grizzlies ran into a difficult situation with their sales of corporate boxes. Unfortunately, the Grizzlies franchise was granted so far into the construction of GM Place that their sibling team, the Canucks, had already significantly tapped into the corporate market. The Canucks had sold out their boxes before the Grizzlies had been granted a franchise. So, the corporate marketing people for basketball were left in the difficult position of having to go back to those same corporations to ask them to pay again if they wanted to keep their luxury box for Grizzlies games. This was disconcerting for many of the companies, as they were being asked to contribute another $90,000 to $150,000, on top of what they'd already paid to the Canucks. In the end, fewer decided to sign up for Grizzlies games, and in June, the team still had approximately eight boxes left to sell.

The Toronto Raptors were having their own problems. However, they were selling tickets and corporate boxes at the SkyDome, which would be their temporary facility, until their own arena was built. But corporate Toronto was willing to be part of the new sport in town. By the end of the summer of 1995, the Raptors Vice-President of Business Development, Brian Cooper, said the team had sold 71 of 104 available corporate boxes. "Some go for $80,000 a year, some are at $100,000 and it goes up to $160,000 a year at the top end, with a commitment required for 10 or 15 years. You put down 50 percent," said Cooper. "People said we'd have trouble, but look at what we've sold just since March—71 boxes at an average of $1.8 million for the term [of the lease]."

The Raptors can, of course, use that deposit money as they wish, as it is not required to be in trust. John Bitove Jr. says Air Canada Centre boxholders will be given "good seats" at SkyDome while the team is playing there. Originally, ticket buyers were told that the first season of Raptors games would be based at SkyDome, but by the end of the Pro-Line dispute, the Bitove group was saying that it would now likely be two seasons at SkyDome before the team's new arena would be built. They might even have to stay at their temporary headquarters at SkyDome for three seasons, much to the chagrin of their fans who paid their money expecting a new arena after one season, certainly not two or, even worse, three years at SkyDome.

There were other problems with SkyDome beyond those of the Raptors themselves. A group of luxury-box owners had formed an association and filed a lawsuit against the Bitove Corporation, which was run by Tom Bitove, John Bitove Jr.'s brother. The Bitove Corporation is the main caterer at SkyDome, and in 1990, the Independent SkyBox Association sued the Bitoves over the food and beverage prices that they were being charged in their luxury box. For example, the boxholders alleged they were being charged around $88.18 for a case of domestic beer that retails at $18.20, a markup of about 384 percent. A 1,000-ml. bottle of L'Epayrie wine cost $29.70, as of August 25, 1994, a markup of about 367 per cent. A pot of coffee was $11.45, a markup of 922 percent, according to a price comparison prepared by the SkyBox Association.

In September 1994, the SkyBox Association sent out a survey to the 160 SkyBox holders. One respondent wrote back that many boxholders were not going to renew their leases because of the so-called price-gouging. "I appreciate anyone who wants to make a buck," writes the anonymous boxholder. "My hat's off to them. But it's the assumptions and petty little service charges, 15 percent gratuity etc., that tick me off. That nickel and diming us to death is going to cost Stadco [the organization that operates the SkyDome] in five years. Because nobody is going to renew."

THE COST OF SKYBOX SERVICE

Comparison of LCBO trade prices with prices charged by Bitove to SkyBoxes as of Aug. 25, 1994.

	LCBO trade price	BItove price including 9% S/C	$ markup	Per cent markup
Case of 24 beer				
Heineken	$28.29	$111.51	$83.22	294.17
Molson	18.20	88.18	69.98	384.51
1,000 ml. bottle wine				
L'Epayrie wine	$6.36	$29.70	$23.34	366.98
750 ml. bottle liquor				
Canadian Club whiskey	$15.93	$67.04	$51.11	320.84
Beefeater gin	16.28	67.04	50.76	311.79
Smirnoff vodka	15.77	67.04	51.27	325.11
Chivas Regal scotch	29.81	92.92	63.11	211.71
Grand Marnier	31.73	105.73	74.00	233.22
Coffee (1 pot package)	$1.12	$11.45	$10.33	922.32

Box licensees store, staff, serve, wash up and provide what is, basically, a retail function for the serving of these beverages.

Source: *Independent SkyBox Association/Globe and Mail.*

In response, Tom Bitove defended his company's business practices, saying the questions in the survey were "skewed" to make his company look bad. He said that the catering prices at SkyDome were the norm in the business and were not excessive.

The SkyBox Association's lawsuit has not been decided in the courts, but it appears that some luxury boxholders are taking other routes to express their dissatisfaction with the way things are run at SkyDome. Part of the SkyBox Association's survey dealt with the leases for the luxury boxes, which are up for renewal in 1999. Of the 60 luxury boxholders who responded to the survey, 52 percent said they were not planning on renewing. Of the 52 percent who said they were not renewing, 68 percent said the reason was because of the high markup on food and beverages. Sixty-seven percent said the rental fee was too high. (The boxes have annual fees ranging from $100,000 to $225,000.)

The issue of the leases is also being challenged in the courts. Tru-Wall Group Ltd., a housing construction company based in Concord, Ontario, is challenging the legal validity of the lease agreement on behalf of the Independent SkyBox Association. The lawyer for Tru-Wall has argued that the leasing arrangements became null and void when SkyDome was sold by the Ontario government to a private consortium in March 1994. Therefore, the new owners of SkyDome, who include the Canadian Imperial Bank of Commerce, Coca-Cola Ltd., The Sports Network and Ford Motor Co. of Canada, would have to renegotiate the agreements or find new tenants.

Meanwhile, many of the luxury boxes sit empty these days. Some companies have gone bankrupt and SkyDome has been unable to find other corporations to take their places. There are often ads in Toronto newspapers with offers to rent SkyBoxes. An advertisement last year in the *Globe and Mail* offered a package including 16 tickets and a hostess for six games for $15,000 plus GST.

If the Raptors don't spend any more than a couple of years at SkyDome, they may not be directly affected by the ill-will the luxury boxholders harbour for the Bitove catering operation and the management of SkyDome. But then again, they could be: the

SkyBox Association, led by President David Butler, called for a boycott of luxury-suite rentals for the Raptors games. "We don't like the treatment we've had from the Bitoves," said Butler in 1994.

The Raptors have always bragged that selling luxury boxes would be a piece of cake in the centre of corporate Canada and they may be right. As they were preparing to start their first season, they were enjoying the use of over $4.5 million from the 50 percent deposits on boxes sold. But the experience at SkyDome with unhappy boxholders may mean some corporations will be demanding fairer treatment for their investments, and this may be a headache at times for the Raptors.

Things were looking good for the Grizzlies in their ticket and box sales as the inaugural season drew near. By the end of the summer of 1995, they had just under 14,000 season tickets sold, with a 30-game combination hockey and basketball package being the hot seller (15 Grizzlies' games and 15 Canucks games for between $1,080 and $1,500, depending on where the seats are). The Grizzlies originally had 88 luxury suites to sell, but had to convert two into TV studios, so they had 86 available and sold them all.

The deal on the suites included access to all events, including Grizzlies and Canucks games, concerts and shows for $120,000 on 5, 7 or 10-year leases. A luxury suite for just the 45 basketball games sells for $40,000, again on the 5, 7 and 10-year terms.

Chapter Eleven

WHO'S IN CHARGE? HIRING A GENERAL MANAGER

"A few months into their existence, [the Raptors] are big on flash but light on substance. While they have a cute name and a pretty logo, there isn't much yet to suggest that they might become an NBA force."

—Neil A. Campbell in *The Globe and Mail*, May 1994

People who don't like his style often describe Raptors President John Bitove Jr. as "starstruck." They point to his association with NHL star Wayne Gretzky, with whom he is a partner in the trendy sports restaurant Gretzky's in Toronto. The restaurant is full of autographed sports memorabilia, just the kind of stuff that turns the crank of a sports fan like Bitove Jr.

That's where Isiah Thomas comes in.

The Toronto Raptors called a big news conference in May 1994 to introduce their new general manager. Everyone knew earlier that morning that it would be the 33-year-old former NBA playoff MVP and perennial all-star, Isiah Thomas, recently retired from the Detroit Pistons. Still, the team went ahead with a glitzy introduction.

The Raptors held the news conference at Gretzky's, of course, and snuck Thomas into the restaurant wearing a tall white chef's hat, as if a group of sports reporters wouldn't still recognize one of the best-known players in the NBA. Then, Isiah Thomas burst through a giant Raptors logo made of paper, wearing a leather Raptors jacket and carrying a basketball. He looked good, but reporters instantly wanted to know why Thomas was qualified to become the first retired player ever to step right off the court into a general manager's job.

At the news conference, Thomas handled himself well. He saw no reason why he wasn't qualified for the Raptors job, though it means building a team from scratch and hiring a coach, players and front-office staff.

"That doesn't frighten me at all," said Thomas. "I've been involved with basketball all my life. I started playing when I was three. Things that happen on the basketball court, things that make people good players, that's second nature to me."

Isiah Thomas had a storybook career in basketball. In 1981, he led the Indiana Hoosiers to the NCAA championship, then jumped to the NBA after just two years of college ball. In the NBA, he became one of the best point guards in the league's history. He was a 12-time all-star, and played his entire career with the Detroit Pistons. Thomas was the Pistons captain and a pivotal part of the team when it won back-to-back championships in 1989 and 1990. He was also the president of the NBA Players Association for several years, so he has seen the league operations from that side of the fence. In April 1993, a ruptured Achilles tendon ended his playing career, and Thomas suddenly found himself looking for work. (One newspaper columnist suggests that if it weren't for the injury, Thomas would make a more useful aging point guard than he does a non-experienced general manager.)

Almost everyone expected that Isiah Thomas would end up working in the front office of the Detroit Pistons. He had played his entire career there, and he had a high profile in the community. In fact, in January 1994, the Pistons called a press conference to announce that Thomas had been offered a job with the team once he retired and would be "a Piston for life." The deal, according to *Sports Illustrated,* reportedly included some equity in the team as well as the general manager's job, and would be worth $55 million. Isiah Thomas' reaction was simple: "This is one of the happiest days of my life."

But things didn't work out as planned with the Pistons. Thomas' career came to a sudden halt with the Achilles injury, and there was no job for him. As Pistons President Tom Wilson said in *Sports Illustrated*: "Things got a little strained. Mr. Davidson [managing partner of the Pistons] wasn't prepared to make Isiah an offer of ownership, and rumours about the deal seemed to have a life of their own.... The stress made it uncomfortable."

With the Pistons no longer an option, Isiah Thomas was in the market for a new opportunity, particularly one that would offer him the kind of equity ownership that he had been looking for in Detroit. Along came John Bitove Jr. and the Toronto Raptors.

Unlike some athletes who don't think about the future until their playing careers are over, Isiah Thomas had spent a lot of time during his days with the Pistons planning for the future. Thomas was featured on the cover of the December 19, 1994 issue of *Forbes* magazine, sitting in the stands with his laptop computer while some players practised shooting hoops in the background. According to the article, Thomas used to sit in the locker room before practice, checking his e-mail and getting updates on his investments, and that used to raise a few eyebrows from his fellow players. But Isiah Thomas has some big goals in business: "I want to make $1 billion," he told *Forbes*.

He started working towards that goal while he was still playing. "I believe that the leverage you have, the accessibility you have to people while you're playing, is a hundred times greater than when you quit."

The year before he retired, Thomas and business partner Rick Inatome, a computer industry entrepreneur, started I.I. Ventures. Their first acquisition was American Speedy Printing Centers, a chain of 600 print shops, which was bankrupt when they bought it in 1993. The company, which only cost $40 million, was making $150 million in gross revenues by the end of 1994. Thomas also bought equity in, and is now a director of, OmniBanc Corporation, an African-American-owned holding company in the U.S.

In its profile of athlete investors, *Forbes* estimates Isiah Thomas' value at $15 million, including his share of the Toronto Raptors. Part of Thomas' deal in joining the Raptors was the option to buy into the ownership of the team. Sources say that Isiah Thomas put up $4 million to buy into the Raptors, and will eventually end up with a nine percent share of the team. (The other partners in the Raptors agreed to give up a percentage, so that the ownership breakdown would remain the same once Thomas bought in. Now, John Bitove Jr. has 40 percent (down from 44 percent) Allan Slaight of Standard Broadcasting also has 40 percent (also down from 44 percent), Scotiabank is down to 9 percent (from 10 percent), and David Peterson and Atlantic Packaging remain at 1 percent apiece.)

Thomas' deal is obviously a very lucrative one, especially considering that he has absolutely no experience. That's what seemed to rile many Toronto sports columnists, as they raised some serious questions about the suitability of Isiah Thomas for the job of general manager. Neil Campbell of the *Globe and Mail* called Thomas' hiring "the sort of stunt one might expect from a Harold Ballard or a George Steinbrenner." He called Thomas "a bizarre and risky choice," a "Dave Stieb trying to be a Pat Gillick."

The Pat Gillick analogy is an interesting one. Ironically, John Bitove Jr. had also invoked the name of the World Series-winning general manager of the Toronto Blue Jays when he first talked about hiring a general manager. In October 1993, Bitove told the media: "We're hunting for the name of the best qualified basketball person who will move to Toronto. That's not necessarily a big name. Pat Gillick of the World Series champion Blue Jays was not a household name when he was hired."

But the Raptors did decide to go with a household name, one with absolutely no management experience. What Isiah Thomas does have, however, is a great smile, and a good amount of experience with, albeit not always a great love for, the media and the public. On the corporate "schmooze" circuit, he will be fine. He is, as one Bay Street lawyer put it, "eminently presentable."

Isiah Thomas also has, of course, somewhat of an historical connection with John Bitove Jr. During Bitove's days at Indiana University, Isiah Thomas led the Hoosiers to the NCAA championship. Later,

Bitove Jr. attended law school at the University of Windsor, just across the river from the home of the Pistons. Still, the Raptors President denies that his personal connections to Thomas played any role in the hiring. "In the end," said Bitove Jr. at the news conference introducing his new general manager, "the fan element becomes zero and practicality is 100 percent."

Michael Farber of *Sports Illustrated* compared Thomas' hiring to that of some other ex-athletes who had gone on to become general managers. Yes, he points out, Bob Clarke of the Philadelphia Flyers and Serge Savard of the Montreal Canadiens have gone on to become general managers of their former teams, but those were established franchises. Again, the name of Pat Gillick is given as the kind of general manager that might have been more appropriate for a new team, or someone like Cliff Fletcher, who has worked to rebuild the Toronto Maple Leafs. That's the kind of general manager that Torontonians have become used to.

John Bitove Jr. obviously didn't agree. He told *Sports Illustrated*: "In basketball, the skills are apparent, but you have to know the psyche of the individual. Nobody understands players better than Isiah. I always thought Isiah was shrewd."

Isiah Thomas recognized right away that there would be some doubters. "I've had to live with every kind of cynicism," he said at the opening news conference. "I can take it again."

As to what kind of team he was going to build, now that he had the job, Thomas seemed to have all the right things to say, starting from Day One. "Our goal is to win a championship, hopefully in our sixth or seventh year. We'll be cautious and conservative, not do crazy things. We don't plan to be winning 40 games one year and then 20 games the next.... It's one thing to make the moves required to become competitive in the short term. It's quite another to build a championship team."

In his first year on the job, Isiah Thomas proved himself to be the kind of person who does his homework. He talked to executives around the league about how they do their jobs. He helped design a computer program for scouting future Raptors players, working with the same Kanata, Ontario software company that designed a scouting package for the Ottawa Senators of the NHL.

Thomas travelled to games around the league, with his scouts, his assistant Glen Grunwald, and Director of Scouting Bob Zuffelato. At the games, he can often be seen whispering into a tiny tape recorder, perhaps recording his comments about a player's attitude as well as his basketball skills. If Isiah Thomas feels his lack of experience at all, he has made up for it by surrounding himself with people with lots of experience, some of them with personal connections from his Pistons days.

Bob Zuffelato is the Raptors Director of Scouting, and at 56, he had already logged a lot of time watching basketball games before he even started looking for his first Raptor. Zuffelato had worked previously as assistant coach of the Dallas Mavericks from 1990–93 and with the Minnesota Timberwolves in their first year, the 1989–90 season. As Zuffelato was being introduced at a news conference, General Manager Isiah Thomas talked about his new scout: "One of the things that really appealed to me about Bob was his experience in expansion with the Timberwolves. He's been through a start-up; he knows what it takes to get an expansion team up and running."

Those familiar with the pathetic record of the Minnesota Timberwolves may wonder if being associated with that team is necessarily a good thing. Some of Zuffelato's other assignments were no better. He served as director of player personnel for the Milwaukee Bucks and as an assistant with the Golden State Warriors. Then again, these posts on mediocre teams may have given Zuffelato the patience and thick skin he might need in Toronto if the Raptors play the bad basketball associated with early expansion experiences.

Some of Thomas' other personnel decisions have had more personal connections. His brother, Larry, has done some scouting for the Raptors, and former Detroit Pistons TV person, Curtis Emerson, is working for the team's video services. Thomas again turned to the Pistons connection when he made his most important hiring decision, signing on former Pistons' Assistant Coach Brendan Malone as the first-ever coach of the Raptors.

This decision was assailed by the media critics who said that the Raptors took the cheap route here, as Malone will earn about $300,000 for a three-year contract. That is peanuts in NBA coaching circles. The prevailing theory is that Malone was "hired to be fired." In other words, it doesn't matter who coaches the Raptors for their first few years, and while a coach can't be blamed for an expansion team's early troubles, someone will have to take the fall, and a change will have to be made to show fans that winning is still an objective. Brendan Malone has decent NBA credentials, but he is not a long-term investment.

There are still some questions, though, about the choice of Isiah Thomas and what it indicates about the degree of influence that John Bitove Jr. is going to exert over the basketball operation. Again, Neil Campbell of the *Globe and Mail* had some foreboding thoughts about the way Bitove Jr. had handled Thomas' hiring, saying that Bitove Jr. was showing tendencies of a "never-win, always-interfere" owner. Thomas exacerbated those fears when he was first hired by saying, "I'm very confident in John's ability to look at basketball talent."

The close tie-in between Bitove Jr. and his new general manager can be seen in these two quotations, with Thomas seeming to adopt the "party line":

John Bitove Jr. in *Sports Illustrated*, November 7, 1994: "A Raptors player is one who plays with an aura of confidence, a hungry player, a team player, one with Raptor purple in his blood."

Isiah Thomas in the *Globe and Mail* advertising supplement on NBA basketball, December 9, 1994: "Our players will clearly connect with our logo. The Raptors will play with an aura of confidence. They will be hungry players. They will be tough and competitive players, who fill their roles in our team's concept."

In contrast, the Vancouver Grizzlies ownership people have shown a much more hands-off approach in their choice of Stu Jackson as general manager. Part of that professionalism may come from the years that Arthur Griffiths has spent with the Vancouver Canucks. It is a lesson that he learned the hard way.

The two, Isiah Thomas and Stu Jackson, have somewhat different styles, and attitudes on accessibility, but both are extremely enthusiastic about their new jobs, about the players they have drafted, and about the opportunities to mould something by their own hand. It remains to be seen who will turn out to be the better choice, and, given the differences in the markets, maybe those choices needed to be motivated by different things. For Toronto, Isiah may be the right stuff—the big name, the instant recognition and, in some people's view, instant credibility for the team in a market that demands things be done in a big, splashy, world-class way. For a more laid-back city like Vancouver, Stu Jackson, who is lesser known, less flashy, but no less earnest and certainly well respected in basketball circles, seems like a good call.

We shall see.

CHAPTER TWELVE

SELLING THE SIZZLE: THE TORONTO MARKET

"It was as if one morning Toronto woke up, raised the shades, and saw the Empire State Building pushing through the smoke of Manhattan across the street."

—Larry Millson, *Ballpark Figures: The Blue Jays and the Business of Baseball*

Torontonians love thinking of their city as "world class," to use a time-worn expression, and the arrival of Major League Baseball in 1977 gave them that world-class feeling in spades. That in turn, has reshaped the city's sports scene.

While the Blue Jays did not threaten the historical popularity of the Toronto Maple Leafs, which persisted even through the dreary Harold Ballard era, the arrival of American baseball has contributed to the erosion of Canadian football in the Toronto market and has left that sport on the verge of extinction. It is into this crowded and complicated marketplace that the Raptors will be clawing out their niche. The key will be maintaining their momentum after the novelty wears off and the losing continues. The team would do well to follow the blueprint of the Blue Jays and to wisely avoid the pitfalls of the recent years of the Toronto Argonauts. As for the Maple Leafs, there are interesting ties between the storied team and the new kid in town, the Raptors. At one point, it looked like the NHL franchise and the new NBA team would be sharing an owner and a home: a marriage of historical success and marketing moxy that had the potential to transform the Toronto sports market.

The arrival of the Blue Jays on the Toronto scene has many parallels with the genesis of the Raptors. By the mid-1970s, there were four groups in contention to bring Major League Baseball to its second market in Canada. (The Montreal Expos had been playing in the National League since 1969, and by this time, the Olympic Stadium was under construction.) Labatt Breweries of Canada was always the front-runner in the bidding race to bring a team to Toronto. Its rival, Molson Breweries, had a long and high-profile association with the Montreal Canadiens and "Hockey Night in Canada," and Labatt was looking for a similar tie-in. Peter Widdrington, who would go on to become a member of the board of the Blue Jays, was then President and Chief Executive Officer of Labatt. In Larry Millson's *Ballpark Figures,* he is quoted as saying: "In the beer business, there has always been a strong association with sports. We had been tied up with the Canadian Football League, and on a minor basis there was a long association with sports, but we didn't have a strong affiliation with a major franchise."

A pro baseball team seemed a perfect fit for the brewery. A Labatt corporate newsletter published in 1977 extols the virtues of becoming involved with the baseball franchise: "Baseball came along as one of those opportunities that would move us to the centre stage in Toronto and that was what we wanted. Owing to the fact that a Toronto baseball franchise was a sound business proposition in its own right, when you add the synergistic effect to the beer business it becomes a major breakthrough."

Labatt was joined in its bid for a Toronto team by Montreal financier R. Howard Webster, then Chairman of the *Globe and Mail,* and by the Canadian Imperial Bank of Commerce. Labatt and Webster were the majority partners, at 45 percent each, and the bank was limited through the Bank Act to 10 percent.

Webster had originally been part of the Toronto Baseball Company, headed by Syd C. Cooper, before he joined forces with the brewery. The third prospective ownership group was headed by Lorne Duguid, of Hiram Walker and Sons, and allegedly included Harold Ballard and Maple Leaf Gardens. A fourth group was headed by Phil and Irving Granovsky, of Atlantic Packaging, who were thought to be fronting for the third Canadian brewery, Carling O'Keefe. Trevor Eyton was acting as lawyer to the fourth group.

The four groups are interesting from an historical perspective because of the many cross-references with the Raptors' ownership. Trevor Eyton is a close family friend of the Bitoves, and Phil Granovsky now owns a small share of the Raptors. The Ballard/Maple Leaf Gardens connection seems always to be present in any potential sports deal. The Labatt–Canadian Imperial Bank of Commerce partnership was also a player in the bidding war for an NBA franchise in Toronto.

While the Labatt group lost out on the Raptors, they were the successful recipients of a Major League Baseball franchise. But it was not a smooth path to eventual success. The group's first attempt to get a team met with failure. On January 9, 1976, it was announced that Labatt, Webster and the bank had bought the ailing San Francisco Giants for $13.5 million. But before the celebrations could begin, George Moscone, Mayor of San Francisco, obtained a temporary injunction to stop the deal. Bob Lurie, a Bay area financier, was willing to put up half the money to keep the team in San Francisco. But as spring training approached, Lurie had still not found anyone to put up the other half of the necessary $8 million. Two and a half hours before the deadline, Lurie found another investor and the franchise stayed in San Francisco. (According to Larry Millson's history of the deal, a few people still have Toronto Giants signs from the planned January 9 press conference.)

While the Toronto hopefuls had always wanted a team in the National League to capitalize on a natural rivalry with the Montreal Expos, the American League became the more logical choice after the league expanded in February 1976 to include Seattle. The American League now needed another expansion team for balance. Toronto was the obvious answer to the league's dilemma and the only remaining question was which group would actually win the franchise.

The Granovsky–Carling O'Keefe bid had a solid connection with Jerry Hoffberger, Chairman of the Baltimore Orioles. Hoffberger had owned National Brewing, which had just been taken over by Carling O'Keefe. But, as the Bitoves showed with the NBA, it was the personal lobbying that swayed the vote in favour of the Labatt group. Don McDougall, then President of Labatt, and Herb Solway, then the lawyer for the Toronto Argonauts, spent a frantic couple of days personally calling and persuading each of the American League owners, other than Hoffberger, that theirs should be the successful consortium. The Labatt group won 11–1, and Major League Baseball was coming to Toronto.

The new Toronto baseball franchise had a couple of things going for it that the Raptors do not. For one thing, they had a stadium to play in. During the first half of the 1970s, Metro Toronto had put $17.8 million into renovations at Exhibition Stadium, creating 14 luxury boxes and seating for 40,000 fans. The province put up half the money for the work at Exhibition Stadium and gave Metro an interest-free loan for the other half, against profits generated by baseball. SkyDome and all its controversies would come much later.

There was another more intangible advantage that the new baseball team had in the Toronto market, and that was the sport's historical roots in the community. In the early part of the century, Babe Ruth had played ball at Maple Leaf Park, on an island across from downtown Toronto, and scored his first professional home run there. In the 1920s, the city built a new stadium at the foot of Bathurst Street which, with 20,000 seats, was considered the "jewel of the minor leagues."

More than three million fans came out in the 1950s to watch baseball during the glory days of the Maple Leafs, the baseball team in the Triple-A International League. The team's owner, Jack Kent Cooke, a Torontonian who would go on to own the Los Angeles Lakers of the NBA, the Los Angeles Kings, and then the Washington Redskins, tried several times to buy a major league franchise. He tried to move the Boston Braves, but they went to Milwaukee, and the St. Louis Browns went to Baltimore. The popularity of the Maple Leafs, however, did not last once the flamboyant Cooke was gone, and after the 1967 season, the team folded and Maple Leaf Stadium was demolished.

By the time the Blue Jays arrived on the scene, Torontonians were again ready to support baseball. The exposure of the Montreal Expos had stimulated national interest in the sport and the fiercely competitive Torontonians were prepared to show that they too deserved to be part of the world of major league baseball. The team was wildly successful in those early years. The Blue Jays drew 1,701,052 fans in their first season, a record for a major-league expansion team in its first year.

There were several reasons for the team's success, going beyond the novelty of the franchise, and they have primarily to do with "selling the sizzle," a style of marketing that has carried the Blue Jays, at least until recently.

Peter Bavasi was the flamboyant leader of the Toronto Blue Jays for the first five years of their existence. Bavasi learned the baseball business from his father Buzzie Bavasi, who in 1968 was a part owner and Chief Executive Officer of the San Diego Padres. When the team ran into financial problems, Ray Kroc of McDonald's bought the team and made Buzzie Bavasi President and Peter Vice-President and General Manager.

In *Baseball Figures,* Larry Millson writes about the impact that Ray Kroc had on the young Peter Bavasi, and how that influence shaped his approach to marketing the team in Toronto. "Soon after he arrived in Toronto, he [Bavasi] talked about 'selling the sight, sound, taste, touch and smells of major league baseball.' It was something Ray Kroc had taught him. 'Ray always said to look at a product through the eyes of the consumer. He was a big fan of selling the sizzle if you don't have the steak ready. It works the same with baseball as it does with food.'"

Ray Kroc's advice has equal resonance for a fledgling NBA franchise. The NBA as a league has already perfected "selling the sizzle," which should give the Toronto Raptors and Vancouver Grizzlies a solid base to build on.

One of the first tasks for Peter Bavasi in Toronto was to find a name for the new baseball team, and surprise, surprise, the franchise decided to have a name-the-team contest. There were 30,000 entries and 4,000 potential names, including the infamous Toronto Towers, which would also be rejected for the basketball franchise.

(Other rejects included: Bay Street Ballers, the Toronto Island Ferries, Toronto Lumberjacks, Beavers, Trilliums, Blue Sox, Blue Shoes and Blue Birds.) The winner was the Blue Jays because, as one owner put it, the jay is "strong, aggressive, inquisitive and it dares to take on all comers."

As much as anything else, the name Blue Jays was selected for its marketing potential. Some analysts even speculated that the Jays ownership was hoping that newspapers would use the shortened form Blues for the team. Blue, of course, is one of the most popular of the Labatt brand name beers, so the newspapers insisted on shortening the name to Jays, which has stuck.

The Toronto Blue Jays also worked hard on creating a logo that would be highly marketable, and settled on the head of a blue jay in light and dark blue. The American-born Bavasi insisted on a maple leaf as well and claims that he got "a lot of hooting and hollering by our Canadian staff." But the maple leaf stayed. In a brilliant marketing move, Bavasi struck a deal with Irwin Toy and made that company the manufacturer and supplier for the team. The company reportedly sold $13 million worth of Blue Jay items in the first two years of the team's existence, of which the Jays received 10 percent of the wholesale price. Peter Bavasi would brag that the sales of ballcaps were more than $2,500,000 over the first three years. The results were impressive, in the pre-NBA, pre-Nike era of sports marketing. (In contrast, the Raptors have sold about $20 million in official merchandise in their first year.) Bavasi said later: "We didn't make a lot of money off the deal as it turned out. But what we did was have this widespread, walking billboard across the country."

In many ways, the Toronto Blue Jays are like an early, less-refined blueprint of many of the concepts of the NBA marketing machine. For example, the team had a strict code of conduct, right down to a dress code. As Larry Millson writes in *Ballpark Figures*, Bavasi was "obsessed with image, and the image he wanted his new Blue Jays to project was squeaky clean, mom-and-apple-pie. On the road there was a strict dress code: players had to wear blazers, grey slacks and team ties. Jeans were not allowed. Players could not sport beards, moustaches, or long hair."

The Toronto Blue Jays have already proved an inspiration for the fledgling basketball team. The Raptors have put together a package of photocopied newspaper articles from 1977 talking about some of the successes and some of the struggles of the Jays in their first season. Apparently, the Raptors take comfort from the fact that the wildly successful baseball franchise also suffered its share of bad press and controversy in those early years.

In particular, many of the clippings in the collection chronicle the faux pas by General Manager Peter Bavasi. By April 30, 1977, just a few weeks after opening day, there were giant cracks beginning to rip apart the front office of the Blue Jays. In a copyrighted article in the *Globe and Mail*, Christie Blatchford detailed some of the problems, including the high rate of turnover in the Jays office. According to Blatchford, two people had been fired and three had quit in the months leading up to the start of the season. She also quoted a memo telling staff to stop drinking so much free coffee and urging them to drain their cups thoroughly or they'd be forced to pay for it. In "The Blue Jay Style," a handbook for employees, ushers were told to put their hands over their hearts during the playing of both national anthems. Blatchford also published a memo asking Jays' employees to phone in to a poll conducted by *The Toronto Sun* about whether players should be allowed to have long hair or beards. They were told not to state that they worked for the Blue Jays.

The strikes against the Blue Jays management were minor ones but in total, they projected the image of a team in disarray. Peter Bavasi replied to Blatchford's charges by saying, "I did things that are not in the management textbook, but the results are there." (It has also been reported that Bavasi attempted to have Blatchford fired, but to no avail.)

Despite his abrasive style and bad personal reviews from the media, Bavasi continued to work marketing marvels in that first season. By July 22, 1977, the team had drawn over one million fans to Exhibition Stadium. They celebrated in style with "Thanks A Million Night," with five cars and 20 television sets up for grabs. Later in the season, the Jays also planned "Hockey Stick Day," "Toque Night" and, for the last game of the season, "Fan Appreciation Day." The promotions worked like a charm and by the end of the first year, the Blue Jays had shattered all previous attendance records for an expansion team. Despite the worst record in major league baseball, the Jays would make a profit of almost $2 million and pump an estimated $62 million into the city's economy.

The early years of the new Canadian basketball teams will also be filled with enthusiasm as the novelty overwhelms any nagging doubts about the quality of the teams. The crucial point will come when the fans begin to weary of always losing. Making the critical transformation from "new team" to "winning franchise" will be the greatest challenge for the Raptors and the Grizzlies, with particular pressure on the Raptors in the jam-packed sports market of Toronto.

For the Toronto Blue Jays, that transformation happened in the fall of 1981 with the departure of Peter Bavasi as the team's leader. He was replaced by Pat Gillick and Paul Beeston, two names that would become synonymous with the great years of triumph of the Toronto Blue Jays.

Years later, Garth Iorg, a member of the Jays since 1976, recalled the team's metamorphosis: "When Gillick and Beeston took over, that's when the team did an about-face. Toronto had been living on the novelty of having major-league baseball. The product had been bad on the field. Attendance was down. Guys didn't want to go to Toronto. Nobody wants to go to a team that's bad."

Obviously, selling the sizzle only goes so far, a difficult lesson that the Canadian NBA teams may someday have to learn.

There is a simple reason why Pat Gillick and Paul Beeston have been so successful with the Toronto Blue Jays. At the time the Jays were hatched, many of the other baseball franchises were largely playtoys for rich men who constantly interfered in the daily operations of the team and lost lots of money. The Toronto Blue Jays would be different. "From the start, the board decided to let the baseball people run the baseball team. It's a basic business principle: hire people who know what they're doing, let them do it, and make them accountable," writes Larry Millson.

Using that principle as a premise, Pat Gillick was a brilliant choice for the job of Vice-President of Player Personnel for the fledgling Blue Jays in 1976. Gillick was a former Triple-A pitcher and a former scout who was working for George Steinbrenner and the New York Yankees when he received a call from Peter Bavasi. Steinbrenner wanted Gillick to become the next general manager of the Yankees, but Gillick wisely chose Toronto instead. In Gillick, the Jays had the essentials of a general manager: experience, savvy and an integral knowledge of baseball.

It would take Gillick a decade but he would build the Toronto Blue Jays into the two-time World Series champions. Along the way, the team would be a financial triumph and would dominate the Toronto sports marketplace.

A large part of the Blue Jays success on the field can be attributed to Pat Gillick and to the team's hefty payroll ($43 million in 1994), which helped them assemble a stable of stars and bought them some high-priced pitching talent late in the season. But it is because of SkyDome that the Blue Jays could afford such winning habits. During the World Series years, the Jays were virtually sold out and put over four million paying customers through the turnstiles every season.

From a marketing perspective, SkyDome is a gigantic money-maker and the envy of every sports city. Ontario taxpayers may disagree. It's fortunate for the Raptors that they plan on building their basketball facility with private funds because the province of Ontario is not the place to be asking for government money to finance a new arena. All three political parties took a bath on SkyDome at various points in its history and there are some lessons to be learned from the SkyDome experience.

On November 15, 1991, SkyDome was sold to a consortium of eight private businesses including The Sports Network and a group of pension funds led by Penfund Capital No. 1 Ltd. Stadium Corporation, or Stadco, the Crown corporation that had owned SkyDome, set a purchase price of $151 million. It was not until 1994 that government documents were filed showing the overall loss on the SkyDome deal: a whopping $262.7 million. That's because the facility had cost a total of $608.9 million, more than two and a half times the original figure contracted for 1986. (If it's any consolation to people in Ontario, the total cost of the Olympic Stadium in Montreal was $1 billion, making it the most expensive sports complex in North America, with SkyDome second.)

There have been volumes of analyses as to why SkyDome turned into such an expensive proposition. Looking back now, that seemed inevitable, even though, at the time, there was guarantee after guarantee from Charles Magwood, President of the Stadium Corporation of Ontario, that the dome would be built on budget, that the hotel would "not cost a dime of public money" and that "the new price tag (then $338 million) will be the last price tag for the project."

One of the biggest concerns when SkyDome was being built was that it would sit empty for the six months of the year outside the baseball season. It's a dilemma that the Raptors are grappling with as well: aside from the 42 home games of the basketball team, what can they put in their new building when it's finished? That has been the impetus behind the team's discussions with the International Hockey League and, most recently, with Garth Drabinsky of Live Entertainment. They absolutely must have other tenants to make the building financially viable.

In the case of SkyDome, the management of the dome went to the Liberal cabinet early in construction and argued that they needed to build a multi-use facility that people would visit every day. The Liberals agreed and that decision led to several design changes and additions that eventually included a hotel and fitness club. The changes added $110 million to the original price tag of $150 million announced by Conservative Premier Bill Davis in January 1985. (The addition of the health club and the hotel were great news for the stadium's tenants like the Bitove Corporation and McDonald's who already had negotiated sweetheart leases. McDonald's got the exclusive fast-food deal at the bargain price of $5 million for 97 years.)

SkyDome has lived up to one expectation. In 1993, it was occupied for a record 256 event days, the highest number of any stadium in North America. (That was negated by the event days lost the following season because of the baseball strike.) In 1993, Stadco reported an operating profit of $35.5 million, again the highest of any stadium or arena in the U.S. or Canada. However, because of the construction debts, taxes and depreciation, totalling $49.7 million, the company was left with a net loss in 1993 of $14.2 million.

The moral of the story? The Raptors should build wisely and with forethought to avoid the enormous cost overruns that have plagued SkyDome and saddled the Ontario taxpayers with a huge bill. SkyDome's legacy means that there will be no public appetite for any government funding for the Raptors and it would be a public relations fiasco for any group to ever approach the taxpayer for public monies to build an arena or stadium in Ontario.

The superb attendance figures and profits have, however, become just a memory for the management of the Toronto Blue Jays. They have experienced a setback since the baseball labour problems began. They may have been the World Series champions but the fortunes of the Toronto Blue Jays plummeted during the 1994 campaign. Not only did the team stink on the field, but the walkout by the players and the subsequent cancellation of the World Series seems to have had a devastating effect on the fan base of the Blue Jays.

As the 1995 campaign began, one published report said that the Jays had almost no group sales booked. Traditionally, groups accounted for anywhere from 10 to 60 percent of the non-season-ticket base at SkyDome. In April, the team projected that group ticket sales to Jays' games would be off by 25 percent, which adds up to a loss of more than $7 million.

The reality turned out to be much worse. On April 18, 1995, the Jays drew only 31,073 to a game against Oakland. That was the reported crowd, though there were about 10,000 season tickets included in that number even though the ticket holders were not present at the game. It was the smallest baseball crowd since 30,105 fans attended a May 26, 1989 game at Exhibition Stadium and it was the tiniest crowd ever at SkyDome. Empty seats have become the norm at Jays games compared to the traditional sell-outs. "It's probably the first time I ever looked down the lines from the dugout and saw empty seats," said Manager Cito Gaston after one of the April games.

By the All-Star Game break, the average attendance at major league ballparks was down by about 25 percent, and empty seats were blatant reminders of the sagging fortunes of the former world champions. In years past, getting tickets to a game, particularly towards the end of the season, depended on whom you knew, how much you were willing to pay or dumb luck. Now, the Jays are so desperate they even cut the price for beer by $1, down to a still-princely $3.75 for a 341-ml cup and took 50¢ off most of the popular food items. The team was not helped by bizarre incidents like sound panelling falling on fans and a death threat to Jays second baseman Roberto Alomar.

The magical hold of the Blue Jays on the Toronto marketplace seems to be ruptured, perhaps permanently, creating a unique opportunity for the new NBA franchise. The two seasons would not intersect in the fall, but would in the spring, as the NBA season goes into June. Had the Jays been making another World Series run in 1995, it would have been interesting to watch the fledgling basketball franchise battling it out for media coverage with the wily veterans of the baseball team, but as circumstances would have it, the Toronto media are desperate for something to talk about other than the sad performance of the Blue Jays.

The stumbling Blue Jays are still not as badly off as the city's Canadian Football League franchise, for whom the last few seasons in particular have been painful ones. The story of the Toronto Argonauts contains many warning signs for the rookie Raptors.

There is no question that the turning point for the Toronto Argonauts came in 1989 when the team moved to SkyDome. While it's a state-of-the-art entertainment facility and the Jays have been successful there, the Argos have struggled since they moved there. Only one game since 1989 has drawn anything close to a sell-out and that was the 1991 Eastern Division final. In 1994, the team's average attendance was 16,841 in a facility that seats over 52,000. To say that there is no atmosphere at an Argos game is to overstate the obvious.

There are a couple of factors that have contributed to the fading fortunes of the Boatmen. The Canadian Football League itself was in decline in the early 1990s and has gone through a radical transformation with a focus on expansion to the U.S. as the primary goal. Secondly, the team would perhaps have been better off staying at Exhibition Stadium to play its games. *Globe and Mail* columnist Marty York has even gone so far as to suggest that the Argos should consider moving to Varsity Stadium on the campus of the University of Toronto. With 22,000 seats, the team would be far more likely to sell out, particularly with the added appeal of real grass and real air to lure more traditional football fans.

(The failure of the Argos at SkyDome is ominous for the Toronto Raptors in a couple of ways. For one thing, the team has said it will play at least two seasons at SkyDome, which is no better a basketball facility than it is a place for football. While the league and the team have put lots of effort into making the place as basketball-friendly as possible, fans who've attended NBA exhibition games at SkyDome can attest to the unsuitability of playing basketball there. Basketball needs a more intimate setting and the cavernous SkyDome could throw off some first-time basketball fans. The other places the Raptors looked at were Hamilton's Copps Coliseum and the ancient Maple Leaf Gardens. Again, neither is a basketball-specific facility. In the end, Hamilton was considered too far away, at 60 kilometres, from downtown Toronto, and Maple Leaf Gardens is too old a building, without the fancy scoreboard and sound system and other enhancements that a new basketball-only arena would have, or that GM Place in Vancouver can boast.

As the Raptors try to make their name in the Toronto market, they realize their best years will be the ones they spend in the new building that they own themselves. Making the wrong choice of venue can be terrible, as the CFL's Argos can attest.)

The Toronto Argonauts have also had a string of owners that have each taken their toll on the overall well-being of the ballclub. One of the most loathed owners in the history of the Argos was Harry Ornest, a colourful sports figure whose name will come up again later in this chapter. Ornest is a 72-year-old entrepreneur who is currently vice-chairman of Hollywood Park Inc., a racetrack in California. (He grabbed international headlines in 1990 when he got into a racetrack brawl with actor John Forsythe.)

Ornest has had many sports affiliations during his business career. His roots in sports can be traced back to his days as a hockey referee. In 1977, after making money in the vending-machine business in Western Canada, he started the Vancouver Canadians baseball team. He ran the team for four years and then sold it. His next sports venture involved the St. Louis Blues of the

National Hockey League. Ornest purchased the Blues in 1983 for $12 million US. Though considered a penny-pincher as an owner, Ornest nevertheless is credited with reviving the Blues fortunes before he sold them for a profit.

His next endeavour involved the Argonauts and his record there is controversial, to say the least. Ornest was behind the team's move to SkyDome in 1989. He quickly fell into the bad books of SkyDome management over a lease dispute in 1990. Earlier in the season, Ornest had battled with SkyDome and the Bitove Corporation over a $3 fee that the restaurants were charging for fans to watch the Argos games while they ate.

In 1990, the Blue Jays had struck a deal with Stadco and the Bitove group that paid the team $3 per game for every seat at the Hard Rock Cafe, Windows and Sightlines. Bitove included the $3 in the eating and viewing packages at the three restaurants and passed the money on to the Jays. Stadco applied a similar $3 fee for Argos games, but Harry Ornest wanted more, saying that the football seats cost more in the stadium and the restaurants were taking away too much business from the football games.

Meanwhile, the Jays were also receiving a set amount of money for every occupied room facing the ball diamond at SkyDome. Ornest wanted a similar deal, but Stadco President Richard Peddie said the Argos were not enough of a draw to warrant an extra charge.

Eventually, Harry Ornest became tired of all the battles and announced he was selling the team. Already struggling to draw people to SkyDome, with an average of only 18,000 per game, the Argos seemed on shaky ground.

In 1991, the Argos were purchased by a trio from Los Angeles with significant Canadian roots. Bruce McNall, Wayne Gretzky and John Candy purchased the Argos for a reported $5 million. They had an immediate impact on the Toronto sports scene. The flamboyant trio rolled into town in a stretch limo, mugged for the press and "bragged about turning around the fortunes of the sagging Argos while rejuvenating interest in the Canadian Football League," said a newspaper article at the time.

Argonauts' games became spectacles, with Hollywood stars lining the sidelines and marching bands and lots of fancy special effects to liven up SkyDome. John Candy and Dan Aykroyd, another Canadian, revived the Blues Brothers at intermission along with special guest Mariel Hemingway. On the field, the Argos were equally impressive, led by experienced quarterback Matt Dunigan and flashy superstar, Raghib (Rocket) Ishmail, the $18 million man in his first year out of Notre Dame. Attendance for the opening game was an impressive 41,178 spectators.

The average attendance that season was up to about 36,000 a game, though there was just one sell-out: 50,386 at the Eastern Final. Candy wore himself out travelling across the country promoting Canadian football: he was a charming and omnipresent ambassador for the sport he loved. The team had a Cinderella season, winning the Grey Cup on a snowy field in Winnipeg, with Candy, Gretzky and McNall in snowmobile suits on the sidelines cheering their team on.

But as suddenly as they arrived, the Hollywood trio were gone. Candy's movie commitments limited the time he could spend on the Argos, though at the time of his death, he was still the most committed of the three partners to making the franchise work. Gretzky's back problems distracted his attention, and Bruce McNall's financial empire was about to fall apart.

The triumvirate had lost $3.4 million in that wonderful winning season and faced the prospect of more losses. Over the winter, McNall had threatened to end his group's association with the CFL, saying they were unhappy with their lease agreement with SkyDome. After they worked things out with their landlord, the team jacked up ticket prices. Then, things got really ugly when the CFL received a bill for John Candy's goodwill tour of the league cities and refused to pay. McNall said the teams had agreed to foot the $225,000 in expenses and was incensed that they were reneging. "They agreed well in advance to pay his expenses and all we charged was $250,000," said McNall. "We could have asked for $2 million, at least. I mean, this is a man who makes a lot of money. He gets millions of dollars for his time ordinarily."

The CFL eventually agreed to pay up and McNall and Candy, at least, were back on side. The Argos stumbled and struggled both on the field and off in 1992. Team management let the efficient and marketable Dunigan get away as he signed with Winnipeg for more money. The crowds averaged around 31,000, slightly off the pace from 1991. Despite a flashy rookie year, it looked as if 1992 would be the last season for the Rocket whose appeal had fizzled. McNall tried to put on a brave face: "Last year, with all the hype, we knew we would have that first rush. But this year, we're not seeing it, and that's disappointing. At least, though, it's not as bad as it was two years ago."

By mid-1992, Wayne Gretzky was reportedly growing tired of the Argos. "He's having a tough time coping as an owner. I mean, he hates losing," said McNall. "He's very intense. He can't control himself when he sees the Argos fumbling or losing. He loses his temper a lot. As a hockey player, he can go out and try to do something about losing. But, as an owner, what are you going to do? You just have to take your losses." (Perhaps this is good advice for Isiah Thomas who may be compelled to step back onto the court when he watches his team losing in the early years of the Raptors.)

The losing continued and the fans stayed away in droves in 1993 and by the end of the season, it was too much for the Great One. "The fact is, the people in Toronto don't want the CFL. It's crazy. It's like being addicted to something. Do you keep going until you die, or do you stop halfway? I've told Mr. McNall I think it's time to sell, but he wants to hang on. But if Toronto doesn't want it and we can't sell it, what's the alternative? As far as I'm concerned, time's up," said Gretzky to a group of Toronto reporters before a Maple Leafs–Kings game in Los Angeles in November 1993.

By the spring of 1994, John Candy, the most stalwart supporter of the team, had died suddenly of a heart attack. Bruce McNall was the subject of a criminal investigation of his finances, and he later pleaded guilty to fraud and watched his empire crumble in 1994. Wayne Gretzky was long gone. The Argos were again on the selling block.

The experience of the Argos could in some ways be considered prophetic for the Toronto Raptors. The Toronto sports fan, though extremely knowledgeable, is also very fickle. The glitz and glamour of the McNall–Gretzky–Candy triumvirate did not seem to wash with the Toronto sports consumer. It was not dissimilar to the entertainment formula of traditional NBA teams and there is concern about how well that formula will translate north of the border. It didn't work for the Toronto Argonauts who, admittedly, were marketing a league that was on a downhill slide. The Argos were also playing in a facility that isn't necessarily well suited for the sport. But there are some interesting cautionary notes for the Raptors management in the untimely demise of the Toronto Argos under their L.A. ownership group.

The ownership of the Argos is again in question after the recent takeover of John Labatt Limited by the Belgian company Interbrew. In June, media reports suggested that a multimillionaire land developer in Florida named Norton Herrick was potentially interested in the team. He had recently been involved with attempts to buy the Pittsburgh Pirates and the San Diego Padres of Major League Baseball and the National Football League's Tampa Bay Buccaneers, but none of the deals had worked out. He was then reportedly shopping around for a CFL team, possibly with the intention of moving a franchise to Orlando. The Argonauts continued to struggle on the field and at the gate throughout the summer of 1995. They even resorted to closing the 500 level in SkyDome in an attempt to make the stadium's emptiness less obvious. But it's a stopgap measure at best and the future of the Argonauts in Toronto remains uncertain.

There is another reason why the history of the Toronto Argonauts could prove profoundly important for the Toronto Raptors and that is because of the expected arrival in Toronto of the NFL by 1999. With only eight or nine home games, the National Football League would represent only a minor scheduling conflict for the Raptors, as the two seasons would only overlap for about two months of the year. But the NFL would be a significant rival in marketing and merchandising and has a base of hard-core supporters in Toronto.

There has been talk of the NFL expanding to Toronto for years but those talks seem to be getting closer to fruition now than ever before. In May 1995, the Commissioner of the National Football League, Paul Tagliabue, and a sizable entourage of NFL personnel travelled to Toronto, ostensibly to promote an exhibition game at SkyDome in August. But there is evidence to suggest that this was a scouting trip with much greater ambitions.

Paul Tagliabue was quoted extensively by the Toronto media about the possibility of an NFL franchise coming to T.O. "We're very interested in this market," said Tagliabue. "We know how much interest there is here in the NFL and we have equally as much interest. We can foresee NFL teams in a number of foreign countries and Canada would have to be the top of that list along with Mexico."

For many years, the alleged reason for the NFL not coming to Canada was the existence of the CFL. Out of respect, the NFL did not want to intrude. However, with the CFL's ambitious expansion into the U.S. in the last few years, that caveat is removed. There had also been concern about seating capacity at SkyDome, which at 54,000 seats is smallish by NFL standards. But the league has now changed its tune on SkyDome: "I think it's the quality of the stadium rather than the size of the stadium," said the Commissioner after a tour of the facility.

A sell-out exhibition game on August 12, 1995 between the Dallas Cowboys and the Buffalo Bills only added to the sales campaign by the Toronto NFL contingent. Two of the NFL's marquee players made favourable comments about the possibility of expansion north of the border. Said Dallas quarterback Troy Aikman: "Toronto certainly should be a city that should be up for a team. The city of Toronto, the people of Toronto, have certainly done everything they could to bring a team here."

"There's no doubt that Toronto would be a great city for the NFL," added Jim Kelly of the Buffalo Bills.

The flamboyant Cowboys owner, Jerry Jones, endorsed the idea, as did the much-loved and much-respected TV analyst, John Madden, while in Toronto. "This is an amazing structure, this SkyDome, and the fans here are great, so's the city. It's a proven sports city. I can see the NFL going international to Mexico and to Toronto with its next expansion in a few years," said Madden on national television.

If the high finances of the Toronto Raptors seem a little breathtaking at times, an NFL team has an even steeper price tag. Yes, there would be a ready-made facility for a new NFL franchise, but the expansion fee would be anywhere from $175 to $200 million US. (The Jacksonville and Carolina franchises paid $160 million in expansion fees. Since then, the Tampa Bay Buccaneers, the league's worst team, was sold in January 1995 for $192 million US, driving up the value of all the existing franchises. Now experts predict that a Canadian expansion team in the NFL would cost $300 million, with operating costs included.)

Some familiar names figure prominently in any discussion of the NFL coming to Canada. Even the Bitoves would be beneficiaries by virtue of their exclusive contract for food and beverage services at SkyDome. There is, however, some dispute about rights in the market. The Sports Network (TSN) appears to own the football rights at SkyDome by virtue of being the largest investor in the refinanced SkyDome consortium. (TSN put up $30 million of the $150 million deal.) However, the waters were muddied because of the recent takeover of TSN's parent company, John Labatt Limited, and the subsequent auctioning off of various Labatt components, including TSN. To further complicate the situation, Labatt's rival Molson also claims to own the NFL rights at SkyDome. Molson took over Carling O'Keefe, which had been part of the original consortium financing the construction of the Dome and had "insisted on exclusive football rights inside the building." Under the original deal, Carling could bring in a successor to the CFL on a couple of conditions, including if the Argos fold or the Canadian Football League is significantly altered, which some may argue it has been because of American expansion. Paul Godfrey, one of the prime movers behind bringing the Jays to Toronto, has also been actively pursuing the NFL, but so far, it's not clear what a potential ownership group would look like, should the NFL expand north to Toronto.

Again, as with the Blue Jays, the Raptors are spared the competition of a potent rival, at least for now. The first five years of the Raptors' existence in Toronto will be critical to establishing the team's presence. If the team doesn't do well at solidifying its market before the NFL arrives, the Raptors could be overwhelmed by the hype that would accompany the arrival of American football. The demographics may be slightly different: the basketball audience is much younger than the NFL fans. But in a battle for the sports fans' dollars, the NFL would likely win.

The timing has worked out perfectly for the Raptors with the Blue Jays struggling and a Toronto expansion team for the NFL still in limbo. But there is one other delicious bit of timing for the team, involving another pro sports franchise, that could have far-reaching implications for the future of the Toronto Raptors. The Raptors have positioned themselves as a key player in a high-stakes battle for control of the Toronto Maple Leafs hockey club and Maple Leaf Gardens. It is a complicated conflict, including feuding cousins, a thwarted son and a feisty former hockey referee.

The controversy begins with the death in April 1990 of Harold Ballard, the long-time majority owner of the Maple Leafs and the Gardens. In his March 1988 will, Ballard appointed three executors of his estate: Steve Stavro, President of Knob Hill Farms Ltd., Donald Crump, former Commissioner of the Canadian Football League and Donald Giffin, a long-time Ballard associate. When Giffin died in 1992, he was replaced by lawyer Terry Kelly. Previous to this, Ballard had set up the Harold E. Ballard Foundation, consisting of seven charities including the Ontario Crippled Children's Centre and the Salvation Army. These charities were named as beneficiaries in Ballard's will.

In January 1991, a $20-million loan to the Ballard estate from Molson Cos. Ltd. was due and Steve Stavro offered to pay off the loan in exchange for the option to buy the estate's shares in Maple Leaf Gardens Ltd., which represented about 60 percent of the company. The executors asked an Ontario court to approve the deal, which it did. That decision was then appealed by Bill Ballard, but he lost his appeal. Later that year, Molson gave Stavro the right to buy its shares in the Gardens, which represented just under 20 percent.

In 1993, the executors hired Burns Fry and RBC Dominion Securities to appraise the value of Maple Leaf Gardens Ltd. They came up with a value of around $110 million, which would put the price of individual shares between $25.83 and $34. Those appraisals were dated October 1993. With that information in hand, the executors began to negotiate to sell the shares to Steve Stavro.

By March 1994, Stavro had lined up investors to provide the $125 million needed for the takeover and formed MLG Venture Ltd. The Ontario Teachers' Pension Plan Board was the largest partner, along with TD Capital Group Ltd., a subsidiary of the Toronto Dominion Bank. On April 2, 1994, Stavro's new company bought the estate's shares and the Molson shares for $34 a share. (He originally offered the estate $29, but bought them at $34.) Shortly after the deal was announced, the Ontario Public Trustee asked for information about the sale and began a three-month investigation of the deal.

The day before a meeting of the company's shareholders that would have given final approval of the deal, the Ontario Public Trustee went to court and won an injunction. The Public Trustee announced it would fight the Stavro takeover, arguing that the deal was not in the best interest of the charities, which are protected under the Charitable Gifts Act.

The judge who granted the injunction, Mr. Justice Sydney Lederman of the Ontario Court's General Division, said that the executors of the estate, including Steve Stavro, were obliged to get "the best price available in an open and informed market."

This is where the Toronto Raptors enter the picture. Included in the court documents was an affidavit from David Peterson, Chairman of the Board of the Raptors, stating an interest in purchasing Maple Leaf Gardens Ltd. The Raptors ownership group, according to Peterson's affidavit, "has been interested, for some period of time prior to April 1994, in either a proposal for a joint-use facility or in acquiring the shares held directly or indirectly by the estate. At no time were we informed that the shares of the estate were for sale [to Stavro]. Had there been a solicitation for bids, the Raptors Basketball Club would have been prepared to make an initial bid which was significantly higher than the $34 a share that was paid to the estate by [Stavro]."

The Raptors interest in Maple Leaf Gardens Ltd. has several ironic twists to it. The family connection is particularly fascinating. John Bitove Sr. and Steve Stavro are cousins. They both have strong connections in Toronto's Macedonian community, though the cousins are reported to like to compete. Some insiders predict that, should Steve Stavro lose his court case, he would still stay in the bidding on the open market just so he could outbid any offer from the Bitove group.

There is another family connection. Harold Ballard's son, Bill Ballard, also filed an affidavit stating that if Maple Leaf

Gardens Ltd. had been put up for sale, he would have bid more for it than Steve Stavro did. Ballard is, of course, a two-time loser in the bidding wars for an NBA team and was beaten out by the Bitove group. Ballard had been a minority owner in Maple Leaf Gardens Ltd. for years, but sold out in 1991 for about $21 million. There was some speculation that Labatt would back a Ballard bid to buy the Gardens and the Leafs but the new ownership of Labatt has changed the dynamics. (Labatt would dearly love to get into Maple Leaf Gardens, which for years has been the sacred turf of its rival, Molson.)

The third significant figure in the battle over Maple Leaf Gardens Ltd. is former hockey referee and former Argonauts owner Harry Ornest. He owns about $4 million in Gardens' shares, making him the second-largest shareholder after Stavro. He has fought the Stavro deal all the way, and along with another shareholder, Jim Devellano, a senior executive with the Detroit Red Wings, even received intervenor status in the lawsuit against Stavro, much to Stavro's chagrin.

In their defence, lawyers for Stavro and the other executors said that there was no obligation to actually test the market price because they had independent assessments done. Donald Crump, one of the three executors, also denied that he received any other offers to buy the shares. "At no time did Mr. Ornest tell me that he had an interest in purchasing the shares," Crump states in his affidavit. "At no time did Mr. Peterson communicate to the estate any interest of the Raptors in making a bid for the shares."

The initial assessment of the value of Maple Leafs Gardens Ltd. was done before the NBA franchise was announced and the lawyer for the Ontario Public Trustee, Frank Newbould, argued that the presence of the Raptors had increased the value of Maple Leaf Gardens Ltd. That made the original assessment dated, argued Newbould, backed up by another assessment, this time from a Montreal-based business valuator, Richard Wise.

A decision on the fate of Stavro's takeover and the future of Maple Leaf Gardens Ltd. was expected sometime in the fall of 1995. Some observers have speculated that the Raptors held off construction

Shaquille O'Neal of the Orlando Magic is one of the younger generation of rising superstars in the NBA. He has propelled the Magic far beyond the other expansion teams of the 1980s.

The Minnesota Timberwolves have struggled since joining the NBA in 1988.

The Charlotte Hornets have played to packed houses since joining the league but have had some problems off the court.

Arthur Griffiths poses with a model of GM Place which opened in September 1995.

Bringing Pat Quinn into the Canucks' organization was one of the shrewdest moves made by the young Arthur Griffiths.

Vancouver Canucks' president Arthur Griffiths poses with his mother, Emily, and Canucks' captain Trevor Linden, as the team advances to the 1994 Stanley Cup.

Professional volleyball player Gabrielle Reece models the new Grizzlies' uniform for Vancouver media, along with team General Manager Stu Jackson. May 18, 1995.

The Grizzlies sign their first player Kevin Pritchard. It would be months later, after the lockout, before they would sign other future Grizzlies. June 1, 1995.

Stoody/Canapress

Bryant "Big Country" Reeves is the Grizzlies' first pick at the college draft in Toronto. He poses at SkyDome with NBA Commissioner David Stern. June 28, 1995.

Damon Stoudamire was the Raptors' first pick, seventh overall, at the college draft. June 28, 1995.

Robertson/Canada Wide

High school sensation Kevin Garnett was selected by the Minnesota Timberwolves in the 1995 college draft.

Workers at SkyDome polish up the official Raptors floor which will be unveiled at the college draft on June 28, 1995.

Loek/The Toronto Star

of their new arena for as long as possible, waiting for the court decision to be announced, in hopes of a ruling against Stavro. The team could then actively pursue buying Maple Leaf Gardens Ltd.

It's not hard to see why buying Maple Leaf Gardens Ltd. had appeared so appealing to the Raptors. By buying the Leafs and the Gardens, the Raptors ownership group would get the Leafs, a debt-free building, and, according to *The Financial Post*, as much as $25 million. Even if the Raptors paid $44 a share, $10 more than Steve Stavro was offering, the Maple Leaf Gardens deal would only cost $163 million, close to the price tag for a new arena. Some analysts think that all the publicity surrounding the court case may start a bidding war, should the Gardens go up for sale. Speculation is that the price could go as high as $50 a share, which would add up to $185 million for Maple Leaf Gardens Ltd. Owning the hockey club would give the Raptors the second tenant they need in their new building.

Whatever happens next with the Maple Leafs, there are a couple of very interesting years ahead in the Toronto sports market. There has not been a new pro franchise in the city since 1977 and the arrival of the Blue Jays. Now, suddenly, the NBA has arrived and the NFL is not far behind. The Toronto sports market is now being divided in more directions than ever before with millions of dollars in ticket revenues, broadcast deals and merchandise sales at stake. With the costs of buying and running a team in the hundreds of millions of dollars, the Toronto teams will be pushing even harder over the next five years to grab their niche in the market and hold it. The more established teams will be watching closely to see where the Raptors' support comes from and how much the new team is going to eat into their share of the Toronto scene.

Chapter Thirteen

THE DRAFT

Toronto's SkyDome bills itself as the "World's Greatest Entertainment Centre." It is fitting, therefore, that it played host to the 1995 NBA College Draft. What was once a simple formality whereby all the league's teams hooked up by conference call to make their choices from the year's crop of college talent has now become a carefully orchestrated, televised, live entertainment extravaganza. First, it moved onto TV. Then, it became an event. The 1994 draft was held at the Hoosier Dome in Indianapolis and attracted over 19,000 fans.

As a newcomer to the league in 1995, Toronto was determined to put on a great show, to demonstrate to the rest of the league and the other NBA cities looking in that it was indeed a good choice for an NBA franchise, and that it knew how to stage things in a "big-league" way. Toronto did the job all right. More than 22,000 people showed up on Wednesday, June 28 at SkyDome to be part of the excitement of a new sport to the city and to the country, and to celebrate the first-ever draft picks by the hometown Raptors and the Vancouver Grizzlies.

Toronto had been awarded the right to host the draft as part of the NBA's deal with the Ontario government on the Pro-Line lottery issue. A shrewd demand by the Bob Rae administration, it was an opportunity to showcase the city and the province, as well as providing an economic injection of several million dollars since league and team officials, international media and players and their families all flocked to Toronto for several days surrounding the draft. The Bitove people relished the idea of putting their operation in the NBA spotlight, and set about planning several days of activity surrounding the draft. They came up with "Raptorfest," a huge festival that began on the preceding Friday and featured a 3-on-3 tournament outside the Ontario Legislature, a three-point shooting contest, a slamdunk competition, and, of course, a weekend full of merchandise and memorabilia sales, ticket sales and ticket giveaway contests in anticipation of the big event at SkyDome.

On the Monday, two days before draft day, players and their families started arriving from the far-flung places that spawn basketball talent. They came from unheard-of hamlets like Glans, Oklahoma and Quitman, Mississippi, from the big cities of Detroit, Chicago and Philadelphia, and from rural parts of Ohio and North Carolina. Many were wide-eyed about travelling to Canada and being in a structure like SkyDome, to say nothing of being part of the NBA draft.

Also arriving in Toronto several days before the draft was the NBA marketing and entertainment machine. Scores of workers, officials and organizers scurried about the SkyDome complex armed with cellular phones and walkie-talkies, barking commands and requests as they set things up to the NBA's requirements and the Raptors public relations desires. The new basketball floor the Raptors would be playing on was to be laid down as part of the set. It would be an "unveiling" as fans would get their first look at the stylized paint job on the floor, complete with "raptor footprints" trailing along the playing surface. The massive stage was erected where the NBA teams would set up shop with a couple of representatives each, and where the giant board would list the teams and their picks as the draft progressed. At one end of the stage was the TV booth, for use by TNT (Turner Network Television), the group that had negotiated with the NBA for TV rights to broadcast the draft live. Next to that was another booth for NBA radio, a league-run operation linking a string of U.S. stations that were picking up live play-by-play of the draft proceedings. Behind the stage was the so-called "Green Room," an area set aside for the players and their families and friends who sat at tables, were served a lavish meal and awaited the calling of the names. In front of the stage was a smaller, elevated platform that would serve as a mini TV studio; it had three chairs on it, two for the "in-house" hosts and one for a guest. This would be the "in-house" broadcast where two NBA-appointed anchors would do live play-by-play of the draft on the giant screen known as the Jumbotron; the people in attendance at SkyDome would form a studio audience of more than 20,000.

But the in-house show was much more than a series of interviews on the big screen. Three people from NBA Entertainment were assigned to "produce" this part of the event. It would include highlights rolling on the big screen, blooper tapes, commercials and celebrity greetings, while on the new basketball court there would be the debut of the Raptor mascot and dance team, the finals of a three-point shooting contest and the finals of a slamdunk contest.

One of the key attractions for the fans at SkyDome would be to see and hear from the players close up after they had been picked. After his name had been called and he had received the congratulatory hugs and high fives from friends and family in the Green Room, each player would make his way out, receive a hat with the logo of the team that had just chosen him, and make his way up the stairs onto the big stage. He would walk out, shake the hand of Commissioner David Stern and would then be ushered quickly to the TNT television booth for an interview, then to NBA radio for another, then to a small, makeshift set for a quick chat with Canada's youth channel, YTV (which was the only TV operation interested in carrying the NBA production live in Canada) and then to the in-house set for an interview in front of the SkyDome crowd with Ron Thulin and Leo Rautins, Canadian basketball legend and former NBA player now turned broadcaster. After that, the players would be ushered past a noisy crowd and down into the bowels of the SkyDome to a football dressing room that had been converted for the night into a series of mini TV interview booths. Here, the newly chosen pros would be interviewed by other major networks that were not rights holders for the broadcast. TSN, CBC, CNN, NBC, ESPN and CBS would all have their crack at interviewing the players one-on-one, as they were shepherded around by a person from the NBA. Only after these interviews could the players go back up into SkyDome and talk with officials from the team that had drafted them, or celebrate more with their families.

Everything was to run smoothly; everything would be carefully orchestrated and meticulously managed to allow for maximum exposure of the product, the newest NBA stars, with the league looking very slick and in control.

The NBA Draft had been held for many years in New York City, but in 1992, it became a "road show. That year it was held in Portland's Memorial Coliseum. The 1993 draft was at the Palace of Auburn Hills, the home of the Detroit Pistons; in 1994, it was a huge hit in the Hoosier Dome in Indianapolis. Then came Toronto in 1995, the league's first foray outside the United States.

Many of the top draft picks over the years have gone on to stardom in the NBA, and many have been what are termed "underclassmen," players who decided to leave school early and make themselves available for the NBA teams who were looking over the college and European club team talent. Some of the biggest names in the game took that route—Michael Jordan, Magic Johnson, Isiah Thomas, Charles Barkley, Clyde Drexler, Hakeem Olajuwon and Shaquille O'Neal all left school early for the big dollars and high-level challenge of the NBA. Once upon a time, players who left college early for the NBA were known as "hardship cases" and had to demonstrate financial need to become eligible for the NBA draft. But the courts ruled in 1976 that the league could not deny a person the right to earn a living by placing on him a set of financial-need criteria. So, since 1976, the draft has been wide open to underclassmen, and many have made the leap.

(In 1987, the draft became a lottery-style situation, where it was no longer simply the last-place team that got to choose first. Under the new arrangement, the lowest nine teams in the league all had an equal chance at getting the number one pick in the draft. In 1989, through the collective bargaining process, the draft was cut down to two rounds. Eventually, the players union would like it cut down to one round.)

Early entry candidates have been picked first overall for the last few years—O'Neal out of Louisiana State by Orlando in 1992, Chris Webber out of Michigan by Orlando in 1993 and Glenn Robinson out of Purdue by Milwaukee in 1994. By being chosen first overall by Golden State in the 1995 draft, Maryland's Joe

CONTRACTS SIGNED BY TOP 10 NBA FIRST-ROUND PICKS.
1. Chris Webber (Golden State) 15 years, $74.4 million
2. Shawn Bradley (Philadelphia) 8 years, $44.2 million
3. Anfernee Hardaway (Orlando) 13 years, $65 million
4. Jamal Mashburn (Dallas) 7 years, $32 million
5. Isaiah Rider (Minnesota) 7 years, $25.5 million
6. Calbert Cheaney (Washington) 6 years, $18 million
7. Bobby Hurley (Sacramento) 6 years, $16.5 million
8. Vin Baker (Milwaukee) 10 years, $15 million
9. Rodney Rogers (Denver) 6 years, $12 million
10. Lindsey Hunter (Detroit) 7 years, $11 million

Source: Toronto Star.

Smith made it four straight for the underclassmen. The 1995 draft saw a surfeit of young talent "coming out," as the expression goes. Many were hoping to beat the rookie salary cap that would inevitably come. As it turned out, they did not.

So for the 1995 draft, there were 18 still-in-school players who had applied to the NBA by the May 14 deadline to be included on the draft-eligible list. Maryland's big man, Joe Smith, dominated at the NCAA level as a sophomore. A smooth and powerful 6'10" forward, Smith scored 20.8 points per game and averaged 10.7 rebounds and 2.9 blocked shots per game on his way to being named Player of the Year in the Atlantic Coast Conference. He was also named the National Collegiate Player of the Year by two different organizations.

"He's a relentless rebounder with great quickness in his leaping. He gets off the floor quicker than his opponents. He runs very well and has shown great improvement and made great strides from his freshman to his sophomore season," said John Nash, Vice-President and General Manager of the Washington Bullets.

"I think he's going to be a great player. He's shown throughout a short college career that he can score and rebound with anyone at the college level. Also, I think he's a good kid. He projects well into the NBA as far as his skills and his intensity go," said Jeff Weltman, Director of Scouting for the Los Angeles Clippers.

Since two teams picking in the top four said how impressed they were with Joe Smith, the Golden State Warriors decided they should take Smith with the first pick, and they did. So with Smith a Warrior, attention turned to the lowly Los Angeles Clippers. They also chose an underclassman in Alabama sophomore forward, Antonio McDeyss. Then Philadelphia chose University of North Carolina's superstar guard–forward, Jerry Stackhouse, also a sophomore. The Washington Bullets were next and took Stackhouse's UNC teammate, Rasheed Wallace, a 6'10" sophomore forward. With the fifth pick, Minnesota's Timberwolves went out on a limb and chose Kevin Garnett, a 6'11" high school phenom from Chicago. Rarely had anyone made the leap from high school to the NBA, but scouts on several teams felt that Garnett, although raw, could enter the pro ranks, apprentice for a few years and then be a star.

Those first five picks were interesting and brought noisy reactions from the crowd at SkyDome as the players were chosen, then interviewed on the Jumbotron and as the picks were analyzed by the in-house broadcast teams. But what these picks really did was serve as an appetizer for the sixth and seventh picks, which were owned by the Vancouver Grizzlies and the Toronto Raptors respectively.

The Grizzlies had brought several of the young collegians to Vancouver in the weeks leading up to the draft to work them out in a gym, talk with them and put them through some physical testing. All teams do this kind of "tire-kicking" as a way of looking at their potential choices in a setting different from the game tapes and highlight reels everyone sees.

Vancouver liked what it saw in Bryant Reeves from Oklahoma State. He's very solid, a seven-footer who weighs in at about 250 pounds, and a proven player in college where he took the Cowboys to the NCAA Final Four in 1995.

"What we also liked was the fact he was a senior," said Grizzlies General Manager Stu Jackson. "He had those extra couple of years of college basketball, and an extra couple of years of maturity, physically and mentally. We liked what we saw in him as a person, in his work ethic and in his commitment to what we're trying to do here."

The Vancouver Grizzlies took Bryant Reeves with the number six pick. The choice was greeted with great cheering in SkyDome. The crowd was clearly enthusiastic about the first choice by a Canadian team, and about the player chosen.

The reaction would not be the same when it came time for the Raptors to choose a player. Like the Grizzlies and the other teams, Toronto had brought in several high-profile players to work out, be interviewed and generally audition. Among those they had brought in were UCLA's Ed O'Bannon, star of the Bruins 1995 NCAA championship team, Michigan State guard Shawn Respert, and Bryant Reeves. They had talked about the young high schooler Kevin Garnett, and there had also been a huge article in a Toronto newspaper the morning of the draft suggesting that Duke centre, Cherokee Parks, might be the Raptors choice. With Garnett and Reeves already gone, the crowd at SkyDome was clearly favouring UCLA's O'Bannon. As Commissioner David Stern stepped up to the microphone, 20,000 fans were chanting "Ed, Ed, Ed...."

Stern read, "With the seventh pick, their first ever pick, the Toronto Raptors choose Damon Stoudamire from the University of Arizona." A chorus of boos followed, and the cameras caught kids holding their noses and giving the "thumbs-down" sign. The crowd wanted O'Bannon and was clearly disappointed. Later, it was suggested that this Toronto crowd did not get to see much PAC-10 conference basketball, where Stoudamire was a star. Toronto viewers get mostly regional NCAA action from the Big East on TV, via the Buffalo stations. Of course, they had been able to see Ed O'Bannon and the UCLA Bruins because the Bruins marched all the way to the NCAA championship and were highly visible on TV.

Stoudamire is a 5'10" shooting guard and a great scorer. It did not go unnoticed that he is, in fact, in the mould of one Isiah Thomas—short, quick, smart and a good shooter and playmaker. But is he the type of player to choose when you're an expansion team, just starting out? Is he the player around whom you build your team? Is he a marketable commodity? Will his presence excite fans and help sell tickets? These were the questions and criticisms the Raptors faced immediately after making Stoudamire their first pick.

Thomas defended his choice, saying Stoudamire was the one he had wanted all along, assuming the big names would be gone by the seventh pick. Like some other clubs, he was worried about Ed O'Bannon's knee. O'Bannon had torn the anterior cruciate ligament and had surgery in 1990. O'Bannon claims the knee is fine and his strong four years of college ball is testimony to that. But the feeling among some NBA clubs was that an NBA schedule of 80–100 games is a lot tougher on a knee than a 40-game college schedule. Thomas wanted someone he could consider a 10-year investment. "We wanted Damon, and I'm sure he'll show the fans here and the rest of the league that he was a great choice. We had to play some chess moves to get him. We knew Portland wanted him because he's from there. The Blazers traded to get up to the eighth spot, thinking they'd get Damon because we leaked out some false stuff about us going for Cherokee Parks with the seventh pick," said the Raptors General Manager.

With their second pick in the two-round draft, the Raptors chose another guard, Jimmy King out of Michigan, once a member of the "Fab Five" that led Michigan to the Final Four twice in the 1990s. (That "Fab Five" was Chris Webber, Juwan Howard, Jalen Rose, Jimmy King and Ray Jackson.) So the Raptors chose two young guards in the college draft to go with their expansion draft choices, who were mostly big men left unprotected by their teams.

By virtue of the coin toss with the Grizzlies, won by the Grizzlies who opted to pick ahead of Toronto in the college draft, the Raptors had the first pick in the expansion draft on June 24. They chose veteran guard B.J. Armstrong, who had been part of three championship teams in the 1990's with Chicago. Armstrong went to Toronto the Monday after the draft and did the required public relations things, spoke to reporters about liking the city and being happy to be chosen, etc. Really it was all a smokescreen. In confidence, Armstrong had told Thomas immediately after the draft that he didn't want to play for the expansion Raptors but wanted to be dealt to a team that had a chance at contending. So, in secret, Thomas cut a deal with the Golden State Warriors who coveted

Armstrong. The Raptors would give Armstrong to Golden State in exchange for two players off the Warriors roster, Victor Alexander and Carlos Rogers, plus three of the four picks Golden State would make in the second round of the draft.

Reporters were miffed on the night of the draft at SkyDome because Thomas only gave a couple of quick interviews after the Raptors first pick, then disappeared to the team's "war room." Afterwards, it became clear why he had been so unavailable. He was, in fact, directing the Golden State people on whom to pick in the second round, since three of the players chosen would actually become Raptors property. For the record, those picks were forward Dewayne Whitfield from Jackson State, Martin Lewis from Seward County Community College and Michael McDonald from the University of New Orleans. This deal had been made, but not formalized, when the NBA labour problems arose, effectively freezing all transactions.

Also obtained in the expansion draft were John Salley, veteran centre from Miami who had played with Isiah Thomas on the NBA championship Detroit teams in 1989 and 1990; Andres Guibert, a former Cuban star who was on Minnesota's roster; Tony Massenburg from the L.A. Clippers; centre Oliver Miller from Detroit; young forwards Acie Earl from Boston, Dontonio Wingfield from Seattle and seven-foot centre Zan Tabak from Houston; veteran forwards Ed Pinckney from Milwaukee, Jerome Kersey from Portland, Willie Anderson from San Antonio and 25-year-old Doug Smith from Dallas, once a first pick of the Timberwolves; and guards Keith Jennings from Golden State and B.J. Tyler from Philadelphia. Eventually, Smith, Kersey and Wingfield left the organization before training camp began.

On the players he got as discards from other teams, Thomas was philosophical: "I think we got a good mix. We wanted to find people with winning ways. We did not want to get bogged down with a lot of big contracts. I like where we are."

The man who will have to work with this talent, and who helped in the selection process, is Coach Brendan Malone.

"I like the height we got," said Malone. "We'll be OK inside. We'll be able to rebound and defend. We got some players with some experience, we kept the cap down, leaving room to sign our college pick."

As for the Grizzlies, they also got some proven NBA talent in the expansion draft. New York Knicks guard Greg Anthony is 27, with four years in the league, all in the media mecca of New York and all of it under the very successful Pat Riley. Anthony went to the NBA Final with the Knicks in 1994. Some of the other recognizable names grabbed by the Grizzlies include 6'8" forward Kenny Gattison from Charlotte, with nine years in the NBA; 6'6" guard Gerald Wilkins from Cleveland, who's played 10 seasons but was injured for all of 1994–95; 7' centre Benoit Benjamin from New Jersey, with 10 years experience; and 6'4" guard Byron Scott, a key part of the powerhouse Lakers teams in the '80s, who arrived in Vancouver at age 34, after playing for Indiana in 1994–95.

General Manager Stu Jackson said he was pleased with the players he was able to pick up, again, like the Raptors, being particularly mindful of the spending. "When you look at the players we chose, I like the mix of youth and experience. But we're also comfortable with the dollar amount committed, even in the long term, to some of these players. It was a factor in our choices. We needed to save some to sign our college players as well."

In addition to Bryant Reeves, the Grizzlies also got a proven scorer in the second round of the college draft, taking 6'5" shooting guard Lawrence Moten out of Syracuse. He holds the school's all-time scoring record with 2,334 points, having surpassed current NBA stars Derrick Coleman and Sherman Douglas.

CHAPTER FOURTEEN

JOHN BITOVE JR.: ANSWERING THE CRITICS

John Bitove Jr. breezes into a meeting on the rooftop patio at Gretzky's restaurant in Toronto. He is late, and apologetic. It's all right that he's late. The man lives an unbelievably hectic life, moving from meeting to meeting, putting out fires here, cutting deals there, doing PR, keeping in touch with the NBA and his staff, sitting on boards, fighting off litigation and still working hard at being a good husband and father.

John Bitove Jr. is a very likable guy, but make no mistake—behind the friendly demeanour and the big smile, the affable, chatty man who leads the Raptors' organization is a "shark" when it comes to business. He is driven and ambitious and totally passionate about sports. That's admirable, but it may at times be his undoing when it comes to handling the NBA's Toronto franchise.

The way Bitove conducts himself at public functions shows he has spent time in the political arena. He's cool and confident, working a room with ease, carrying on several conversations at once, interrupting one for a moment to respond to someone's greeting or query, then picking up where he left off, leaving no one offended. He's as comfortable with the media as he is with the barons of Bay Street. He can switch gears from a hard-edged business meeting where the conversation involves millions of dollars to a goofy gab-session with the local all-sports radio station via his car phone.

"It's funny, I never wanted that role," says Bitove. "I never wanted the limelight. I know people think I love it and bask in it, but I don't. In fact, I told Russ Granik and David Stern that I'd be happy to lead this project, but that I didn't want the public attention that went with it. They had little sympathy and they told me, 'John, are you up for this or not, because if you're not...'. so I realized right then I'd have to live with it. But really, all it is for me is the fact I love business and I love sports, and this combines the two perfectly, so it's a perfect fit. The limelight I could do without."

Bitove has been an avid sports fan and participant since he was very young. His choice of universities was based on a desire to play football at an elite level. "I went to high school at York Mills in Toronto, played football there and always wanted to go on to play Big Ten football. So I went to Indiana University, hoping I could make it there as a walk-on," says Bitove, shaking his head and smiling at the memory and, presumably, at his naivete. "I didn't make it, but I enjoyed the school a lot, so much so that when I got into the University of Windsor law school while at Indiana, I went to Windsor, completed my law degree, but spent my summers back at Indiana, finishing the degree I had started there as well. So I was a graduate of Indiana, class of '83, and a Windsor LLB, class of '84. That was a hectic time."

After a year of articling with the Ottawa law firm Gowling and Henderson, in 1985 Bitove went to work for then Conservative Cabinet Minister Sinclair Stevens. "I was excited about that job because it was going to be a great chance to learn about the inner workings of the politics and business that ran our country. But I was just a month and a half into that job and suddenly things got messy," says Bitove, in reference to the scandal in which Stevens was accused of breaching conduct rules regarding a blind trust and his company, York Development. Bitove was immortalized in a photo that was picked up by newspapers across the country. In it, he was shown holding the reporters and photographers at bay with one arm while holding open the door to a limo so that his besieged boss, Sinclair Stevens, could escape the throng.

After that, Bitove went to work for Don Mazenkowski, then Deputy Prime Minister. "What an education that was!" says Bitove. "Mulroney was busy fending off the political stuff and getting himself in and out of trouble, and meanwhile, Maz and his staff were running the country. He taught me a ton about how to handle crises, how to pick your battles, when to make a stand, and about what people to go to and what channels to follow to get things done without the political hassles and delays."

With this kind of driven, ambitious personality, business acumen, political connections and a love of sports that would send him to an expensive American school in pursuit of his dream of playing football, John Bitove Jr. certainly seemed to have the credentials necessary to be a sports entrepeneur. The question was: Were there others with some money who thought so too, and would the NBA moguls think so as well?"

"When I realized the NBA was going to expand to Canada, I went to my family and asked for the money to finance the bid process," says Bitove. "It was six figures. So it was a good chunk of money, but they believed in it with me, and they thought we could be successful."

And so it began—John Bitove Jr. heading up the group known as Professional Basketball Franchise Ltd., and working to be the winning team, the one that would be granted the franchise when the NBA came to Toronto. Asked why he thinks his bid won out over the Palestra group and the Ballard–Cohl group, Bitove says simply, "Preparation. I don't think there's any one issue. I just think we worked the hardest. A lot of time and preparation went into it. I and my family had been planning for this for the better part of five years. We weren't vocal about it, that's not our style and still isn't. Even when I thought we were ahead, I didn't say it."

In fact, insiders say that the NBA liked the Bitove group and the word in the NBA circles was that Commissioner David Stern had said it was the Bitove group's to win or lose during presentations. "I hadn't ever heard that," says Bitove. "We had felt that, but certainly wanted to keep on it, dot every i and cross every t, take care of every detail."

It's clear Bitove is proud of his work at the 1994 World Basketball Championship in Toronto, and believes that work went a long way to helping secure the NBA franchise for his group. "In the fall of 1992, it became clear that the 1994 Worlds were going to be pulled from Yugoslavia. I put together a bid group and worked with Basketball Canada, with Joe Halstead, Deputy Commissioner of Sport and Fitness for Ontario, and with the Metro Toronto Visitors and Convention people. I was vice-chairman and we went over to the FIBA meetings in Munich, put in a bid to host the event and wound up beating out seven other countries. I think that may be one of the intangibles about why our NBA bid group was selected. We showed we were committed to bringing those World Championships to Canada and to grow the sport of basketball in Canada even before there was talk of the league expanding here."

Bitove shrugs off the opportunity to comment about why the other groups were unsuccessful. There is the suggestion that the control-crazy NBA resented the fact the Palestra group may have approached them with a bid before they were asked for one.

"No, I don't believe that," says Bitove.

He does admit, though, that the league was wary about just who and how many people would come forward. "They were apparently ready at the 1993 All-Star Game in Salt Lake City to announce that they were coming to Toronto with an expansion franchise. But they didn't want to open it up and have a free-for-all, with 10 guys throwing in 10 grand each and saying 'Let's see what happens.' So, in an effort to disguise it a bit, the league simply said it was expanding to Canada, without being any more specific. I hear there was no thought of Vancouver at that point. But, hearing the league say it was expanding to Canada, Arthur Griffiths put in a bid, and lo and behold, now we have two Canadian franchises.

"And we won ours because we worked at it. It's like any other business competition. You have to work on the contacts, you work on the financial, and you work the business plan. It's not any one thing, it's all of those elements. People say, 'Oh, you won out because you had a relationship with the league already from the World Championships.' I say, 'Forget it.' If we didn't do everything else right, we wouldn't have won it simply for that reason."

Another one of the whispers about the Bitove-led group centres on the question of the franchise fee. The suggestion is that when it came time to talk about money and what each bidding group would be willing to pay for an expansion franchise in Toronto, the Palestra group and the Ballard–Cohl group both named figures they thought were reasonable. The story goes that when it came to John Bitove Jr., he pretty much offered a blank cheque and said he'd leave it up to the NBA to decide what was fair.

"That's not true," says Bitove. "What we were asked was, 'Would you pay 125 million?' "And our response was, 'It depends what 125 million gets us.' We didn't know what was in the deal. We had heard that they were planning to exclude us from the NBC-TV money available to all teams. There was merchandising, licensing, all kinds of factors that we had to understand what they were talking about before we could say whether we would pay that or not. But we definitely did not say 'We'll pay whatever you want' to the NBA.

"Now, I heard all kinds of conjecture and talk from third parties about what happened with the other groups. I've had only one direct conversation about it, and that was with Bill Ballard about a week after the presentations in New York. He said to me, 'Did they ask you the big question?'

"And I said, 'Which one is that?'

"He said, 'If you were willing to pay one two five.'

"I said, 'Yeah, why? Did they ask you that?'

"He said, 'Yeah.'

"So I quickly said, 'And what did you say?'

"He said, 'Well, of course. What did you say?'

"I said, 'Well, I told them it depends on the deal and all that stuff.'

"So that's what happened. Yes, we got the question about 125 million, but so did Bill. Now I know there was another group out there saying they never would have paid it, and the most they would have paid was 85 million, and that we said 'Here's a blank cheque.' That's not true. Again, our response was to ask what we would get for the 125 million if that's the price."

Bitove said he had heard from Canadian broadcast executive John Hudson that the NBA was cutting out the NBC broadcast rights money, and that Canadian teams would only get Canadian rights revenues. He had also heard that the Canadian franchises wouldn't get in on the revenues from the sale of licensed NBA products. In fact, the Bitove group got a sweet deal regarding revenues from licensed goods—90 percent of the Canadian-generated revenues.

Another of the "word on the street" rumours was that some of the key figures on the NBA expansion committee were "thanked" by a grateful group in Toronto. One rumour had a couple of people getting new houses in Aspen, Colorado, among other "gifts."

"Of course not," says Bitove, bristling. "I'm young, so I haven't done a ton of business deals, and I worked in government for a time, and people always talk about that sort of thing going on. But I don't think so. When it happens, those people usually get nailed. And when they do, of course people say it goes on all the time. Maybe I'm naive, but I just don't believe the world can work that way, because if you do that stuff, you're going to get nailed."

When reminded of the "courting" of International Olympic Committee members that goes on when cities are bidding for the Olympics, Bitove says that's different. "That's part of doing business. Didn't Conrad Black court Ken Thomson like crazy before he bought his newspapers? It's part of doing business."

And was there courting of the NBA kingpins by the Toronto Professional Basketball Franchise people?

"What's courting?" asks Bitove.

Was there any taking of people on ski holidays or that sort of thing?

"No. Those people are above reproach on that sort of stuff. Did we wine and dine them up here? Sure, when they came up for their due diligence visit, but in fact, I almost screwed up on that one. We had heard that Vancouver was going to whisk the NBA expansion guys over to Victoria by helicopter to meet the Premier. So we figured, if they're putting on that kind of a show, we'd better do it, too. In the interim, though, the guys on the committee said they didn't want the helicopter ride to Victoria, suggesting Premier Harcourt could come to Vancouver if he wanted to meet them. Now, their visit to Toronto was first, so in they come—Russ Granik, Jerry Colangelo and league general counsel Joel Litvin. David Peterson and I got security clearance to go right out to the plane and meet them, and we had the helicopter waiting. Granik said, 'What's this?'

"I said, 'Well, it's the easiest and quickest way to get us downtown, Russ. Let's go.'

"He said, 'We told the Vancouver people no helicopter ride.'

"Eventually, we talked them into the helicopter, but they were not happy because they had instructed the Vancouver group and us not to do anything excessive. I didn't know they had said no to the helicopter. I thought it was a good idea because I had heard Vancouver was doing it and I had read that the Colorado Rockies had done it. It almost backfired on us."

One of the most frequently heard allegations against the Bitove group regarding the handling of the NBA franchise is that the "name game" was bogus, and that Raptors was the name all along, and that it had been so ordained by the league marketing people. The team ran a nation-wide contest and allowed Toronto newspapers to conduct reader polls as to what names they would like for their new NBA team. Insiders say that was all to generate publicity, and really there was no intention of naming the team anything else but Raptors.

"Absolutely not true," says Bitove. "Quite frankly, we had our favourites. T-Rex was my favourite all along. Any time we heard a name we liked, we registered it, to the point where we had about 18 names legally registered. I could show you the legal letters to prove it. It's too bad the *Toronto Star* wrote that piece about our rigging the contest, because they based their conclusion on the fact that we had legally registered the name Raptors months earlier, when really we had all of them registered, just to be safe.

"We had five or six names that we always considered the frontrunners—Grizzlies, Bobcats, Dragons, Raptors, T-Rex and one other I can't recall. At the time the vote was going on, NBA Creative Services was working on logos for all of the names. Three or four started to emerge as good names. So while the vote was going on, we invited the presidents of Starter, Nutmeg Mills and Pro Player, three of the biggest licensees in the country, and we threw all the logos and all the colour combinations and everything else out on the table. I remember David Beckerman from Starter saying, on Raptors, that: 'You guys will be either heroes or the biggest putzes that ever lived if you go with this.'"

So, the dare was there. But Bitove says he and his people were getting feedback that suggested Raptors was a good choice. "We were doing focus groups, predominantly with kids, throwing all the logos and stuff up on the wall and asking them to go through them. Our people were going around to the schools, showing the stuff, and the kids there loved Raptors. At the same time, we were continuing the legal registrations around the world for all the names, and the *Toronto Star* had a huge phone poll—I think their biggest ever. They had 350,000 and I think 70,000 respondents said they liked Raptors. As for the logos and the colours, Dragons and Raptors were the best. Registration-wise, Raptors was the cleanest, and also, it won the vote. Again, I liked T-Rex best, but all the research, the votes and all the rest generally pointed to Raptors."

But the ever-vigilant NBA had to approve, of course, and Bitove says the league heavyweights had differing levels of enthusiasm for the name Raptors. "Rick Welts, President of NBA Properties, thought it was great," says Bitove. "Russ Granik said, 'I can't believe you're going to be this bold.' But I told him this is what the kids are into now, it's on the heels of *Jurassic Park* and all that. But believe me, this is the most researched name in pro sports, and our choice was the right one because we're seventh in licensing sales now, without even having our jersey out there. Of the $3 billion in licensing sales the NBA does, half is from the sale of jerseys, and we don't even have our uniform out there yet. So we're hoping we'll be in the top four and stay up there. Part of the success is the colours, but a big part of it is the concept. We get newspaper articles and photos sent to us from all over the world showing kids in Raptors T-shirts. It was the right choice, it was legitimate and we did our homework. In fact, it wasn't until 72 hours before our press conference to unveil our logo and colours that we actually made the final choice. We needed at least 72 hours to get the stuff printed up and get it ready.

"We did not have a rigged contest; Raptors was not the choice months in advance. We had many names registered in advance; in fact, we eventually signed the name Grizzlies over to the Vancouver people. And no, we did not get our arms twisted by the NBA."

Another source of strong criticism of Bitove was the hiring of former NBA star Isiah Thomas as his general manager. A great player in his day, Thomas had many who liked him during his playing days, but also many who didn't. Now, popularity with players or with fans or the media is not necessarily a hiring criterion, but there were many eyebrows raised when Thomas got the nod. The main reason was that he had no experience in running the business of a team. Not many have made the move directly from being a player to being a general manager without serving some sort of apprenticeship first. So why Isiah?

"Well, when I began my search, I kept saying that to me, the epitome of a general manager in sports is Pat Gillick," says Bitove. "But, after I began talking to some veteran players, Joe Dumars of the Pistons being the one who really crystallized it for me, I began to realize that the NBA was not like baseball. In baseball you want to find a pitcher who has a good fastball and you hope to teach him a slider as well. You find a great young fielder and hope you can teach him to hit. It's about identifying young talent and moulding it. Basketball, I came to understand, is not about diamonds in the rough as much as it's about getting talented players to raise their game to another level while under great pressure and scrutiny. So, it became apparent to me that understanding the psyche of a player is more important than discovering raw talent. People will tell you that the kids coming into this game have such incredible raw talent that the only difference between the ones who make it and the ones who don't is all up in the head. So, now that I understand this, there's a big change in what we're looking for. It's no longer a Pat Gillick."

NBA sources say Bitove had a list of about eight candidates, including the likes of Chuck Daly, Brad Greenberg, Dave Twardzik and Gary Fitzsimmons. All were deemed unsuitable for a variety of reasons: Daly is in his 60s and might have been inclined to look at such a post as simply an annuity as he heads towards retirement; Greenberg's reputed management style may have eliminated him; Twardzik did well enough in Charlotte, but there were some eyebrows raised around the league when he took over in Golden State, and there were questions about Fitzsimmons' credentials, about whether his father, Cotton Fitzsimmons, got him the job, and about whether he'd ever make a general manager. Bitove may or may not have interviewed these people, and may or may not have rejected them for some or all of these reasons. He won't say. But he does admit that the Isiah Thomas idea came about as the result of a "thank-you" call.

"I was in my office one night about 8:30. Isiah Thomas was on the phone calling to thank me for getting him on Dream Team 2. We had lobbied the NBA to get him on that team for the World Championships because the Pistons were sort of the closest team to Toronto and Isiah and the Pistons had a lot of fans here, and we thought he would be a good draw. So he and I talked for about 20 minutes and that was it. Then I called him back about a week later and said I wanted to bounce some things off him. I asked him to describe what he thought the perfect general manager would be like. And Isiah was the first one who was progressive. He told me he thought it was very difficult in the NBA right now because there isn't a lot of young depth in the management side. He pointed to football and all those coaches and scouts, the depth of their staffs. In basketball, he said, only recently have teams employed full-time scouts. So, his view was that in the '80s, the sport grew up as a business, but the basketball side was way behind. So, he told me I had to look for someone who had more of a broad approach, who was not stuck in the old ways, someone who recognized that Europe was a lot more important to the league than it used to be. So, suffice to say, he impressed me as being progressive in his views."

But again, the criticism is legitimate that a once-great player who may have revolutionary or progressive ideas does not necessarily translate into a solid general manager and someone who can run the basketball operations of a brand new team. Shouldn't it have been someone with a track record in that regard? Someone who's been a general manager, or at least an assistant general manager, someone who's made some deals, drafted some players, hired some staff?

"Well, don't forget, Isiah ran the players union for five years," counters Bitove. "In terms of guys in management Commissioner David Stern talks to about the whole negotiation with the league, Isiah is in that group. He knows the ins and outs of the league. He knows the players, the agents. He pretty much engineered the deal that saw Don Chaney hired to coach the Pistons, he negotiated the deal for Davidson. So he's been a part of a lot of that stuff. Plus, it's accepted knowledge that Isiah pretty much ran the Pistons at times, he helped in the player moves, he put together the Agguire deal. So it's not the case of a guy being a player, then just shifting over.

"Here's a guy who has his own businesses, who's made money. You saw how well prepared we were for the expansion draft. I mean I was shocked. He had his staff going every night until 2 a.m. or later. They had that thing nailed down perfectly. We did better than we had anticipated, because we had it all there. All the scenarios, all computerized, and Isiah was the one who got all the scouts on-line by computer. They sent their stuff in by modem to a central machine that only Isiah and Glen Grunwald had access to, and they could send stuff back to those guys. But, it's all in the way he thinks. Isiah is a process guy. So when you go through the progressive outlook side, when you go through the experience side and what he did with the Pistons, when you look at the players association experience and the fact he understood the salary cap and the things in contract negotiations that are important, why not Isiah?"

Bitove knows about the immediate reaction to his choice, about the criticism that the Raptors had done this just for the immediate publicity lift of having the great Isiah Thomas as part of the organization. But he says that was not in his thinking at all; in fact, it was just the reverse. "You know what? We almost didn't hire him because of that. We worried that people would think we're copping out and going with this guy because he's a name. But when I looked over the other available candidates, and when I thought about our conversations with him, he seemed light years ahead. And we are an expansion team. He may not be Jerry West [General Manager of the L.A. Lakers], but we have time."

On the subject of the Pro-Line gambling dilemma, Bitove says it was not the PR fiasco it was made out to be, but it did irk the NBA to have to deal with, and eventually bow to the wishes of, the Bob Rae government. It also definitely set the team back in its arena plans.

"There was a lot of posturing and a power play by both sides, with us in the middle. We were the meat in the sandwich, just the bystanders to an issue between the league and the province," says

Bitove. "It was a case of the government not wanting to appear to have let these Americans come in here and tell us what to do, and of course, the NBA doesn't like to be pushed around. It's a league that is used to having people co-operate. I had a meeting with the Premier at Larry Bertuzzi's house and said that we had to get a deal done on this, and soon."

An arbitrator–negotiator hired by the Rae government, Bertuzzi then went to New York for a meeting with the NBA commissioner.

"Bertuzzi met with Stern. It was a horrible meeting, and it was going nowhere," says Bitove. "So we worked the middle and made some progress, but the situation was escalating in the media and so the Premier said he wanted a meeting with all the partners. Everyone was getting very nervous at that point. So we met at Slaight's house, and Rae said he wanted to get a deal done but wanted the province to be protected. So, what happened was, we negotiated with the province, then we negotiated with the league, keeping both sides away from each other until it was done. In the end, it was just that the province asked for the sky and the moon, and at the end of the day, they got realistic and asked for what was doable. Of course, the spin on the story in the media was that the Raptors were screwing up again when really, it had nothing to do with us, and, in fact, if anything, the Raptors resolved it all."

Do the Raptors have cash-flow troubles?

"We do not," answers Bitove flatly.

The suggestion has been made that the Raptors used the ticket deposit money and licensing fee money to make the final payment on their expansion fee. Bitove categorically denies it. "In our agreement, it states clearly that we cannot use ticketing money to pay for expansion. At some point, our sponsorship money from Air Canada and Ford, our ticketing money, and our TV revenues all become one pot, and we take from that pot to build an arena, pay for players salaries and run the team. But, I repeat, our agreement with the NBA does not allow us to use ticketing money to pay the bill when we closed on the expansion fee. I don't know where the *Globe* got that."

Suggestions of cash-flow troubles surfaced again through the month of July 1995 when the Raptors battled with certain factions of the Toronto City Council over a small parcel of land the team needed for its arena site. There were differing estimates from each side about what the oddly shaped triangle of land was worth. No other parties were interested in developing it. The Raptors needed it for bus parking and the like. They balked at paying $4 million for it, and offered a package of "contra" instead. The package included 450 game tickets a year for 20 years, six stadium dates a year for 20 years and $80,000 a year for community and anti-drug programs. After a messy couple of weeks of having it debated in the media, the Raptors had their proposal overwhelmingly accepted by the council.

Bitove says, "It was not cash-flow troubles that prompted us to offer that package instead of paying hard cash for the land. The whole issue was that the city asked us to pay for a whole bunch of things in our plan to develop that arena site. After a certain point, we said, 'OK, $20 million is enough.' We had agreed to $20 million worth of development in the city without any of those things being essential to our arena. I mean the Washington Bullets are saying to the local governments there that they have to pay for the land and for all the infrastructure before the team will build an arena. Any of us who has ever negotiated a deal to buy a car or whatever, at a certain point, says, 'Look, enough is enough, this is as far as I can go.' It had nothing to do with cash flow or what our resources are."

Yet rumours persist that the Raptors will need a deep-pocketed partner if they are to make it. Perhaps a brewery or a broadcasting organization or a wealthy out-of-towner as was the case in Vancouver?

"No. We're fine," says Bitove. "When you've generated over $200 million in ticket sales or sponsorship commitments, when you're going to be in the top five in the league in season-ticket sales and top three or four in the league on sponsorships, you're going to be a very healthy franchise."

Still, there are some big expenses associated with that franchise: $125 million for the franchise fee, salaries to pay, an arena to build. Is the money there? People who know about these things say there is no way the Raptors can make it with basketball only in their building, and that they will have to lure the Leafs or an IHL franchise, something they admit they are trying to do. But Bitove remains defiant.

"One sport can make a building work. Look at Montreal and Ottawa and Vancouver before they had the Grizzlies...all arenas being built and financed for one sport. With us, the 45 basketball nights drive 80 percent of our business over the 365 days in a year.

"Yes. We've got $14–15 million a year in broadcasting revenues from the league; we'll have 17,000 season tickets sold and the sponsorship money. My family, Allan Slaight, the Bank of Nova Scotia—all run successful businesses. They know what profit and loss is, and this deal was scrutinized thoroughly. It had to work or we wouldn't have stepped forward and said we could do it."

CHAPTER FIFTEEN

THE LABOUR SITUATION

On May 11, 1995, the Raptors and the Grizzlies had made the necessary payments and were allowed to join the NBA and the 27 other franchises as full members in the league. Originally, the acceptance of the two expansion teams was supposed to have been contingent on the league's reaching a new agreement with the Players Association. That agreement was still not in sight but the expansion draft scheduled for June 24 and the college draft a week later were looming on the horizon. So the league agreed to speed up acceptance of the two Canadian teams and to go ahead with their participation in the two drafts so they could be ready to play in November 1995. Unfortunately for the Raptors and the Grizzlies, the money was paid before the NBA labour situation went sour; for the summer of 1995, it looked like the two teams had chosen the worst possible moment to join the world of the NBA.

On July 1, 1995, the NBA owners locked out the players. Suddenly, the 1995 season was in jeopardy. The Raptors and the Grizzlies were frozen in time, unable to sign contracts with players, hold summer training camps or make trades. They were not even able to talk about the labour situation as all teams were under a gag order from the league, which reportedly threatened a one-million-dollar fine and the loss of a draft pick for any team that spoke out about the labour strife. "We closed the franchise deal with the NBA in the spring because we believe the league office and the Players Association will get this collective agreement done," said Raptors President John Bitove Jr.

The Raptors and the Grizzlies had based their optimism for a labour settlement on the previously amicable relations between the league and the NBA Players Association. The July 1 lockout was the first job action in the league's 49-year history and it was just bad luck and bad timing for the Canadian teams that they happened to be caught up in it.

The NBA had broken new ground in the labour relations of pro sports when, in April 1983, the Players Association agreed to a salary cap. (The association was then headed by the late Larry Fleisher. Charles Grantham would take over as executive director in 1988.) A salary cap had originally been proposed in the NFL where the Players Association agreed to the concept but the owners turned it down. However, the salary cap would become the salvation of the NBA in the mid-1980s as the league struggled back onto its financial feet. NBA Deputy Commissioner Russ Granik has referred many times to the salary cap as "the cornerstone" of the league's current financial success. "What made it happen in basketball was that the players and management were in the gutter together," said Charles Grantham, former Executive Director of the NBA Players Association, in 1993. "Everyone saw how necessary it was for both sides to work together to survive."

In exchange for agreeing to a salary cap, which in effect restricted the amount of money that teams could offer players in salaries, the league offered the players a 53 percent cut of gross revenues. That included gate receipts and local, network and cable television fees. Once the two sides agreed to this idea of revenue-sharing, it provided an incentive for both sides to work hard to promote the league. If the NBA did well, the players prospered. Many observers feel that this deal laid the groundwork for a more conciliatory relationship between the players and management than in other pro leagues where the players do not get a share of the revenues. The next decade of labour relations in the NBA was relatively calm, especially compared to the labour squabbles in baseball, football and hockey. There were no strike threats, no scab games, no arbitration hearings, no lockouts. There had, however, been clouds on the labour horizon for about a year before the stormy summer of 1995. The last six-year agreement expired at the end of the 1993–94 season and the summer of 1994 featured a particularly vitriolic court battle between the NBA and the Players Association. U.S. District Judge Kevin Duffy reprimanded both parties for using the court "as a bargaining chip in the collective-bargaining process."

Originally, the union had threatened to sue the league over the issue of free agency. The NBA filed its own lawsuit first and then the union counter-sued. In his ruling, Duffy was highly critical of the NBA's suit, even though he had ruled in the league's favour. He said the NBA lawyers, in filing the suit, had shown "sharp and shady practices of the type that most ethical lawyers shun" and he urged both sides to stay out of court in the future.

Duffy's ruling, however, re-affirmed that the NBA's salary cap, college draft and right of first refusal were legal. (The right of first refusal means that a team can keep a free-agent player with fewer than four seasons from going to another team simply by matching the salary terms offered by another team.) The Players Association had argued that the salary cap violated antitrust laws. But as Duffy pointed out, at least three other legal rulings had already given pro sports a wider latitude to work out labour agreements outside the parameters imposed on other businesses.

Despite the legal wranglings, the NBA and the players appeared to want to put the court case behind them and head back to the bargaining table. The NBA's Russ Granik said he hoped "now the players will come back to the bargaining table so we can move forward." The union had a similar reaction.

"The most important point that Judge Duffy wanted to make is he wants us to settle this thing at the collective bargaining table," said Buck Williams of the Portland Trail Blazers, President of the Players Association. "It may take a good while but eventually that's what's going to happen."

But by the fall of 1994, with the start of the season around the corner, there was still no deal. Meanwhile, the NBA and the players were very aware of the impact that labour strife was having on two other professional sports. The World Series was in jeopardy and the NHL season was about to be postponed. The two sides in the basketball talks decided to take a different route: they agreed to a no-strike, no-lockout pledge for the duration of the 1994–95 season. (This wasn't unusual for the NBA. For three of four labour deals, the negotiations had gone into overtime and twice, 1979–80 and 1982–83, the players had played an entire season without a collective bargaining agreement in place.) Again, the NBA and its players appeared like marketing geniuses in contrast to the poor public relations that the other leagues were suffering as their players sat idle.

The lack of a new collective agreement was a minor annoyance for the Canadian franchises. They would be putting together their teams without knowing what would be happening to the salary cap and to the rules of free agency. Still, they were able to continue with their preparations for their inaugural seasons.

"The [no-strike, no-lockout] pledge doesn't punish the fans—it doesn't put us in the same boat as baseball and hockey and that's terrific," said Grizzlies GM Stu Jackson. "The relationship between the Players Association and the owners has always been a good one, and the negotiations are ongoing. All those things are positive and really lead me to believe an agreement will be done. There isn't the venom that there is in the other sports. The venom was still to come. As winter wore on, the negotiations seemed to be going at a snail's pace. By the All-Star break in the 1994–95 season, the two sides were still far apart.

"Definitely, we're on a collision course," said Charles Grantham, at that time executive director of the union. He pointed to the owners' reluctance to identify and share the additional revenues generated by the league, such as from licensing and merchandise. The league estimated that it would do about $3 billion in retail sales over the 1994–95 season. Under the previous agreement, the players got $500,000 of that revenue, while the league's take was close to $125 million.

The union also chafed at owners' attempts to close loopholes in the salary cap. While the 1994–95 salary cap was just under $16 million per team, those loopholes allowed the teams to pay more than that and the average payroll in the NBA was actually closer to $21.5 million. In fact, if he had had his way, Grantham wanted the salary cap to be more than loosened up, he wanted it eliminated. "There was a time when the salary cap in our business was necessary and it helped stabilize our league," said Grantham in *Forbes* magazine, June 1993. "Now the business has matured. The revenue streams have increased and the marketing of the sport is different. We are all now in a position to resume as a business without restrictions."

The NBA, however, was adamant that the salary cap should stay. As far as management was concerned, the salary cap wasn't even on the table. "The salary cap is the envy of every sports league," replied Orlando Magic General Manager Pat Williams in *Forbes*. "It is one of the pillars of this league. We will never let it go."

With such a substantial point of disagreement, the talks between the union and the league appeared to have stalled by February 1995.

"We're agreeing a little bit. We're disagreeing a lot," said David Stern in a state-of-the-league interview at the All-Star weekend in Phoenix. "But we're working hard. Our history is that we probably will make a deal. I remain the optimist."

In April 1995, there was a new twist to the labour situation as Charles Grantham suddenly resigned as executive director of the NBA Players Association. Grantham had held the position since September 1988. In announcing his departure, he and the union cited "irreconcilable differences over internal matters."

It didn't take long for speculation to start about the nature of the disagreement between Grantham and the union and there was even discussion of a cover-up. Player agent Marc Fleisher, speaking on behalf of several of his clients, demanded more information. "A number of my players have expressed concerns over the way in which Charlie's resignation has been handled and the apparent attempt by the union leadership to sweep the whole matter under the table," said Fleisher, whose father Larry had headed the Players Association before Grantham.

Grantham replied to the allegations in an interview with *The New York Times*. "If you allow speculation to generate this thing, it clearly could take on a personality of its own," said Grantham. "There's no truth to any of the rumours. Grown people can differ about how things should happen and be governed. We reached a point where those differences became a distraction. How many organizations have you seen change leadership? It's never one thing; it's a series of several things. Leadership wanted to go in one direction, I in another. There was a disagreement. I chose to resign."

The past history of Grantham's replacement as executive director also raised a few eyebrows. Simon Gourdine had served as the union's general counsel before taking over as executive director. Before that, he had worked as a deputy commissioner for the NBA during the David Stern era. Now, he would be negotiating with his former employer, something which irked some of the player agents. One agent told *The New York Times:* "It's fair to say no one expects Simon to be the one negotiating with David Stern." There were even questions asked about how exactly Gourdine had been given the job as executive director because there was no evidence that the issue was ever put to a vote of the executive board of the union.

The upheaval in the union's leadership came at a critical point in negotiations with the league. The replacement of Grantham signalled the first murmurings of dissatisfaction with the Players Association and the first questions were starting to be asked about who was running the shop on behalf of the players.

By mid-May, the union and the league had met three times in three weeks but suddenly broke off negotiations. "We're very far apart," said NBA Deputy Commissioner Russ Granik. "It's rather discouraging right now."

The union was slightly more optimistic, saying the two sides simply needed to step back and re-assess the situation. The players had been making some progress in an area key to their interests. One of the league's proposals had suggested that the NBA and the players move to a 50–50 split of the league's gross revenues. (In the previous agreement, the players received 53 percent.) However, the league had agreed to include more sources of income in the split, such as arena advertising, luxury-suite revenue and international TV-rights fees. This had been a key tenet in Charles Grantham's negotiating position: to get the players a bigger share of the other league revenues. However, it appeared that the union was no longer pushing to have the salary cap removed, an issue that Grantham had eloquently argued in a column in *Sport* in January 1995. "Why should the players agree to keep the salary cap in a time when the league is more successful than ever? Yet that is precisely what the owners want to do—place a set limit on how much money their players can make," wrote Grantham. "It's unfortunate that it must come down to this kind of a fight with the owners, but the time has come to eliminate a salary cap that is limiting the players' options in the short and long run."

However, five months later, Grantham was out of the negotiating picture and it appeared the players had conceded that the salary cap would stay. After negotiations broke down in May, Grantham's successor Simon Gourdine told reporters, "It comes down to money relating to the salary-cap proposal. If we can reach agreement on that number, while not conclusive, it would move the process along."

By mid-June, the labour picture had not improved and with the Houston Rockets about to sweep the Orlando Magic to claim the championship, the league apparently issued an ultimatum to the players to make a deal or they'd be locked out within 24 hours of the completion of the NBA Finals. No one with the NBA would confirm or deny the report and Commissioner David Stern had put a muzzle order on the teams.

"We've been asked not to comment and I'm going to adhere to that," said Vancouver GM Stu Jackson.

The timing was critical for the Canadian teams. The expansion draft when they would select the bulk of their team's prospects for the 1995 season was only 10 days away and the all-important college draft was just a few days later. At this point, the Grizzlies had only signed one player, the Raptors none and both teams knew that a lockout would grind their preparations to a halt.

Finally, however, there was a breakthrough in the labour talks. Late in the evening of June 21, the NBA and the Players Association announced that they had reached an agreement. Under the deal, the union had agreed to a rookie salary cap, something many of the older players had been lobbying for. Rookie contracts would be limited to three years, after which the player would become an unrestricted free agent. The rookie cap would involve using the player's draft position and would be calculated on the average salaries of the players drafted in that position over the last seven years, plus a 20 percent raise. This would put an end to some of the exorbitant deals that recent rookies had negotiated, like the 10-year, $68-million package of 1994 first pick Glenn Robinson. Similarly, the top player chosen in 1993, Chris Webber, had signed a deal worth $74 million over 15 seasons. Those kinds of long-term, big-dollar deals would no longer be allowed under the proposed agreement.

There would still be a team salary cap, though it would rise incrementally from $15.9 million to the end of the agreement. But the most controversial element of the deal was the inclusion of a luxury tax that would go into effect if the percentage of NBA revenues going towards salaries rose over 53 percent. Under the luxury tax, teams granting salary increases of more than 10 percent would be taxed 50 percent in 1996–97 and 100 percent for the rest of the deal. The luxury tax was something that many of the players had vehemently opposed when it had been suggested in the past. They argued that it basically restricted their salary level and was a disincentive for teams to pay them their true market value. While the players had been aiming for more free agency, the luxury tax in effect gave them less.

Even before the final terms of the agreement were announced, the damage was done. A group of the league's marquee players and their agents had sprung into action and were about to rock the NBA to its foundation. Hours before the June 21 deal was announced, Michael Jordan, Patrick Ewing and 15 other players filed legal papers with the National Labor Relations Board in a move to decertify the players union. Fifteen of the league's most powerful player agents combined to form an advisory committee to their clients, including Jordan's agent, David Falk, Marc Fleisher, and Steve Kauffman, who together represent dozens of high-profile players. In total, the agents represented about 50 percent of the league's players. Lawyer Jeffrey Kessler filed the petition with the NLRB.

"This is an absolute groundswell of dissatisfaction of players who believe it's no longer in their interests to have the union represent them," said Kessler. "They'd prefer to assert their rights before the league without being encumbered by the union."

The reaction from the league and from the union was swift and fierce. "A disgruntled lawyer, whose firm was terminated by the Players Association, filed the NLRB petition and Marc Fleisher, the self-proclaimed spokesman for the group, represents very few NBA players and seems interested only in ousting the union leadership that replaced his father," said Commissioner David Stern in a statement. "I do not think that the rhetoric of a few people will keep owners and players, who have co-operated in making past agreements work, from considering the current one on its own merits."

"These agents have a fiduciary duty to their clients and have breached it," said Simon Gourdine of the Players Association. "We're going to put on a strong lobbying effort and reach out to as many players as we can."

The public display of disharmony among the league, the union and its superstar players was unlike anything before in the NBA's history. It was startling to watch the marketing magicians at the NBA scramble to get the situation back under control. After all, the league had made its mark largely through its ability to package marquee names like Jordan and Ewing. Suddenly, these same players were accusing the league of trying to rip them off. For an organization that is obsessed with its image, it was a disaster and about to get even worse.

On June 28, the dissident group filed an anti-trust suit against the National Basketball Association in federal court in Minneapolis. The petition was signed by Michael Jordan, Patrick Ewing and five other players. The 27-page class action claimed that the salary cap and draft are illegal because the previous contract had expired and the union no longer represented a majority of the players. The other players who were plaintiffs in the suit were Stacey Augmon of the Atlanta Hawks, Dale Davis of the Indiana Pacers, Alonzo Mourning of the Charlotte Hornets and Howard Eisley and Stacey King of the Minnesota Timberwolves. "The NBA defendants have jointly agreed and conspired to deny plaintiffs the ability to market their services as professional basketball players...through a comprehensive set of anticompetitive restrictions," stated the players in the suit.

Because the courts had already ruled that class-action suits could not be filed by labour unions, the anti-trust suit could only go ahead if the dissident players were successful in their other gambit, the decertification of the union. But by filing the anti-trust suit, which automatically includes a provision for triple damages from the league and the 29 teams (including the two Canadian franchises who had not yet even fielded a team), the players and their agents had significantly raised the stakes in what was already an ugly battle.

"There's a real risk of that [delay of season]," said NBA Deputy Commissioner Russ Granik at a news conference being held in conjunction with the college draft in Toronto. The league had been caught off-guard by the anti-trust suit and it put a tremendous damper on the festivities at the draft as the NBA scrambled to react to the news. The league wanted to send out a strong message to the dissidents and to the other players who might be considering joining them. "The players have to make a real decision, either to join with these people who seem intent on overturning the business, or to play basketball."

"The owners are very united," added Granik. "They spent 18 months trying to get a deal and at the end worked round the clock to get a deal with the union."

Looming over Granik and the owners was the fact that a moratorium on any further labour action until the expansion and college drafts were completed was about to expire on July 1.

There was to be no miraculous last-minute settlement and at midnight on July 1, the NBA locked out the players, the first-ever work stoppage in the league's history. "It's a shame that the success we and our players have enjoyed as a result of working together is now in jeopardy," said Commissioner David Stern in a statement from the NBA.

It was ironic that the players were locked out on Canada Day because it would be the two new Canadian franchises who would be hardest hit by the lockout. "I'm concerned for our fans but we're moving as if it's going to get resolved, based on the track record that they've never missed a game," said Raptors President John Bitove Jr. "It's always hung out there," said Bitove, referring to the work stoppage. "But the reason we closed with the NBA was that in these sorts of matters, we knew it could get done. We at the Raptors are still moving full speed ahead and preparing for October, it's really only the basketball side that's affected by this."

The Raptors could, in fact, continue with some of their plans for the season. They could sell tickets and continue the plans for a new arena. But everything on the basketball side came to an absolute halt. For example, the Raptors were in the midst of a trade with the Golden State Warriors, sending their first pick in the expansion draft, B.J. Armstrong, to Golden State in exchange for a package of players. The deal was frozen until the labour problems were resolved and a collective bargaining agreement was signed. (When the lockout was lifted on September 18, the deal went through.)

The labour stand-off continued five days later at a National Labour Relations Board hearing in New York. Teammates on different sides of the issue faced off across the boardroom. The meeting before NLRB Regional Director Dan Silverman lasted four and a half hours. At issue was whether a vote should be held to decertify the union.

Michael Jordan and Patrick Ewing, who led the group of players dissatisfied with the union, presented a petition signed by 180 NBA players. "This isn't personal," said Ewing. "It's about business."

One of his teammates on the New York Knicks, Charles Smith, disagreed with Ewing and his actions. Smith is a vice-president with the NBA Players Association. "The players are getting bad information from their agents," said Smith after the NLRB hearing. "Buck Williams [NBA union president] and I think that the deal that was made is the best for both sides. The agents are trying to ferment this because they are worried about things like the rookie cap, which would affect their commissions."

The stand-off was becoming an increasingly bitter fight between the agents and the NBA, with the players caught in the middle. The vitriol was flying at the NLRB hearing as the two sides jockeyed for the support of the players. "Of the 180 signatures supplied, 146 of them were faxed to agent Jeffrey Kessler," said NBA attorney Howard Ganz. "This creates a suspicion of some sort as to their legitimacy."

Kessler denied any impropriety on his part, and his client, Patrick Ewing, denied any undue influence from the agents. "I'm my own man," said Ewing. "I'm going to listen to what my adviser says and make up my own mind."

Both sides took advantage of the hearing to argue how many players should be allowed to vote and when the vote should be held. Everyone agreed that the players should have to vote in person to guard against any impropriety. At the end of the meeting, Dan Silverman of the NLRB said he would issue a ruling on an election and guidelines in two weeks.

As the summer passed, time was running out for the Canadian franchises who would now be hard pressed to put together teams for November. The Raptors had a free-agent camp scheduled for four days in July in Toronto. That was cancelled. They had put together a team of players and registered for a summer league in New York. Again, the league was cancelled because of the lockout.

While the players and the league waited for the ruling from the National Labor Relations Board, the two sides agreed to resume contract talks. Again, however, the negotiations went badly as they continued to disagree on the issue of a luxury tax. In a media briefing after the first day of the talks, Russ Granik of the NBA said there was "an overwhelming" gulf between the two sides on the luxury tax. Simon Gourdine of the Players Association told the media that he had a "clear mandate" from the players to eliminate the luxury tax or there could be no deal. (The luxury tax was one of the key points of criticism by the dissident players. The concept of a luxury tax had also been part of the reason for the breakdown in the labour negotiations in baseball, so the idea carried baggage that went beyond the NBA talks.)

However, the union was dealing with internal problems as well. Just before the negotiations resumed, Simon Gourdine had accepted the resignation of W. Charles Bennett, a financial consultant for the Players Association during the negotiations. He claimed that Simon Gourdine had misrepresented the revenues of the NBA teams in a letter that was sent out to the players explaining the June 21 labour deal. The letter claimed that the team profits wre declining because of escalating salaries. Bennett said he had never undertaken that financial analysis and in his resignation letter said, "I have no basis for believing that the conclusion of declining profits in the NBA is correct."

Simon Gourdine struck back. He accused Bennett of "a very serious breach of trust and ethics" and said Bennett had misrepresented the NBA teams' revenues. "If you knew something that we didn't, we wish you would have brought it to our attention earlier," wrote Gourdine in a letter released to the media. "We were convinced that the owners were paying out money at a much greater rate than they were taking in revenues and we had to address that reality in bargaining."

What is amazing about the internal strife within the union is that Bennett's allegations did not become a bigger issue. They seemed to go unnoticed amidst the ongoing turmoil in the league. However, it is hard to believe, considering many of the NBA's other statements about its increasing revenues in merchandising, TV deals and overseas sales, that the league had actually experienced a decline in profits. Either the league had been misrepresenting the financial health of the NBA and the league's income had dropped, or the numbers were being manipulated to make it look like the union should receive a smaller share of the profits. Either way, it is surprising that the dissident players were not able to exploit this opportunity to make the union leadership look bad.

As the NLRB decision came closer, the breakaway players and the union were busy trying to win the public relations battle over who best represented the interests of the players. The Players Association organized a press conference featuring four Hall of Famers—Oscar Robertson, Bob Cousy, Dave DeBusschere and Bob Pettit—who all spoke out against possible decertification of the union and chastized the players like Michael Jordan and Patrick Ewing who were trying to break the union.

"Their greedy and destructive behaviour makes me ashamed and a bit resentful that I played a role in starting this," said Cousy, who helped found the union in 1955. "A small dissident group is trying to destroy something we've all—management and players—built a good living from. Our response is from the heart."

"It makes no sense to wreck something, kill the goose that laid the golden egg," said DeBusschere. "No one knows what will happen if the union is decertified."

The former players also pointed to their own experiences, before the union existed, to warn of the possible consequences. When Cousy founded the union, the association was asking for an increase in meal money from $5 to $7 and his starting salary was $9,000, which included two dozen exhibition games before the season started. Years later, the situation had only marginally improved, and Robertson had taken part in a boycott of the 1964 All-Star Game to force the NBA to pay the players' pensions and other benefits. He ultimately had to go to court in a landmark case that established the premise of free agency. The older players said they found it hard to relate to the complaints of a bunch of multimillionaires who had reaped the benefits of their earlier labour battles.

"We have the highest-paid players, we have the highest visibility and we have players who are wealthy individuals today," said Robertson. "I don't think we can sit idly by and let this great game deteriorate."

"If you can't get by on $2.3 million playing a child's game for eight months of the year, you need serious counselling," added Cousy, who said he now lives on an annual pension of $15,000.

The union scored some valuable points with the Hall of Famers news conference. Union President Buck Williams of the Portland Trail Blazers and the other players on the negotiating team were also doing the media circuit trying to plug the union's position. On July 25, Williams talked to the newspaper *USA Today,* about the dissent in the union. "Sometimes I feel betrayed because everything I've done has been for the union and for the good of the game," said Williams. "If Michael, Patrick and these guys had approached me and wanted to discuss things like decertifying the union, I would have said, 'Fine, let's sit down and talk about it.' But the way things were done takes on a whole different perspective, because this is something the agents initiated. I'm president of the union and I never heard of agents trying to overthrow a union. I can't understand that."

Williams also defended the deal that the union had negotiated, despite the concessions that the players had made like the rookie salary cap, the end to balloon salary payments (such as the one that Patrick Ewing had received that season) and the imposition of a luxury tax. "The average salary, by the final year of the agreement we had

[2000–01] would be about $3 million. [The average salary last season was about $1.35 million.]... Basketball is in its prime and ready to take off even more, and we will be a bunch of fools if we haven't learned anything from the other sports. Being in the league for 14 years and finally getting to this level of success, and then you're going to erode it just because the agents are greedy? I think that is very wrong," argued Williams, who was elected president of the Players Association during the All-Star break in 1994. (The other players on the union's executive committee are Charles Smith and Herb Williams of the New York Knicks, Danny Manning of the Phoenix Suns, Jimmy Jackson of the Dallas Mavericks, Dikembe Mutombo of the Denver Nuggets, Detlef Schrempf of the Seattle Supersonics, Mark West of the Detroit Pistons and Tyrone Corbin of the Sacramento Kings.)

On July 27, the dissident players led by Michael Jordan and Patrick Ewing got their wish. The National Labor Relations Board announced there would be a vote on whether to decertify the union. A majority vote of the 422 eligible players would be needed to dissolve the Players Association and strip it of its power to negotiate on behalf of the players. The vote would be a secret ballot at regional NLRB offices across the United States. Any player who was on an NBA roster, including injured players, and anyone signed for more than ten games the previous season would be eligible to vote.

Jordan and Ewing were pleased with the board's decision. "I'm glad we're going to have the opportunity to vote quickly," said Ewing. "I just wish the vote weren't necessary, and that everybody would jump on board so we could get the right leverage we need to get a deal done."

"We're not being greedy here," said Jordan. "We're not trying to make sure the league starves or doesn't become successful. We just want an equal opportunity to make our value."

For its part, the NBA had some harsh words for the players about what was at stake in the election, which was scheduled for late August. "The league and the teams are going to have to provide players with adequate information on what's transpired," said Russ Granik of the NBA. "We will explain that if the union is decertified, we are putting at risk at least part of the season. That's the choice the players are going to have to make."

Meanwhile, the union and the NBA announced they would be going back to the bargaining table in an attempt to get another deal before the decertification vote. The Players Association knew it had to convince the league to drop the luxury tax if the union had any chance of surviving the decertification vote. Otherwise, the momentum was definitely in favour of dumping the union.

"We probably will end up treating the election as a referendum on a new collective-bargaining agreement," said union Executive Director Simon Gourdine. "I remain optimistic we'll be able to make a deal with the NBA and that deal will be good enough for our players to approve."

Time was running out for everyone in this dispute. By August 4, the union and the NBA had broken off their discussions again. The main sticking point was still the luxury tax. The union had suggested a number of loopholes to allow teams to go over the proposed salary cap of $23 million US, including a $1.5 million pool of money over the cap to pay free agents, a provision to allow teams to use half an injured player's salary to sign another player and another provision that would allow players who have played for the same team for two years to re-sign at double the salary. The league, however, was still not budging on the luxury tax that would kick in if the players' salaries went over a certain level.

The NBA Players Association decided to turn up the heat on the negotiations. It announced that if there was no deal within 72 hours, the union would voluntarily relinquish its authority to negotiate on behalf of the players. That, of course, was what the dissident group wanted. However, the NBA said it would then call off all negotiations and the season would be sacrificed. "If there's no union, the owners won't play the '95 season," said NBA Commissioner David Stern. "The owners will keep the players locked out."

"If we don't get a deal done," said union leader Buck Williams, "I definitely feel the next season is in jeopardy."

The breakaway group of superstar players had created a bizarre three-way dynamic in these negotiations. The union and the NBA had now been forced together, in opposition to the dissident group, at the same time as they were on opposite sides of the negotiating table. Both the union and the league were now turning up the rhetoric as it appeared more and more likely that there would be no deal and no season.

The NBA fired another eleventh-hour salvo in the direction of the dissident group. On August 4, the NBA went to the National Labor Relations Board and filed an unfair labour practice complaint against the 14 player agents who were affiliated with the dissident players. The league accused the agents of interfering with player negotiations.

There was to be still one more dramatic development. At a few minutes to midnight, the NBA and the union announced they had reached a revised agreement. The league agreed to drop the much-hated luxury tax proposal, but the rookie salary cap would stay and multimillion-dollar balloon payments at the end of contracts would be abolished. The overall team salary cap would rise to $32 million by the end of the six-year deal and the average salary would be $3 million by the 2000-01 season. Bowing to the demands of the dissident group, the college draft would be reduced from two rounds to one in year four of the agreement. There would also be a $1 million exemption over the salary cap to sign free agents, as well as the provision to use half the salary of an injured player to sign another and the provision that said a player could re-sign for double his salary after two years with the same team. In a concession to the owners, the union did agree that if salaries exceeded a certain level after three years, the salary cap would be lowered by half a million dollars.

David Stern announced the deal at a midnight news conference, surrounded by 25 players. "Our indications are that it won't be a difficult sell," said Stern. "We don't think it's going to be a problem."

"It gives more people freedom to move from team to team," said Danny Ferry of the Cleveland Cavaliers, one of the players at Stern's press conference. "The players should feel this is fair and reasonable."

But the reaction from the dissident players was predictably hostile to the new agreement. "This is a real shocker," said Jeffrey Kessler, a lawyer for the breakaway group. "There are terms from the June 21 agreement that no one ever knew before, in many cases. Some I would characterize as bombshells."

Kessler claimed that the league was trying to include a clause that would bar players and teams from negotiating contracts downwards, something that's common in the NFL as a way to bring in new players under the salary cap. (It was also, in the past, done in the NBA. The player who negotiated down his contract would then be paid the money in a balloon payment at the end of his contract or in his next deal.) Kessler's group said the NBA was trying to close all the loopholes in the salary cap and players would be the ones to suffer. Kessler added that the agreement was still "too good for the owners at a time when the Knicks are charging $1,000 a seat."

With the decertification vote set for August 30 and September 7, the public relations battle was on. The union was able to convince some high-profile players to speak out on its behalf to balance off the tremendous profile of Michael Jordan and Patrick Ewing on the opposing side of the debate. Karl Malone, Charles Barkley, Hakeem Olajuwon, David Robinson and Shaquille O'Neal all said publicly that they favoured the new deal and would vote to accept it by saying "no" to decertification on the NLRB ballot.

"The new collective bargaining agreement may not be that great for the players," wrote O'Neal in a statement released by his agent. "But I support it because we have to learn from what happened in baseball.... We owe it to the fans, sponsors and ourselves to not lose any of the season. Accepting the compromise is the only way to ensure doing that."

The NBA also made sure that the players knew just how real its threat was to cancel the season, starting with various exhibition games. Days before the first day of voting on the proposed deal, Commissioner David Stern told players that the McDonald's Championship, scheduled to begin October 19 in London, England, would be cancelled immediately if the vote went against the union.

"We're looking down into an abyss that's larger than we've ever contemplated," said Stern of the impending vote. "It gets your adrenalin going, that's for sure. If the season is not played, it's going to be a disaster," warned the Commissioner.

The main target for the NBA continued to be the agents it claimed were the masterminds behind the group of dissident players. Stern went as far as saying that Michael Jordan's agent David Falk would "stop at nothing" to derail the labour agreement.

"I don't take it personally," said Falk in response to Stern's verbal attack. "It shows a level of desperation. I respect David Stern for doing a great job. Our complaint isn't against him, it's against the union."

Meanwhile, the NBA had put its marketing muscles to work, lobbying the more than 400 players who would ultimately decide the fate of the 1995 season. General managers were enlisted to work the phones, calling players to argue the merits of voting in favour of the deal. The players were sent faxes and letters from both sides. The dissident players even put out a video that was sent to all potential voters, featuring Michael Jordan, Patrick Ewing and Reggie Miller explaining their point of view and why the union should be disbanded.

"Just the stature of the players on that video was impressive," Grant Long of the Atlanta Hawks told *Sports Illustrated* after viewing the video. "What they said made some sense. I was right back where I was to begin with—on the fence."

The legal wrangling continued in the days leading up to the vote. On August 28, Mitch Richmond of the Sacramento Kings decided he too wanted to file an unfair labour complaint with the National Labor Relations Board. He claimed that the NBA was coercing the players into voting against decertification by "threatening publicly to cancel the season and continue the current lockout if the players vote to decertify." In his complaint, Richmond argued that the election should be stopped or the results should be sealed. We saw what happened to baseball," said Richmond. "We want to play basketball. Hopefully, we can still save this season."

"I'm in the middle. I want the season, I do not want to decertify," Richmond told reporters. "It's just a lopsided deal and we don't like it. This is an ugly situation."

The NBA's response was that the league had done nothing improper in saying that the season could be cancelled if the labour dispute was not settled. "It is simply a fact that the only way to assure that the 1995–96 season will begin on time is a 'yes' vote in the election," said Russ Granik, Deputy Commissioner of the NBA. "Unfortunately, the owners had no choice but to declare a lockout, and that lockout will continue until there is a collective bargaining agreement in place."

It appeared that the league was winning the public relations battle. On the first day of voting, approximately half of the league's players showed up at NLRB offices across the United States to cast their vote. Some arrived in limousines—an incongruous image in a struggle where the players were claiming that they were not getting a good deal. (Both the union and the league had offered to pay transportation costs for players to get to and from voting sites across the country. Apparently this was one of John Bitove Jr.'s suggestions, something he remembered from his days politicking with the Progressive Conservative Party of Canada.)

Speaking to the media after voting, many of the players seemed, above all, to want the season to go ahead as scheduled even if they didn't necessarily like everything in the proposed labour agreement. "It's just what we saw in baseball and hockey," said Marty Conlon, a free agent who played 1994–95 in Milwaukee. "If basketball drops the ball here, it could be dangerous."

"I'm for the union," said Derrick Coleman, one of the league's highest-paid players. "I think we should settle down and vote for the union. I think it's been good to us all these years. We can compromise. We can't get everything we want, but I think it's a good proposal for us. I think we just should learn a lot from what happened with baseball."

"I felt there really wasn't a choice," said Dan Majerle of the Phoenix Suns. "I don't think decertification is what anybody wants, because it's untested waters, and I want to play this year. Madison Majerle, my little baby, wants me to play this year, so I voted yes. Baby's got to eat."

Only a couple of the players admitted publicly to voting for decertification. (Some players did apparently tell reporters off the record that they feared retribution if they were seen to be opposing the league, even if the vote was a secret ballot.)

It appeared as if the agents and the dissident group had not convinced the players that they would be able to work out a deal with the league to allow the season to go ahead once the union was decertified. There was definitely a fear of the unknown, post-decertification, despite the fact that Jeffrey Kessler had also been part of the legal team for the NFL Players Association when it successfully sought an injunction against the NFL to end a lockout in that league.

With the second day of voting over on September 7, the two sides sat back to await the results.

On September 12, the waiting was over. Representatives from the league and the Players Association gathered at the NLRB office in New York to watch the ballots being officially counted. Both sides kept their own tallies as the ballots were taken out one at a time while the NLRB kept track of the votes on a blackboard at the front of the room. Television cameras and photographers crowded in the back of the room while others waited in the hallway for reactions after the votes were counted.

A total of 360 players, out of the 422 eligible to vote, had voted and it soon became clear that the union had won a decisive victory. The final tally was 226–134 against decertification of the union and, by extension, in favour of the proposed collective-bargaining agreement.

"I believe this is a wonderful victory," said Simon Gourdine, Executive Director of the Players Association, whose job had been on the line in the NLRB vote. Gourdine had been personally criticized by players and agents for the way he had handled negotiations with the league. "We are going to savour it and I believe it is the best thing for the union and for the players."

"The turnout by players was very impressive," said an obviously relieved David Stern. "They educated themselves about the issues and they demonstrated that they cared about our fans and the future of our league."

"It's time to put everybody back to work. We still haven't lost a game to a labour problem," added Stern.

There was no immediate reaction from Michael Jordan and Patrick Ewing, whose side had lost the day. (As he cast his vote, Jordan indicated that he would not be pursuing further action against the union. "If decertification doesn't carry, then the players have spoken their minds, and that's all I ask," Jordan told the media.) After the results were announced, lawyer Jeffrey Kessler spoke on behalf of the dissident players. He accused the league and the union of "pressure tactics" in convincing the players to vote in favour of what he felt was a bad deal.

"Of course I'm disappointed by the vote," said Kessler. "I still believe this is a terrible vote for the players and they will regret it for a long time."

The NBA had pulled itself back from the edge of the lockout abyss and appeared to be back on track. Because it had been agreed that the NLRB vote would also be a referendum on the new labour deal, the player representatives now had no choice but to ratify the deal. On closer examination, they may not like everything that they find there, particularly the loopholes in the salary cap that have been eliminated. But the players do owe a debt of gratitude to the dissident group because without them, the league may now have been operating with a luxury tax. If the rebel group had not been there to force the union to go back to the negotiating table and get a better deal, under threat of being decertified, the luxury tax may have remained in the agreement. There is no doubt that the NBA owners will try again for the luxury tax but the players now have six years to re-examine their union and how well it is or is not representing them. As well, the players will now be "cut in" for a much bigger share of the NBA's licensing revenue. The union share increases immediately from $500,000 to $26 million, and will be $47 million by the year 2000.

The NBA owners did all right from this labour deal. They didn't get the luxury tax but they were able to get the rookie salary cap. For the league, though, there has been a stiff price for the concessions they have won. The NBA had always prided itself on staying away from the labour turmoil that plagued other professional sports, but the summer of 1995 changed that. There will obviously be some short-term public-relations damage for the NBA. Fans will not soon forget the images of Michael Jordan and Patrick Ewing fighting with the league or of the players pulling up in their limousines to vote on decertification. The experience of baseball has proven that fans are increasingly unforgiving of the complaints and labour problems of multimillion-dollar athletes.

The league also pulled some extremely stupid moves itself during the summer lockout. In early August, a story in the Fort Lauderdale *Sun–Sentinel* reported that the NBA had ordered teams to return fan letters to their senders during the lockout. "While this dispute is ongoing, the Miami Heat is not able to forward mail to any of our players, and we are therefore returning your letter to you," the team wrote to a sixth-grader in Fort Lauderdale.

The Orlando Magic had returned about one thousand letters written to Shaquille O'Neal and the Chicago Bulls had done the same for hundreds of letters to Michael Jordan. The story was carried on the wire service across the United States and Canada. It was not the kind of public relations move on which the league has made its reputation. Now the NBA will have to work hard to erase the memories of the lockout and mend relations with two of its biggest stars.

"There's been damage from a public-relations perspective, from a licensing perspective, a slowdown in television sales," admitted Commissioner David Stern after the results of the NLRB vote were released. "If we get back to the business of basketball rather than the litigation of basketball, we'll have a chance to grow the game again."

But the two Canadian franchises will perhaps pay the heaviest price of all in the wake of the lost summer of 1995. The two lost months were crucial for the preparation of the expansion teams. They had lost their special rookie and free-agent camps. They would have to scramble to negotiate contracts with the players they had selected in the expansion and college drafts. The two teams had also lost a lot of momentum. The excitement about the NBA coming to Canada had been tempered by the harsh reality of the lockout.

"To say we haven't lost momentum wouldn't be a truism," said Vancouver Grizzlies General Manager Stu Jackson hours after the votes were counted. "But I do think you'll see it pick up again.... We have a lot of catch-up to do. One of the most frustrating things has been the inability to communicate with the players and treat them in the manner we as an organization would like to treat them."

In Toronto, the Raptors General Manager Isiah Thomas figured he was "30 to 40 days behind...We're behind on everything. So instead of things crystallizing for us as far as what we're going to be like, it would have been sometime in early December, but now I figure it'll be sometime in January instead," said Thomas in his news conference shortly after the vote. He added that his top priority would be to sign his two draft picks, Damon Stoudamire and Jimmy King. The new agreement will save the Raptors and the Grizzlies some money in that area thanks to the new rookie salary cap. The most Damon Stoudamire can make as the seventh pick overall is $4.6 million over three years, which is the new maximum length of rookie contracts. Contrast that to the seventh pick in 1994, Lamond Murray of the L.A. Clippers, who has a $13.5-million deal over five years. The Raptors' second pick, Jimmy King, is guaranteed a minimum of $200,000. Vancouver's Bryant Reeves, picked one spot higher than Stoudamire, can earn a maximum of $5 million over three years. Top pick Joe Smith can earn a maximum of $8 million over his three-year contract. In addition to the changes in the rookie salaries, no player can now have a contract longer than seven years, with increases limited to 20 percent annually.

The two Canadian franchises received a further hit from the new collective-bargaining agreement. One of the conditions in the new deal is that the Canadian teams have been given a $15-million-US spending cap, 66 percent of the $23-million cap imposed on the existing teams. (That percentage will rise to 75 percent of the league-wide number and 100 percent by 1997.) So not only have the franchises been severely hampered in their preparations for their debut, they have also been guaranteed several seasons of mediocrity because of their salary cap. (Although because of their finances, the Raptors and Grizzlies may not mind the cap as they may not have wanted to spend more than $15 million on salaries in their first season.)

With the new labour deal in place, the Raptors had to then turn their attention to arranging financing for the outstanding expansion-fee balance of $60 million US that the league had been carrying for the club. But the two Canadian teams put on a brave face as they were finally able to plan for their first season in earnest. It had been a long and bumpy road already but they could now look forward to those opening games.

Chapter Sixteen

VANCOUVER

Vancouver—Canada's gleaming jewel on the West Coast. A city of one and a half million and a mecca for those who enjoy the slower pace of life and a hip, health-conscious, recreational lifestyle in a glorious climate. It has become a focal point for Asian immigration and investment in Canada, and for import and export with the Pacific Rim countries. But is it an NBA city?

Arthur Griffiths and the McCaw brothers from Seattle are counting on it.

When the NBA was being lobbied hard by the Palestra group and by the Bitoves, expansion to Canada was seen as a possibility to be explored sometime down the road, and at no time was there talk of Vancouver. Vancouver had inquired politely about major-league baseball expansion and had been rebuffed. There had been talk of buying an ailing baseball franchise, but that too was dismissed. There had been no hint of Vancouver being in the plans of the NBA when and if it did decide to look to Canada. There were already two franchises in the Pacific Northwest in Portland and in Seattle, and in fact, with Seattle less than a two-hour drive from Vancouver, the very idea was seen as an encroachment by some. But, in March 1993, when the NBA announced it was going to consider expansion bids from Canada, and not just from Toronto, Arthur Griffiths saw his chance.

Griffiths was well acquainted with the ways of pro sports, as his family had been the driving force behind the NHL's Vancouver Canucks since 1974. That team had been community owned for the first four years after entering the NHL in 1970. Then, after falling into financial difficulty, and with the franchise in danger, broadcasting magnate Frank Griffiths Sr., Arthur's father, stepped in and provided the money and the leadership that kept the team in Vancouver. Frank Griffiths Sr. was a chartered accountant who made his big money in broadcasting. In 1956 he bought a radio station and built it into an empire known as WIC (Western International Communications Ltd.) that includes a string of radio operations, eight TV stations, two syndication services and some pay-TV and satellite interests. The company has revenues of more than $350 million a year.

In 1980, as a kid in his early 20s, Arthur Griffiths was working for his dad's team, trying hard to learn the business. He began by working in ticketing and in the souvenir shop before soaring to the post of "assistant to the chairman" in 1981. Stories abound from those days about the 24-year-old kid, working in the front office, but also acting like a starstruck teenager and even suiting up and skating with the players at practice sometimes. In the spring of 1981, the Canucks made it to the Stanley Cup Finals with Roger Nielson coaching, with Dave "Tiger" Williams as the most popular player and with goaltender Richard Brodeur taking the team further than it really should have gone. It was an amazing spring for West Coast hockey fans, but what it did was raise expectations unreasonably. From 1982 to 1987, the Canucks lost more games than any other NHL team, and Arthur Griffiths found himself taking some knocks in the media and in hockey's front-office circles as well. At one NHL Board of Governors' meeting, Griffiths was told to "climb back in your high chair" by the crusty curmudgeon who owns the Chicago Blackhawks, Bill Wirtz. Eventually, Griffiths realized he was not a hockey man but a financier, so in 1987, he hired Pat Quinn, a cigar-chomping, no-nonsense hockey man who had played for the Canucks in their early years, and had been a successful and respected coach and then a general manager in the NHL. Leaving Quinn at the helm of the hockey operation, Griffiths stepped back to concentrate on the business of helping run his father's empire and adding to it.

In 1989, long before the NBA expansion figured into things, Frank Griffiths Sr. had visions for a new arena in downtown Vancouver. The Pacific Coliseum in the city's east end was antiquated and no longer suitable for his hockey team; more accurately, it was unsuited to the revenue stream his company needed to continue to operate the hockey team efficiently. Pacific Coliseum only seats just over 15,000; luxury box space is limited; it is 20 kilometres from the downtown core; and as a tenant, the team's ownership group, Northwest Sports Enterprises, got no cut of the parking and concession fees. In 1992 Arthur Griffiths secured a piece of land downtown, beside B.C. Place Stadium, and began building a new, state-of-the-art, privately funded arena where there would be more seating, more corporate box space, and where he could control the parking and concession revenues. Knowing he'd need another tenant to make the arena viable, Griffiths then began to work towards getting an NBA franchise.

This did not sit well with his family. "My father was never overly excited by the idea of a basketball team," Griffiths told *Canadian Business* in a November 1994 article. Nor was Arthur's older brother Frank Jr., who told *Maclean's* that his family "was not going to make an investment in basketball. That was absolutely clear."

With his family and some local investors leery of the NBA's $125-million US expansion fee, Griffiths had to work hard to get the support he needed, but he got it, and formed Vancouver Basketball Limited Partnership. It included John and Bruce McCaw from Seattle, multimillionaires who had made their money in cellular communications, Allan and Thomas Skidmore of Vancouver who head up Speedy and Apple Auto Glass, and Ron Joyce of Hamilton who owns Tim Hortons Donuts. Griffiths also recruited a sharp young lawyer from Toronto named Michael Korenberg, who had represented the NBA on occasion and who would help guide the Vancouver people through the bid and start-up hurdles as Northwest Entertainment Group's deputy chairman. The group went through the required process, which included the $100,000 fee and formal application to the league, the due-process visit, the lobbying of the NBA Board of Governors, and the bid presentation on September 20, 1993 in New York.

While the Toronto people were told within a couple of months that they had been successful, the league said it had looked favourably on the Vancouver bid but had some concerns it wanted to investigate further. Presumably, those concerns were about market size and about the finances of the Vancouver Basketball Limited Partnership. The league loved the concept of the spanking new arena and the fact that it met the requirement of a team playing in its own building, but the NBA also saw how much Arthur Griffiths was leveraged already with the Canucks and the new arena, so there was caution. But, evidently satisfied over the winter, the NBA Expansion Committee used the occasion of the All-Star Game in Minneapolis to announce on February 12, 1994 that it had unanimously endorsed Vancouver's bid to join the league. To everyone's surprise, the plan was for the Vancouver team to begin play in the fall of 1995 along with the Toronto Raptors. The Vancouver team would play in the Western Conference's Midwest Division with San Antonio, Houston, Minnesota, Denver, Utah and Dallas. (The Pacific Division is where Vancouver would like to be to enjoy regional rivalries with Seattle and Portland, but that division already had seven teams, and the Midwest only had six.)

The Vancouver group was ecstatic and immediately launched a season-ticket campaign with a view to selling what they knew would be the required minimum of 12,500 by the end of the year. Griffiths and his people were already suggesting the name of their team would be The Mounties and had several jackets and caps made up with the name and a logo for the first news conference. In late April, the NBA's Board of Governors formally awarded the franchise to Vancouver, again with the season-ticket requirement and with the demand for a deposit of $12.5 million US. However, some unloading of debt and some financial reshuffling were going to be required in order for Arthur Griffiths to pull all of this off. He would work on it for the next year.

In the meantime, the Griffiths group was in the basketball business and set about gathering the ingredients and the people to make it work. After the initial euphoria about the city getting an NBA team, there was some grumbling among Vancouverites about the name Mounties. *The Vancouver Province* ran a name-the-team contest and got suggestions ranging from Dragons to Rain to Steelhead Salmon to Vipers. Insiders say Vipers was considered for a time by the team but was rejected because Chrysler makes a car with that name, and General Motors was putting up big money to have its name on the new arena. Arthur Griffiths enlisted the help of the NBA marketing department when he realized Mounties was not going to be acceptable to the league or the public, and that the RCMP was going to have a problem with it as well.

With the name situation still in limbo, the Vancouver ownership group turned its attention to hiring someone to run the basketball side of things. When Griffiths made his presentation to the NBA in the bid process, he said he would take the same stance in hiring a general manager as he eventually had done with his hockey team when he handed the reins to Pat Quinn—hire the right guy and stay out of the way. Griffiths actually went to the NBA and asked for a short list of candidates it thought appropriate. "There were other names on that list, but Stu was my first choice," said Griffiths later.

"Stu" was Stu Jackson, who became the Vancouver team's Vice-President of Basketball Operations and General Manager on July 22, 1994, and was quickly accepted by the local media as a good choice. In his late 30s, Jackson, a native of Reading, Pennsylvania, played college basketball in the Pacific Northwest at the University of Oregon. He has a relaxed, affable demeanour. He also has good basketball management credentials; he has been a player and has had coaching experience with the NBA's New York Knicks and the NCAA's University of Wisconsin Badgers, and had a job for two years in the NBA's front office. Jackson quickly moved to Vancouver with his wife, Dr. Janet Taylor, who is a psychologist, and their four young daughters. He wasted no time in getting out and pounding the pavement with Arthur Griffiths to promote the team.

Two weeks later they had a name for their team and it was the Vancouver Grizzlies. The name and the logo were unveiled on August 11, 1994; the team ownership said at the time that "the name represents the culture, geography and heritage of Western Canada," and even drew on aboriginal lore by pointing out that "in West Coast Indian mythology the grizzly bear's nature inspired awe and respect. Some considered the grizzly bear a warrior's warrior. They believed it powerful, aggressive and fearless in battle." The logo depicts a snarling grizzly bear surging out from under the name Vancouver Grizzlies with a basketball in its claws; the colours are Spirit

Turquoise, British Columbia Bronze and Canadian Red. The team trotted out its uniform in a splashy news conference with Nike model and beach-volleyball star Gabrielle Reece modelling the jersey and shorts that the Grizzlies would wear on the court. With the team named and with a catchy, interesting logo on its merchandise, the Vancouver Grizzlies were a hot item for the rest of 1994, reaching ninth in worldwide sales by the end of the year.

Ticket sales were not as great. By November 1994, there were 7,500 season tickets sold with two months to go before the December 31 deadline set by the NBA for selling a minimum of 12,500. The Grizzlies launched what they called the "Drive for Five" campaign in an effort to sell the remaining 5,000 tickets to reach the required minimum. The campaign worked, with some last-minute corporate help, and on December 20, the Grizzlies were able to announce they had 12,624 season tickets sold.

In March 1995, with a balance of $112.5 million US due on the expansion fee, Arthur Griffiths completed his financial restructuring. He sold equity control in his company, Northwest Entertainment Group, which owned 87 percent of the Canucks, 100 percent of the Grizzlies and 100 percent of the new GM Place arena, to John E. McCaw Jr. of Seattle. Already a big shareholder, McCaw paid $110 million US for his extra 30 percent of the company. The transaction saw Arthur Griffiths move from a 70 percent majority ownership position to being a shareholder with a 40 percent minority interest. He would have loved to maintain majority interest and keep 51 percent, but his personal debt load couldn't handle it and he needed the capital. Griffiths and his sister, Emily, were responsible for the $125 million US expansion fee to the NBA and for the $160 million Canadian cost of building GM Place. The three-month hockey lockout in late 1994 had hurt Griffiths' revenues, and as 1995 began he was admitting he needed new money, saying he would seek it either in the form of a new controlling partner, or by taking on limited partners. "I could have cut it off at the hockey team and the arena and kept that for myself," said Griffiths at the news conference announcing the restructuring. "But that would have sacrificed a great opportunity for John and myself to build something special and something strong for this city."

Griffiths kept his posts as Chairman and CEO of Northwest Entertainment Group, and talked of his and McCaw's dedication and determination to see the Grizzlies succeed in Vancouver. "This is not the case of some unknown American coming in and taking control. I've known John for 30 years. He loves Vancouver and he wouldn't be doing what he's doing if the opportunity didn't exist here. If this opportunity existed in a U.S. city, he wouldn't be interested."

Since the restructuring, things have run smoothly for the Grizzlies. They actually signed a player before they had a coach. On June 1, Kevin Pritchard, a free-agent guard who had played on the NCAA championship team at Kansas in 1988, had the distinction of becoming the first player officially signed to play with one of the new Canadian teams. Then, on June 19, the Grizzlies named as their first-ever head coach former NBA guard Brian Winters, a veteran of 18 seasons, and with plenty of assistant-coaching experience in the NBA. The Grizzlies were happy with the players they got in the expansion and college drafts and were set to begin moulding a team when, like every franchise in the NBA, they had to put everything on hold for the entire summer because of the labour dispute. When it ended, Stu Jackson breathed a sigh of relief and admitted being ready to see some on-court action. "We have had a year now of ticket drives, mascot searches, announcing dance teams, colours, logos, nicknames. Now it's time to have some fun and to do what we all came to Vancouver to do, and that's to play the game."

Late in August 1995 Arthur Griffiths was able to stage a sneak preview of his spanking new arena, GM Place, as he took a ceremonial skate around the newly laid ice surface of the $160 million facility. "It's on budget and on time," said Griffiths, beaming for the sponsors and reporters who had gathered for the occasion. "This building rivals anything else in North America." GM Place will seat 20,004 for basketball, 19,056 for hockey and 22,000 for concerts. More than 55 events were booked for the four-month period from the time it opened to the end of 1995, and some 200 events are expected over the first year of operation. Construction of the arena has provided hundreds of jobs at a labour payroll of just under $30 million, and Griffiths expects GM Place's ongoing operation will employ about 1,100 people and will inject over $50 million annually into the Vancouver economy. It has eight levels, more than 80 luxury suites, three restaurants with seating for more than 800, 31,000 square feet of office space and 4,000 square feet of retail space. The literature on the building boasts that it has specially engineered sightlines that are "the best of any new arena" and that a special ventilation system will ensure that during an event, each person will receive 15 cubic feet per minute of outdoor air, allowing patrons to breathe clean rather than recycled air. The arena officially opened on September 19, 1995 with a Bryan Adams concert, followed by a Canucks exhibition game with San Jose on September 23, 1995.

Just before the opening of GM Place, the Northwest Entertainment Group changed its corporate name to Orca Bay Sports and Entertainment, with a new logo showing killer whales in a stylized "O" in red, blue and black. Vice-President and majority owner John E. McCaw Jr. said he hoped the organization "grows to reflect the strength, unity and loyalty exemplified by the orca."

That day in April 1994, when he was officially welcomed into the NBA, Arthur Griffiths said: "I've been very fortunate to be part of a lot of unique opportunities and to be successful at many of them. This is one that is probably as major an accomplishment as anybody could be part of." Still not 40 years of age, and chairman of a huge sports empire that includes the Canucks, the Grizzlies and the new GM Place, Griffiths is not daunted by any of it. "There's an awful lot to be excited about, but there's also a lot to be cautious about," he told *The Vancouver Province* early in 1994. Well, he needn't have worried. Griffiths has pulled it off. The Canucks and the Grizzlies have their seasons under way, they are housed in a beautiful new building and Vancouver is excited. Arthur's father Frank Griffiths Sr. would have been proud. (Frank Griffiths Sr. passed away in April 1994.)

Arthur Griffiths told reporters, "One of the last things he said to me was, 'It's now yours, good luck.' It's gratifying to have that support."

CONCLUSION

"We brought the NBA to Canada, but Bitove got the team because he was in the club already."

—Richard Peddie of Palestra

John Bitove Jr. has done it. At 35 years of age, he has put together a $400-million deal and has brought the NBA to Toronto. Yes, it may have been a bumpy ride between winning the franchise and the team's hitting the court; and yes, there will be losing seasons and more ownership and management fires to put out, but give the man his due. He had a dream, he pursued it and now it's come true.

The NBA will work in Toronto and it will work in Vancouver, but for very different reasons. In Vancouver, it will work because of the ethos and spirit of the community. People will support the team because it is a *Vancouver* team. The city is small enough that there is still some civic pride, and Vancouverites are excited by the NBA coming to *their* city.

"They've done everything right so far, sometimes to a level that has been nauseating," said veteran Vancouver sportswriter Jim Taylor. "They are the kings of the press conferences. They call them all the time to announce this or that, and while many have been not worthy of a press conference, they have the team profile very high. I'm a fan, and I'm happy they're here, but I just don't know how long it will last. The sheer economics of battling for the Vancouver sports dollar will make it tough." Indeed, the owners will find it tough as they make sports fans choose in some cases between the Canucks and the Grizzlies, and in good weather, the Grizzlies will also have to battle against all the recreational opportunities people have on the West Coast. But, over all, after an exploratory trip to Vancouver to try to get a sense of whether there is a palpable excitement, it became clear it is there. There is not the same proliferation of Grizzlies hats and T-shirts being worn by the kids as is enjoyed by the Raptors in Toronto, but there is a genuine enthusiasm in the city about the team and about the NBA. Again, it should work because people will feel a sense of civic or regional affinity and allegiance—it's *our* city and *we* have a team.

By contrast, the NBA will work in Toronto because of the glitz and glamour that surrounds the league. Toronto sports fans, especially the Toronto corporate community that wants to be involved with sports for any number of reasons, love anything American and "big-league." The Raptors have sold 17,000 season tickets. We would venture to suggest that a large number of those are not held by *sports* fans, and certainly not by *basketball* fans. Rather, they have gone to downtown Toronto companies that have bought a pair or more to entertain clients, reward salespeople or do favours by providing a place and an event that is a "hot" place to be and to be seen. It's the same with the good seats at Blue Jays games, where the cell phones are out and the networking is in high gear. We've been to games in those seats in the middle of a pennant race and have seen people arrive in the third inning with a couple of kids in tow, stay for a few innings and leave in the seventh. The gold seats at Maple Leafs games are that way as well. One sees a lot of the "fur coat-and-Rolex" crowd that does not follow hockey with a passion or even a passing interest. But if sitting in the rinkside seats at a Leafs game is seen as a sign of influence, affluence and prestige, the upscale, corporate crowd in Toronto will buy those seats every year, write them off and be happy to have access to "what's hot."

Toronto has a small, devoted basketball following and a ton of kids who love the game, its superstars and its souvenir jerseys and caps. But this is not the Raptors season-ticket and luxury-box crowd. The seats at Raptors games are not priced for Lenny and Billy from Rexdale or Scarborough; they are priced for Gareth and Judith from downtown or from the wealthier suburbs. Lenny and Billy will scoop up the hats and the T-shirts and watch the games on TV.

But the NBA venture will work in Toronto. People will flock to the games to see Michael Jordan or Shaquille O'Neal or Charles Barkley play against the Raptors. It will be like New York and Los Angeles—TV and film stars will sit at courtside and be very visible.

It will be an "in thing" to be at Raptors games, not unlike being at the "hot" new bar or nightclub or restaurant. The NBA will work in Toronto, perhaps in spite of the management and ownership because the control-crazy NBA won't let it fail. John Bitove Jr. is ambitious, driven and confident, and he can cut deals, but the organization is becoming infamous for management mistakes. Three people hired for key jobs left before the first game was played. Public Relations Director Tom Mayenknecht moved across the country to become a vice-president of marketing and communications for the Grizzlies after a year of having to be a paid apologist for the Raptors. Stephen Weber, whom the Raptors hired from the Phoenix Suns in 1994 to be their senior marketing executive, left early, and so did Director of Consumer Products David Strickland. The radio play-by-play team was named just three weeks before the first exhibition game. Just over a month before the season started, no permanent TV play-by-play voice was in sight. The Raptors asked popular Toronto TV sportscaster John Gallagher to be the public-address announcer at home games, but insulted him by offering him *$50 a game* plus two tickets. (The league standard is $150 US per game and two tickets.) Gallagher refused and the Raptors hired a kid from a local broadcasting school. Isiah Thomas has decided not to move to Toronto permanently with his family. His reasons are personal and understandable. His kids were ready to start school in Detroit in the fall of 1995, and with the NBA labour situation still unresolved at that point, he decided not to move them but to commute by Lear jet and to keep an apartment in Toronto. None of this does much for public perception. In fact, one observer who's been close to it all said: "It sure looks as if, when the NBA was passing out the blueprints on expansion franchises and how to run them, the Grizzlies got a copy of Charlotte's and the Raptors got a copy of Minnesota's."

And then there's the arena. People who know their stuff in this field say it'll never fly with one tenant. "Aligning with Garth Drabinsky and putting musical theatre in there doesn't help," says Richard Peddie. "Garth is hugely successful, but he's way too tough and leaves nothing on the table. That won't help their revenues just to have some shows in there a few times a year. They have to get some hockey in there."

But Peddie says the Bitoves can actually do whatever they want on the arena matter now that they have the franchise. "They can stay at SkyDome, they can go to Maple Leaf Gardens, what can the NBA do now? Take the franchise away? Doubtful. They've already spread the expansion money around. They can't ask for it back. The promises the Bitove group made about arenas don't matter. Look at the NHL. When Tampa and Ottawa got their franchises in December 1991, they promised new rinks within two years. Ottawa's only just getting theirs finished, and Tampa's is nowhere in sight. Doesn't matter. It's their problem now, the league has its expansion money."

Should Palestra have been the choice? Maybe. But it was clear that Larry Tanenbaum's group was on its own mission, and that mission was not part of the NBA's imperialistic view. "Stern was looking for some puppets who would be clones of Orlando and Charlotte. He wanted a group that would do as he said," said Tanenbaum.

"But Toronto's unique. It's a city that grew up on hockey. Sure, the kids today have played some basketball and they know the game and its stars. They know Jordan and they wear the stuff, so you have a market there, but not among the adults. They didn't grow up with it. We were of the opinion that we had to sell it to them and do it the *Canadian* way. We showed Stern that plan, the plan to educate and to market the game to Canadians right across the country. I mean there's George Taylor from Labatt in our presentation in New York saying he'd put Toronto Thunder logos on 24 million cases of beer sold across Canada. There's the bank saying they'd have promotions at 1,800 CIBC branches, something about opening an account and joining 'the Thunder Force.' But Stern saw it as a grab by a strong group of people with a vision different from his. His only response was to say, 'What makes you think I'd give you any rights to promote beyond the 75-mile territorial limit?'

"Don't get me wrong, I have no ill will towards the Bitoves. I wish them well. My beef is with Stern. I still feel Toronto wins because we got the NBA here, and I do have a sense of satisfaction about that. I'm disappointed that the NBA didn't pick us. We would have done a great job bringing a Canadian sense to it. We would have been the 'Northern Lights,' just a little different in the way we sold and marketed things. Why, we had $10 million set aside just for marketing and educating Canadians about the subtleties of the NBA, like the Blue Jays did in the late '70s with those commercials explaining what 'sacrifice flies' were and so on. We just saw a different approach. Anaheim and San Jose in the NHL certainly do things they don't do in Montreal or Toronto and they're not discouraged from it. There's no need to be clones. But Stern saw it as a backwater and decided that the successful applicant would be one that would do his and the NBA's bidding to the letter."

It could be a likely scenario that the Raptors will change hands in a few short years. An investor might like the look of things and see some potential, or there might be a fire sale if the current owners are in trouble as many predict they will be. It's interesting to note that three of the four most recent expansion teams have changed hands. In fact, at a cocktail party in the fall of 1995, the Detroit Pistons managing partner, William Davidson, was overheard saying to Palestra's Larry Tanenbaum that he now regretted not supporting the Palestra bid, and suggested that Tanenbaum would be able to buy the Raptors in a few years for "50 cents on the dollar."

But whatever lies down the road, the Raptors and the Grizzlies are a reality now with the owners that made the successful pitches and came up with the money. John Bitove Jr. is like a brash, confident and competent young rookie guard. While not much older than Bitove, Arthur Griffiths has more experience with sports ownership, franchise leadership and dealing with a big-time sports league. The hotshot rookie guard and the experienced veteran guard—coaches would differ on who they'd want to have the ball in the dying seconds of a tight game. But the NBA, dozens of corporate sponsors and thousands of basketball fans in Toronto and Vancouver are hoping each man will be successful in his own game and will hit the clutch shots when necessary.

INDEX

Adidas endorsement, 36
Ainge, Danny, 84
Air Canada, 105, 125, 201
Air Canada Centre, 75, 105, 108–109, 145, 145
American Basketball Assn., 47, 64
Anthony, Greg, 189
Armstrong, B.J., 187–88, 214
Arum, Bob, 85
Atlantic Packaging, 21, 152, 159

B.C. Sports Action lottery, 95
Bahakel, Cy, 74
Bakjer, Vin, 184
Ballard, Bill, 11, 24, 51, 54, 96, 176, 177–78, 194
Ballard, Harold, 46, 51, 101, 152, 157, 159, 176, 177–78
Bank of Nova Scotia, 16–17, 22, 152, 203
Barkley, Charles, 36, 37, 39, 41, 43, 132, 183, 221, 237
Bassett family, 1
Bathos, Tom, 129
Bavasi, Peter, 161–62, 163, 165
BCL Enterprise, 11, 14, 24, 192, 193
BCTV, 128
Becker, Edd, 57
Beckerman, David, 196
Beeston, Paul, 164
Belinsky, Deb, 137
Bennett, W. Charles, 215–16
Bertuzzi, Larry, 201
Bettman, Gary, 95, 120, 137
Beynon, Murray, 97
Bias, Len, 33
Biasatti, Hank, 45

Bird, Larry, 35, 36, 43, 49
Bitove group. *See also* Bitove, John Jr.; Professional Basketball Franchise
 court actions, 6–9
 Pearson Airport deal, 6–8
 SkyBox issue, 145–48
 SkyDome catering, 9, 146, 170, 175
 World Indoor Track & Field Championship, 12–13
 World Championship of Basketball, 12–13, 61, 192–93
Bitove, John Jr.
 and arena site, 96–98, 101–102, 106, 201–203, 239
 background, 4–5, 16, 20, 24–25, 190–91
 Bitove group bid, 1, 4, 11–12, 14–18, 20–27, 192–96, 228, 236
 and corporate boxes, 145–46
 and general manager selection, 149, 151–53, 155, 197–200
 and licensing fee, 140, 201
 ownership of Raptors by, 17, 152
 P.C. connections of, 8, 191–92
 and Players Assn. negotiations, 204, 213, 223
 and Pro-Line gambling, 87, 93, 95, 97, 179, 200–201
 and season tickets, 142
 and team name, logo, 112–13, 116, 117, 196–97

television broadcasts, 122–23, 125–26
and Vancouver bid, 27
Bitove, John Sr., 5–6, 8, 177
Bitove, Tom, 5, 6, 145–47
Blair, Bill, 84
Bolla, Joe, 47
Boston Celtics, 33, 35, 45, 46, 52, 55, 76, 79, 80, 188, 223
Bradley, Shawn, 184
Brisbin Brook Beynon, 97
Brown, Larry, 43
Buffalo Braves, 4, 46, 62
Buss, Jerry, 195
Butler, David, 148

Cadillac Fairview, 96–100
Candy, John, 170, 171, 172
Carling O'Keefe, 159, 160, 175
Carmichael, Scott, 11
Cassady, John, 130
Catledge, Terry, 75
CBC, 182
CBS, 182
CFRB Raptors deal, 127
Chamberlain, Wilt, 14, 51
Champion (uniforms), 118
Chaney, Don, 199–200
Charlotte Coliseum, 68, 69, 74–75, 76
Charlotte Hornets, 41, 50, 53, 54, 62, 63, 66, 67, 68–71, 72, 73–76, 78, 81, 82, 85, 86, 114, 140, 189, 198, 212, 238, 239
Cheaney, Calbert, 184
Chicago Bulls, 32, 37, 41, 42, 55, 62, 63, 68, 70, 75, 105, 140, 187, 226
CIBC, 13, 23, 147, 158, 159
CITY-TV Raptors deal, 121–23
CKNW, 128
CKVR Raptors deal, 121–23

Cleveland Cavaliers, 46, 47–48, 62, 63–64, 189, 220
CNN, 182
Coats, Cari, 133, 134
Coca-Cola, 58, 125, 147
Cohl, Dusty, 51, 52
Cohl, Michael, 11, 24, 51, 53, 96
Cohl, Robert, 51
Colangelo, Jerry, 10, 11, 195
Cole Sports Agency, 114
Coleman, Derrick, 42, 223
Concert Productions Inc., 51, 53
Continental Basketball Assn., 47, 50, 56, 79, 80, 82
Converse endorsement, 36
Cook, John, 124
Cooke, Kent, 160
Cooper, Brian, 109, 110, 145
Cooper, Syd C., 159
Copps Coliseum, 51, 169
Corbin, Tyrone, 80, 218
Corzine, Dave, 75
Cossette Communication-Marketing, 21
Cousy, Bob, 216, 217
Craddock, Eddie, 45
Creelman, Scott, 33
Cross, Jay, 100, 104
Crump, Donald, 176, 178
CTV NBA deal, 128–30
Cunningham, Billy, 64, 65, 66, 67

Dallas Mavericks, 52, 62, 154, 184, 188, 218
Davidson, William, 200, 240
DeFlorio, Larry, 114
Denver Nuggets, 2, 11, 63, 82, 115, 184, 218
Detroit Pistons, 46, 51, 149, 150, 151, 153, 154, 184, 188, 198, 199–200, 240
Devellano, Jim, 178
Donahue, Jack, 61

Drabinsky, Garth, 109, 166, 238
Duguid, Lorne, 159
Dumars, Joe, 198
Dumas, Richard, 33
Dunigan, Matt, 171, 172

Ellis, Steve, 108
Emerson, Curtis, 154
England, Herb, 14
Erhart, Steven, 56, 57, 58
ESPN, 123, 182
Ewing, Patrick, 36, 211, 212, 214, 216, 217, 218, 221, 222, 225, 226
Eyton, Trevor, 5, 8, 159

Falk, David, 211, 222
Felton, George, 68
Fingold, David, 51, 52
Fingold, Paul, 51
Fleisher, Larry, 32, 205, 208
Fleisher, Marc, 208, 211–12
Fletcher, Cliff, 97, 153
Fobasco, 51
Ford, Mike, 141
Ford Motor Co. of Canada, 105, 125–26, 147, 201
Fowler, Keith, 49
Fox Network, 120
Fox, Rick, 55
Freedman, Norman, 51

Gallagher, John, 238
Gardner, Kay, 106, 107
Garnett, Kevin, 185
General Motors of Canada, 35, 105, 232
Giffin, Donald, 176
Gillick, Pat, 152, 153, 164–65, 198
GM Place, 34–35, 75, 105, 136, 144, 169, 232, 233, 234–35
Godfrey, Paul, 1, 175

Godsoe, Peter, 16
Goldberg, Michael, 30
Golden State Warriors, 35, 42, 72, 133, 135, 154, 183, 184, 185, 187–88, 198, 214
Goodman & Goodman, 7, 8
Gourdine, Simon, 209, 210, 212, 215–16, 219, 224
Granik, Russ, 17, 43, 72, 93, 114, 131, 191, 195–96, 197, 205, 206, 209, 212, 215, 218, 223
Granovsky, Irving, 159
Granovsky, Phil, 21, 159, 160
Grantham, Charles, 32, 205, 207–210
Gray, Lisa, 126
Green, Norm, 85
Gretzky, Wayne, 38, 149, 170, 171, 172
Griffey, Ken, 39
Griffiths, Arthur, 10, 27, 35, 95, 127, 128, 131, 142, 155, 193, 228–35
Griffiths, Frank Sr., 127, 229, 235
Grunwald, Glen, 154, 200
Gulf & Western, 16
Gund Arena (Cleveland), 105
Gund brothers, 47, 48
Gutteridge, Barry, 104
GWE, 58

Hall, Barbara, 107, 108
Halstead, Joe, 193
Harcourt, Mike, 95
Hardaway, Anfernee, 72, 85, 184
Harlan, Kevin, 79
Harter, Dick, 74
Hatskin, Ben, 56
Havelock, Jon, 57, 58
Hayman, Lew, 45
Hewitt, Jim, 76
Hoffberger, Jerry, 160

Houston Rockets, 35, 42, 46, 62, 139–40, 188, 210
Howard, Juwan, 187
Howe, Pat, 99
Hubbard, Jan, 23
Hudson, John, 194
Huizenga, Wayne, 67
Hunkin, John, 13
Hunter, Lindsey, 184
Hurley, Bobby, 184

IHL, 38, 101, 109, 166, 202
Inatome, Rick, 151
Independent Sky Box Assn., 146–47, 148
Indiana Hoosiers, 4, 150, 152–53
International Amateur Athletic Federation, 12
International Basketball Assn., 56–57
Ishmail, Raghib (Rocket), 171, 172

Jackson, Bo, 39
Jackson, Ray, 187
Jackson, Stu, 73, 155, 156, 185–86, 189, 207, 210, 226, 232, 234
Jakobek, Tom, 107
Japanese basketball market, 121
Johnson, Larry, 71, 75, 85
Johnson, Magic, 14, 24, 35, 36, 43, 49, 183
Jordan, Michael, 35–37, 41, 67–68, 77, 89, 183, 211, 212, 214, 216, 217, 218, 221, 222, 225, 226, 237
Joyce, Ron, 230

Katz, Harold, 21, 72
Katz, Sam, 59, 60
Kaufmann, Steve, 211
Kelly, Terry, 176

Kelly, Malcolm, 49
Kessler, Jeffrey, 211, 214, 220–21, 224, 225
Kidd, Dusty, 37
King, Jimmy, 187, 227
Knight, Bobby, 70
Korenberg, Michael, 230
Korwin-Kuczynski, Chris, 107
Kroc, Ray, 161

Labatt, John, Ltd., 11, 13, 14, 23, 24–25, 127, 158, 159, 160, 162, 173, 175, 178, 239
Laettner, Christian, 83–84, 85
Las Vegas Sports Consultants, 90
Lashway, John, 35
Lastman, Mel, 98–99
Lean, Ralph, 15, 16
Leiweke, Tod, 35, 82, 138
Leonard, Irv, 3
Lewis, Reggie, 33
Litman, Joel, 19, 195
Lone-Studley, Marlene, 122–23
Long, Grant, 67, 222
Longley, Luc, 83
Los Angeles Clippers, 63, 72, 80, 82, 139, 143, 185, 188, 227
Los Angeles Lakers, 35, 139, 189, 195, 200
Lyons, Terry, 40–41

Magwood, Charles, 166
Malone, Brendan, 154–55, 188
Maple Leaf Gardens, 14, 44, 46, 47, 51, 109, 110, 159, 169, 176–79 , 239
Marathon Realty, 24, 102, 103, 104, 107–108
Markie, Ed, 38
Marshall, Bill, 113
Martens, Alex, 77, 132–33, 134
Martin, Rob, 134–35, 136
Mashburn, Jamal, 184

INDEX • 245

Matthew, Himal, 21
Mayenknecht, Tom, 111, 141, 238
Mazenkowski, Don, 191–92
McAlister, Peter, 96–97, 98, 99, 100–101
McCaw, Bruce, 228, 230
McCaw, John, 228, 230, 233, 235
McCombs & Woods, 2
McCracken, Chris, 123
McDeyss, Antonio, 185
McDougall, Don, 160
McKim Media Group, 129
McMahon, Jack, 70
McNall, Bruce, 11, 170, 171, 172
Megna, Michael, 86
Metro Toronto Convention & Visitors Assn., 92
Miami Arena, 65, 67, 76
Miami Heat, 50, 52, 53, 62, 63, 64–67, 73, 75, 76, 77, 78, 81, 82–83, 86, 123, 188, 226
Milwaukee Bucks, 62, 154, 184, 188
Minnesota Timberwolves, 28, 42, 50, 52, 53, 62, 77–85, 86, 140, 143, 154, 184, 185, 188, 212, 238
Molson Breweries, 50, 158, 175, 176, 177, 178
Mourning, Alonzo, 71, 85, 212
Mulroney, Brian, 8
Murphy, Dennis, 56
Murray, Lamond, 227
Musselman, Bill, 79–80, 81, 82

Naismith, James, 44, 55, 113
Nash, John, 184
Nation's Bank, 16
National Basketball League, 59
NBA. *See also* individual teams
audience, 31, 37–39, 40, 41, 53, 54, 61, 65

Canadian expansion by, 1–4, 10–12, 28, 40, 50–54, 63
college draft (1995), 180–89
and drug use, 33
expansion, expansion teams, 50–54, 63, 64–66
and gambling, 87–95
image of players, teams, 24–25, 28–29, 36–37, 42–43, 70, 118
lottery draft, 71–73, 83
marketing strategy, 30–31, 33–41, 43, 43, 54, 61, 131–32, 134–36, 138
merchandising, 36–37, 39, 40, 73, 92, 114–15, 118, 121, 207, 216
name, logo policy, 19–20, 34
salary cap, 31–33, 205, 206, 208, 211, 219, 220, 225, 227
season ticket sales, 86, 120, 139–40, 143–44
and television, 31, 38–39, 40, 53, 54, 119–30, 216
and "too–black" argument, 30–31
NBA Entertainment, Inc., 31, 182, 120
NBA Players Assn., 30–33
anti-trust suit filed against, 212–13
decertification vote, 218–19, 221–25
negotiations and lockout (1995), 204–27
NBA Properties, 73, 197
NBC NBA deal, 120, 129, 194
Nebiolo, Primo, 12
Nelson, Don, 42
New York Knicks, 16, 41–42, 44, 51, 132, 140, 189, 214, 218, 232

New Jersey Nets, 2, 42, 90, 189
New Orleans Jazz, 62
New York Rangers, 16
NFL expansion to Ont., 1–2, 37, 173–75
NHL. *See also* individual teams
  and Ontario lottery, 94–95
  marketing, 132, 137–38
  strike, 205
  television deal, 120, 122
Nike, 36–37, 118, 162, 233
Northwest Arena Corp., 10, 21, 27
Northwest Entertainment, 35, 95, 97, 105, 127, 128, 136, 230, 233, 234, 235

O'Bannon, Ed, 186, 187
O'Brien, Larry, 29, 48
Olajuwon, Hakeem, 77, 183, 221
Oliver, Gerald, 49
Olympics Dream Team, 12, 40, 83
O'Neal, Shaquille, 37, 39, 42, 43, 72, 73, 77, 85, 124, 132, 183, 221, 226, 237
O'Quinn, John, 85
Orca Bay Sports & Entertainment, 235
Orlando Magic, 29, 32, 39, 42, 50, 52, 53, 62, 63, 65, 71, 72, 73, 75, 76–77, 78, 82, 85, 86, 123, 124–25, 132–33, 139, 183, 184, 208, 210, 226, 239
Ornest, Harry, 169–70, 178
Osmak, Borden, 16, 22

Palestra group, 2–4, 10, 11, 13–15, 18–21, 23–27, 96, 97, 101, 116, 117, 192, 193–94, 228, 239–40
Parks, Cherokee, 186, 187

Peddie, Richard, 2, 3, 9, 23, 25, 170, 238–39
Pepsi–Cola, 125
Perkins, Sam, 67
Peterson, David, 10, 15–18, 22, 27, 93, 109, 152, 177, 178, 195
Philadelphia 76ers, 21, 64, 72, 76, 139, 184, 185, 188
Phoenix Suns, 10, 33, 39, 41, 62, 75, 84, 140, 195, 218, 223, 238
Pickering, Geoff, 58
Pippen, Scottie, 37, 42
Portland Trail Blazers, 34, 62, 76, 89–90, 187, 188, 206, 217, 228, 231
Pritchard, Kevin, 234
Pro–Line gambling issue, 87–89, 91–95, 97, 139, 143, 179, 180, 200–201
Professional Basketball Franchise, 15, 96–99, 101. *See also* Bitove, John Jr.; Bitove group

Quinn, Pat, 229, 232

Rae, Bob, 87, 92, 93, 94, 95, 200–201
Rae, Kyle, 103–104
Ratner, Harvey, 78–79, 81, 85
Rautins, Leo, 182
Reebok endorsement, 39, 43
Reeves, Bryant, 185–86, 189, 227
Reinsdorf, Jerry, 32
Reville, David, 92
Reynolds, Jerry, 75
Rice, Glen, 66
Rice, Jerry, 37
Richardson, Jerome "Pooh," 80, 82, 83
Richman, Ruby, 46, 56–57

Rider, Isaiah, 42, 84, 85, 184
Riley, Pat, 189
Robertson, Oscar, 216, 217
Robinson, Glenn, 183, 211
Rodman, Dennis, 42
Rogers, Rodney, 184
Rose, Jalen, 187
Rose, Joel, 2, 3, 11, 13, 20, 25
Rothstein, Ron, 66
Roxborough, Michael (Roxy), 90–91
Rutledge, Pat, 38, 54

Sacramento Kings, 184, 218, 222
Sadowski, Ed, 45
Salley, John, 51, 188
San Antonio Spurs, 2–3, 42, 188
San Francisco 49ers, 37
Sanders, Deion, 39
Saunders, John, 123
Schaffel, Lewis, 64, 67
Scheer, Carl, 69–70
Sean Michael Edward Design, 115
Seattle Super Sonics, 62, 76, 134–35, 139, 188, 218, 228, 231
Seikaly, Rony, 66, 67
Shinn, George, 69, 71, 73–74
Shoppers Drug Mart ticket purchase, 143–44
Silas, Paul, 30–31
Silverman, Dan, 214, 215
Skidmore, Allan & Thomas, 230
Slaight, Allan, 17, 93, 127, 140, 152, 201, 203
Smith, Charles, 214, 218
Smith, Don, 47, 67
Smith, Joe, 183–84, 185, 227
Smith, Steve, 67
Solway, Herb, 160
Sovran, Gino, 45
Spalding Sports Worldwide, 33

Spencer, Felton, 83
Spoelstra, Jon, 34
Stackhouse, Jerry, 185
Stadco, 147, 165, 166, 170
Standard Broadcasting, 17, 152
Stavro, Steve, 14, 101, 176, 177, 178–79
Stein, Bob, 79, 81
Stepien, Ted, 47–50, 59, 60
Sterling, Donald, 72
Stern, Jon, 39–40
Stern, David, 2, 3, 4, 18–19, 23, 25–26, 27, 28, 29, 30, 31–32, 33–34, 35, 37, 39–40, 41, 60–61, 71, 72, 76, 87, 88, 89, 90, 94, 120, 121, 128, 143, 182, 186, 191, 208, 209, 210, 211–12, 213, 219, 220, 221–22, 224, 226, 239
Stoudamire, Damon, 186–87, 227
Strasser, J.B., 36, 37
Strauss, Albert, 47
Strickland, David, 115, 238

Tagliabue, Paul, 173–74
Tanenbaum, Larry, 1–3, 11, 13, 14, 15, 18–19, 23, 24, 27, 97, 117 , 239–40
Target Center (Minnesota), 81, 83, 85
Taylor, George, 239
Theus, Reggie, 75
Thibodeau, Tom, 82
Thomas, Frank, 39
Thomas, Isiah, 4, 36, 51, 149–56, 172, 187–88, 197–200, 227, 238
Thomas, Larry, 154
Thulin, Ron, 182
Toronto Argonauts, 11, 158, 168–73
Toronto basketball franchise, arena sites, 96–110

Bay & Wellesley, 99
Canada Post, 99–100, 102–110
Eaton Centre, 18, 20–21, 96–100
Exhibition Place, 11, 24, 96
Maple Leafs (shared), Maple Leaf Gardens, 14, 18, 97, 101, 158, 178–79, 239
North York, 98–99
SkyDome, 4, 9, 13, 14, 51, 125, 143, 145, 169, 239
Toronto Blue Jays, 3, 13, 23, 25, 52, 61, 152, 158–68, 240
Toronto City Council, 102–104, 106–108, 201–202
Toronto Dominion Bank, 176–77
Toronto Huskies, 44, 45–46, 47
Toronto Maple Leafs, 153, 158, 176, 179, 202. *See also* Maple Leaf Gardens.
Toronto Raptors. *See also* Toronto franchise, arena site
  charitable foundation, 94, 108
  corporate boxes, 145–48
  expansion draft picks, 180, 186–87, 188–89
  and expansion teams, 62
  general manager selection, 149–56, 197–200
  licensing fee, 25–26, 51–52, 107, 109, 120, 140, 141–42, 207, 225 lockout, impact on, 210, 213–14, 215, 227
  lottery draft, 72, 73
  marketing, 43, 133–34, 136, 162
  media relations, 35
  merchandising, 92, 114, 115
  name, logo selection, 23, 34, 111–18, 196–97
  ownership of, 17
  players, 51, 72, 73, 180, 186–87, 188–89
  and Pro–Line standoff, 96, 139
  radio deal, 127
  season ticket sales, 86, 96, 139–45, 147–48, 237
  television deal, 119–27, 128–30
  uniform design, 115
Toronto Tornados, 47, 48–50, 56, 59, 60
Tru–Wall Group Ltd., 147
TSN, 125, 126, 127, 147, 175, 182
Turner Network Television (TNT), 37, 120, 181, 182

Utah Jazz, 91, 139

Vancouver Canucks, 10, 35, 105, 128, 131, 138, 142, 144, 148, 155, 228, 229, 235
Vancouver Grizzlies, 228–35
  arena site, 34–35, 97, 105
  bid for NBA team, 10, 21, 26–27
  corporate boxes, 144–45, 148
  expansion draft picks, 180, 185–86, 189
  and expansion teams, 62
  general manager selection, 155
  licensing fee, 25–26, 51–52, 107, 109, 120
  and lockout, impact on, 210, 215, 226, 227, 233
  lottery draft, 72, 73
  marketing, 131, 133–34, 135–37
  merchandising, 114, 118
  name, logo selection, 116–17, 118, 197, 231–33
  ownership of, 233
  season tickets, 86, 139, 142, 144–45, 148, 231, 233

television deal, 119–20, 127–30
Vincent, Sam, 75
von Schottenstein, Greg, 35, 133, 135–36, 137

Walker, Michael, 102–103, 104, 107–108
Wallace, Raheed, 185
Washington Bullets, 184, 185
Webber, Chris, 42, 72, 183, 184, 187, 211
Weber, Steve, 129, 238
Webster, R. Howard, 158–59
Weinhauer, Bob, 83
Weltman, Jeff, 185
Welts, Rick, 197
Wennington, Bill, 55
West, Doug, 80, 82
Western International Communications, 127, 128, 229
Weston family, 98
Widdrington, Peter, 158
Wilkerson, Bill, 19, 23
Williams, Buck, 206, 214, 217–18, 219
Williams, Pat, 29, 32, 63, 72, 73, 75, 76, 208
Wilson, Tom, 151
Wingfield, Dontonio, 188, 189
Winnick, Pauline, 65, 66
Winters, Brian, 234
Wirtz, Bill, 229
Wolfenson, Marv, 78–79, 81, 85
World Basketball League, 55–58
World Championship of Basketball, 12–13, 61, 128, 141, 142, 192–93, 199
Worrall, James, 13
Worthy, James, 67

Znaimer, Moses, 122
Zuffelato, Bob, 154